STP 1073

Natural and Artificial Playing Fields: Characteristics and Safety Features

Schmidt/Hoerner/Milner/Morehouse, editors

ASTM
1916 Race Street
Philadelphia, PA 19103

Library of Congress Cataloging-in-Publication Data

Natural and artificial playing fields: characteristics and safety
   features/Schmidt . . . [et al.] editors.
     (STP; 1073)
     Papers presented at the Symposium on the Characteristics and
   Safety of Playing Surfaces (Artificial and Natural) for Field
   Sports, held 6 Dec. 1988, Phoenix, Ariz., sponsored by ASTM
   Committee F-8 on Sports Equipment and Facilities and ASTM
   Subcommittee FO8.52 on Playing Surfaces and Facilities.
     "ASTM publication code number (PCN) 04-010730-47."
     Includes bibliographical references.
     ISBN 0-8031-1296-3
     1. Athletic fields—Congresses.   2. Synthetic sporting surfaces—
   Congresses.   3. Turf management—Congresses.   4. Athletic fields—
   Safety measures—Congresses.   5. Synthetic sporting surfaces—
   Safety measures—Congresses.   6. Turf management—Safety measures—
   Congresses   I. Schmidt, Roger C., 1951-   II. Symposium on the
   Characteristics and Safety of Playing Surfaces (Artificial and
   Natural) for Field Sports (1988: Phoenix, Ariz.).   III. ASTM
   Subcommittee FO8.52 on Playing Surfaces and Facilities.   IV. Series:
   ASTM special technical publication: 1073.
   GV411.N34   1990   90-33013
   796'.06'8—dc20   CIP

Copyright © by AMERICAN SOCIETY FOR TESTING AND MATERIALS 1990

NOTE

The Society is not responsible, as a body,
for the statements and opinions
advanced in this publication.

Peer Review Policy

Each paper published in this volume was evaluated by three peer reviewers. The authors addressed all of the reviewers' comments to the satisfaction of both the technical editor(s) and the ASTM Committee on Publications.

The quality of the papers in this publication reflects not only the obvious efforts of the authors and the technical editor(s), but also the work of these peer reviewers. The ASTM Committee on Publications acknowledges with appreciation their dedication and contribution of time and effort on behalf of ASTM.

Printed in Ann Arbor, MI
June 1990

Foreword

This publication, *Natural and Artificial Playing Fields: Characteristics and Safety Features*, contains papers presented at the Symposium on the Characteristics and Safety of Playing Surfaces (Artificial and Natural) for Field Sports, which was held 6 Dec. 1988 in Phoenix, Arizona. The symposium was sponsored by ASTM Committee F-8 on Sports Equipment and Facilities and ASTM Subcommittee F08.52 on Playing Surfaces and Facilities. Roger C. Schmidt, Halstead Industries, presided as chairman of the symposium, and Earl F. Hoerner, Neuromuscular Diagnostic Service, Edward M. Milner, AstroTurf Industries, and C. A. Morehouse, Pennsylvania State University, served as cochairmen. All four also served as editors of this publication.

Contents

Overview

Over the past several years, there has been a dramatic increase in emphasis in field sports from the point of view of both observers and players. Technical advances in nearly all aspects of field sports have tended to improve both the performance and the safety of the athlete.

With the increased emphasis on field sports has come an enhanced awareness of the problems associated with playing surfaces, since they are related to both the performance and the safety of the athlete. The initial question one must ask is, "What defines the ideal surface for a particular sport from the standpoint of both performance and safety of the athlete?" The playing surface should enhance both the performance and safety aspects of the sport.

Considerable work has been done in several different disciplines—including biomechanics, agronomy, polymer chemistry, and physics—to characterize the properties of an ideal playing surface. In addition, maintenance personnel, officials, and others have studied the subject. Each discipline has previously published results and is currently performing studies concerned with athletic fields, communicating the findings in the publications of its own specific professional field. This Special Technical Publication has been published as a result of the 1988 Symposium on the Characteristics and Safety of Playing Surfaces (Artificial and Natural) for Field Sports, held in Phoenix, Arizona. The symposium was an attempt to begin to communicate and provide information concerning playing surfaces across several disciplines. It was also organized to promote information exchange opportunities, particularly objective data, among these disciplines.

The symposium was the outgrowth of work within ASTM Subcommittee F08.52 on Playing Surfaces and Facilities, a subcommittee of ASTM Committee F-8 on Sports Equipment and Facilities.

It is well known to most individuals involved with playing fields that there are many more variables than constraints to be considered. In reviewing field performance, the player/field interaction and the ball/field interaction are two key factors. Before appropriate standards can be established, test methods must be developed and correlations of test results to actual field performance must be carried out. The test methods established should be applicable to any type of playing surface, artificial or natural. Of course, compromises will then have to be made between player performance, safety, and field maintenance. In an attempt to approach the subject from an objective point of view, the symposium included sections on the following subjects:

(a) playing field standards—studies and recommendations,
(b) surface traction,
(c) testing and correlation to actual field experience, and
(d) state-of-the-art playing surfaces (natural and artificial).

The collection of papers published in this Special Technical Publication has followed the same format. Some papers could have been placed in more than one section, and in these cases, arbitrary decisions were made.

Playing Field Standards

The papers in the section on playing field standards are written with varying levels of technical depth, which provides those relatively new to the area with a general overview of the interaction of a sport with the playing field. The approach taken by these papers would be suitable for any type of playing field or sport. The views of the designer, administrator, athlete, and sport researcher are expressed.

Surface Traction

An integral part of the player/surface interaction concerns the interaction of the player's shoes with the surface and their compatibility with the surface. The papers presented in this section deal with the problems associated with the correlation of laboratory test results and actual field experience. It is extremely important for the footwear designer to consider the movements of the athlete required by the sport in relation to the surface on which the sport is being played.

Testing and Correlation to Actual Field Experience

Various material tests are currently being used to assess the qualities of playing surfaces. In this section, the relevance of these tests to both natural and artificial surfaces is discussed. The majority of the papers presented deal with the problems associated with testing a surface and the correlation of the results to a real field situation. Several techniques for testing, data acquisition, and interpretation of results are discussed. Specifically, test results relating to shock absorption [the ASTM Test for Shock Absorbing Properties of Playing Surface Systems and Materials (F 355-86), the Clegg soil impact test apparatus, and other tests], friction [ASTM Method of Measuring Surface Frictional Properties Using the British Pendulum Tester (E 303-83)], and other tests are reviewed in this section. Several papers deal very specifically with the Clegg tester and adaptations of it. The effects various playing surface management practices have on test results is also discussed. The issue of field maintenance and liability of the operator as a key concern in relation to testing is the topic of one paper.

State-of-the-Art Natural and Artificial Surfaces

Various types of playing field surfaces are reviewed in this section in relation to aspects ranging from composition and construction to end use performance. Modified or enhanced natural surfaces such as Prescription Athletic Turf and the incorporation of randomly oriented interlocking mesh elements are discussed from the aspect of performance improvement. Artificial turf surfaces are reviewed, including their material selection and performance.

The papers briefly outlined here should provide the reader with a good review of the work completed on playing surfaces by several disciplines. A general overview of established standards, test methodologies, and state-of-the-art fields is presented. The symposium committee is grateful to the authors for presenting their work, and to ASTM personnel for their efforts, which have made this publication possible. I would also like to acknowledge and thank my cochairpersons, in particular, Dr. Chauncey Morehouse of Penn State University, who helped organize and present the symposium.

Roger C. Schmidt

Halstead Industries, Greensboro, NC 27410; symposium chairman and editor.

Playing Field Standards

Arthur H. Mittelstaedt, Jr.[1]

Safety Recommendations in the Design of Athletic and Sports Fields

REFERENCE: Mittelstaedt, A. H., Jr., **"Safety Recommendations in the Design of Athletic and Sports Fields,"** *Natural and Artificial Playing Fields: Characteristics and Safety Features, ASTM STP 1073,* R. C. Schmidt, E. F. Hoerner, E. M. Milner, and C. A. Morehouse, Eds., American Society for Testing and Materials, Philadelphia, 1990, pp. 5–9.

ABSTRACT: The planning and designing of playing fields have become focal points of debate. The difference between natural and artificial turf is a part of this debate. However, in addition to the question of the surface material, a host of additional recommendations must be considered as they relate to safety, as well as the performance, operations, and other influences.

This paper addresses safety concerns related to ball fields used for baseball, softball, and junior baseball, as well as football, soccer, lacrosse, field hockey, and related field activities. For ball fields, factors affecting the infield, outfield, and sidelines are addressed, and for football and related fields, factors affecting the sidelines, field, and end zones are addressed, along with factors affecting the general area surrounding the fields. Such factors must become standardized and unified for field activities.

KEY WORDS: playing fields, field sports, planning fields, designing fields, safety recommendations

Athletic and sports fields today are facilities which have undergone years of scrutiny and change. There can be no question that rules of the game, regulations for play, criteria for development and maintenance, and a host of other recommendations abound for such field areas. It is not the intent of the author to repeat what is known about the design and ultimate construction and operation of such field areas, but to highlight those elements that affect the safety of the players and spectators. As a result of the wealth of knowledge compiled to date and our unending quest for further information, personal injuries are becoming less attributed to the care of the owner or operator and more to the recklessness of the players or spectators.

However, when an injury occurs, the victim looks to others to pinpoint the blame. That, plus an aggressive litigation environment and an array of books, criteria, handbooks, and other documents, plus numerous court decisions and theories of negligence, enables specialized experts to have their own "field day." A sympathetic jury makes the final decision, usually in favor of the injured party, which means that the owner/operator cannot afford to make any mistakes. It is imperative that the owner/operator of any type of athletic or sports field recognize that he cannot designate an alternate for the responsibility but must face it squarely. He must ensure and assure that every reasonable effort is and has been made to reduce his exposure. Diligence, not negligence, is the byword.

The focus of the operation of a field is predicated on its design and construction, an integral but yet separate responsibility, and subject to subsequent liability. There is no such thing as a sports field facility that is not designed. Any forethought given to the use of a piece of

---

[1] Administrator and past president, Recreation Safety Institute, Ronkonkoma, NY 11779.

land, whether it is already flat or has to be graded, is considered design. Although every state has licensed professional engineers and landscape architects who have licenses to practice the design of such fields and to certify their correctness, very few fields are certifiable. Only 2% of the sports fields now in existence have been designed with the advice of such a professional. Most have been designed by the owner's bulldozer operator, landscape contractor, athletic administrator, athletic trainer, manufacturer, turf grower, grounds keeper, or other such person. When an accident happens, the "discovery process" ultimately proves negligence, because nobody was charged with the responsibility, or assumed the responsibility, for the care of the fields. Those lay persons usually involved in the design were probably not aware of the state of the art in sports field design and construction. Thus, an accident happens, and, ultimately, a judgment or settlement results in favor of the injured party.

What can be considered exposure today as it relates to athletic field liability? Virtually every aspect of sports field development and management is vulnerable.

This paper addresses concerns related to the design and subsequent construction of the athletic and sports field facility. In order to put into proper perspective the guidelines as set forth, it is critical that a difference be made between those fields used by amateurs for play and those used by professionals for play. These guidelines address fields used for amateur play, although there is no distinguishing difference between spectators of amateur and professional play; thus, the guidelines cover safety for spectators of both amateur and professional teams. It must also be noted that if such guidelines were appropriate to professional play, the U.S. Occupational Safety and Health Administration would be responsible for advancing these safety concerns.

Facility Hazards

The athletic and sports field for amateur play contains a multitude of hazards to the players. These guidelines will address different aspects of the field as it relates to ball fields, that is, softball and hardball, and then to football-related field sports, that is, soccer, field hockey, lacrosse, and others.

The designing of a field for professional sports requires consideration of a variety of other factors that affect safety, which are not dealt with here.

Ball Fields

Ball fields consist of the following components: infield, outfield, and sidelines; each will be addressed separately.

Infield

1. The surface, which may consist of clay and turf or snythetic material, must be free of any large grains, pebbles, rocks, debris, and other foreign objects. (Although various opinions have been expressed regarding the resiliency of clay-turf or synthetic materials and its effect in preventing injury, other papers will address such studies.)
2. The surface must all be of a level or even grade, with no depressions, ruts, mounds, or other irregularities.
3. The pitcher's mound must be of a rubberized or resilient material with rounded edges.
4. The bases must be of a resilient or soft material, with a low profile or quick release capability.
5. The baselines and batter's circle and the turf-clay edge must be straight and even, with no irregularities creating an unforeseen tripping hazard.
6. The baseline and other marking material must not be toxic to the skin or by inhalation.

Outfield

1. The surface, consisting of turf and synthetic material, must be free of any large grains, pebbles, rocks, debris, or other foreign objects. (Although various opinions have been expressed regarding the resiliency of the turf or synthetic materials and its effect in preventing injury, other papers will address such studies.)
2. The surface grade must be even and pitched in one direction, without any depressions, ridges, or other irregularities.
3. The outfield must have a fence of an even arc or radius that can be judged by a player in pursuit of a fly or ground ball, and a 4.6-m (15-ft)-wide warning track of clay or synthetic surface without irregularities.
4. The outfield fence must be at least 2.4 m (8 ft) in height to prevent an adult player, who is jumping up to catch a fly ball, from falling over the fence. Furthermore, no obstructive or protruding material, such as posts and pipes, may be on the inside of the fence.
5. The fence, if chain link material is used, must have the top and bottom of the mesh knuckled (with no barbed or protruding tops).
6. The fence, if made of plastic fabric with bendable vertical supports, must not have any protrusions.
7. The outfield fence must not have any solid wood or metal signs or plates fastened on the inside.
8. The outfield fence, if of a solid material, must have padding mounted on it.
9. The outfield must have no flagpoles, monuments, or other objects that provide impact resistance.
10. The outfield must not have any scoreboards, unless they are padded to provide impact resilience.
11. The outfield must not have any trees or landscape materials.
12. The outfield must not have any drain inlets or catch basins.
13. The outfield irrigation system must often be checked for any pop-up sprinklers that may have had ground settlement around them or that may be without caps.
14. The outfield must have no lighting standards, footings, or stanchions.
15. The outfield must have no drainage courses or structures and must not be shortened by such structures or by roads or jogging/walking paths.

Sidelines

1. The dugout or players' bench must have a protective fence or screen or have unbreakable plastic or glass in front of it.
2. The backstop must have an overhang of sufficient size to contain foul balls that would impact on other areas in use.
3. The backstop must be constructed of 25.4-mm (1-in.) mesh to prohibit climbing.
4. The backstop, where an overhang will not be effective, must have netting utilized to contain foul balls.
5. The backstop must be designed to accommodate the site's specific requirements for protection of spectators, users, and bystanders.
6. The sideline fence between the spectators and the playing field must be 2.4 m (8 ft) in height as specified by the Amateur Softball Association of America (ASA).
7. The sideline fence must extend from the backstop a minimum of 6.1 m (20 ft) beyond first and third bases.
8. The outfield distance must be no shorter than that specified by various organizational rules of the game.

9. The outfield fence, if removable for multipurpose play, must have sleeves at least 0.1 m (4 in.) below the top of the grade of the surface material.
10. The outfield turf or synthetic material must have no joints that could catch a shoe.
11. The outfield turf sod must have no burlap or other mesh materials that could catch spikes.

Football Fields

Football and related field sports consist of the following components: the field, sidelines, end zone, and surrounding area. Each will be addressed separately.

The designing of a sports field also requires consideration of a host of factors that can result in negligence if not considered.

Field

1. The field should not interfere with another facility, track, or jogging path.
2. The field should have no surface drain inlets, pop-up sprinkler heads, metal sleeves, or other obstructions unless these are rubber capped.
3. The field should be lined to the sports regulation size with a nontoxic paint or powder.

Sidelines

1. The sidelines should have no permanent markers or pylons which could cause tripping or falling and should be of a flexible material that cannot cause penetration.
2. The sidelines should have officials' tables no closer than 6.1 m (20 ft).
3. The sidelines should have players benches no closer that 6.1 m (20 ft).
4. The sidelines should have equipment, refreshment, and emergency equipment no closer than 9.1 m (30 ft).
5. The sideline positioning of officials, players, coaches, and related penalty zones or official space should be as per the rules of the game.

End Zone

1. The furthest game line of the end zone shall be no closer than 9.1 m (30 ft) or, if a closer dimension is required, a padded fence or wall shall be installed.
2. The end zone should have no lighting with fixtures directed to the field that could cause a blinding glare when played at night.
3. The end zone should have a high fence, high net, or adequate warnings protecting the public from goals.

Surrounding Area

1. The area around the activity field should be controlled so that there is no interference from the traffic of pedestrians, buses, automobiles, service vehicles, or bikes.
2. The area around the activity field should be planned to give direct access to parking

areas and should not bisect or parallel play areas. Adequate fencing should be installed to separate the areas of use.
3. The area should have an adequate pad and driveway providing a station for emergency vehicles and rapid ingress and egress.

General Site Hazards

The planning of a sports field requires consideration of a variety of factors that affect safety and that can result in negligence if not considered:

1. A field without fencing must not be located directly adjacent to a parking lot, park drive, or road, which might cause play interference or injury.
2. A field must not have unguided or uncontrolled access to it without traffic crossing signs and markings or children playing signs.
3. A field must have access for emergency vehicles and must not be remote from emergency phones.
4. A field must have potable water service and sanitary service.
5. A field must not be unfenced or contain natural hazards for spectators or players.
6. A field must not be near unprotected railroads or power lines.

The designing of a sports field also requires consideration of a host of factors that can result in negligence if not considered:

1. A field must not be oriented so that untrained players can be momentarily blinded when fly balls, line drives, wild throws, or other similar aspects of the game occur that can result in injury.
2. A field must not have obstacles along the sidelines, behind the plate, or in the outfield that are not protected.
3. A field must have fencing in front of the players' benches and parts of the spectator outfield that are not protected.
4. A field must have fencing or a deterrent on top of the backstop or on top of the dugouts preventing youths from climbing them.
5. A field must not have exposed pop-up irrigation or other valves for sprinklers, exposed drainage, inlets, or exposed manhole covers.
6. A field must not have have exposed sharp corners on footings.
7. A field must not have steep slopes in the playing area, rutted outfields, depressed baselines, or holes in the outfield.
8. A field must not have puddles or collect water in the field or along the perimeters, which can cause mosquitos to breed and can create slippery conditions.

These are only a few of the problems that can arise in the planning and designing/engineering stages of playing field development. It is in these stages that the input of the planner, designer/engineer, and operator, working together, can be used to avoid future problems resulting in claims of negligence. The plans and specifications, the change order or other documents, and supervision of the construction and installation are all areas in which the causes of concern can and must be addressed.

Marlene Adrian[1] and Dali Xu[1]

Matching the Playing Field to the Player

REFERENCE: Adrian, M. and Xu, D., **"Matching the Playing Field to the Player,"** *Natural and Artificial Playing Fields: Characteristics and Safety Features, ASTM STP 1073,* R. C. Schmidt, E. F. Hoerner, E. M. Milner, and C. A. Morehouse, Eds., American Society for Testing and Materials, Philadelphia, 1990, pp. 10–19.

ABSTRACT: This paper is a philosophical treatise on matching the artificial playing surface to the player. Questions are raised and answered regarding the field characteristics to be measured and tested. The concept of force-time curves as an approach to better understanding of the requirements of playing fields is presented. Representative patterns of ten basic locomotor activities are described with respect to the forces against the surface. These patterns include walking, running, veering, cutting, stopping, dodging, pivoting, jumping, landing, and lunging. The absorption, traction, abrasiveness, and elasticity characteristics of playing fields are key elements related to the locomotor patterns used by the players of these sports. The problem is a complex one, but biomechanics researchers, materials engineers, and design engineers working together can facilitate the improvement of sports playing fields.

KEY WORDS: ground reaction forces, biomechanics, playing fields, artificial turf

How does one match the playing field to the player? Or, from another perspective, how does one match the playing field to the sport? The process is a two-step one. First, one must analyze the sport—its general play and objectives. Second, one must analyze the specific and common movement patterns of the players. The design of artificial (or natural) playing fields for field sports should be based upon these two analyses.

Since field sports are similar in objectives and general play, there will be common elements in designing all playing fields. One team attempts to move the ball, with or without sports implements, in one direction to score a goal. The other team attempts to control and generate movement in the opposite direction. Since, a relatively wide playing area exists, both teams also move the ball right and left, and at all intermediary angles in between. Thus, the primary principle in matching the field to the sport is to manufacture and install a multidirectional surface. This means that there will be no substantive changes in the characteristics or responses of the playing materials to movement in the multitude of possible directions of foot-surface interaction.

The second requirement for matching the field to the sport is to install a flat field. In order for a player to outmaneuver the opponent, there must be no guesswork as to the height of the playing surface at any position on the field. Removing the necessity to adapt to a changing supporting surface, whether for a foot or a ball, ensures consistency of play and predictability of actions.

It is evident that the answer to the second question posed in the first paragraph of this paper has been easily answered. Playing fields should be, can be, and are flat and multidirectional. But what other characteristics are deemed important and are required for answering the first question—how does one match the playing field to the player? Three main categories

---

[1] Department of Kinesiology, University of Illinois at Urbana-Champaign, Urbana, IL 61801.

of playing field characteristics will be considered: traction, abrasion, and shock absorption. These three are dependent upon the movement patterns of the players and their body weights.

Concomitantly, the player's ability to perform these movement patterns without slipping or falling also must be considered. The frequency and intensity of falling injuries in field sports constitute the data base upon which design characteristics of playing fields are initially developed. In non-contact field sports, falls normally result in impact of the lower body, the arms may be used to catch the body, and the fall is not a catastrophic one. In contact sports (such as football) headgear is required, since falls or blows to the head can and do occur. The playing fields are designed with knowledge of the use of headgear as one of the design components.

How well have playing fields been designed with respect to the common and specific movement patterns being used in field sports? Only if the movement patterns have been studied can one scientifically deduce the interaction between player and field. Ten basic movement patterns are utilized during field sports play. Although within a sport, as well as among field sports, some of these patterns are used more frequently than others, these basic movement patterns appear in all field sports: walking, running, cutting, veering, stopping, pivoting, dodging, lunging, jumping, and landing. Vertical and horizontal forces are generated during the execution of each of these movement patterns. Excess vertical forces may cause compression fractures, bruises, and joint trauma. Excess horizontal forces, commonly known as shearing forces, may cause blisters and other abrasive traumas. In addition, too little traction (slipping) can result in both impact and abrasive trauma.

Enhancement of the effectiveness of matching the player to the playing system also is a more recent development in design of playing fields. The energy return (the elasticity or "spring") of the playing field is the characteristic to manipulate in order to enhance performance effectiveness and efficiency. Playing fields designed to accommodate the ten movement patterns will provide *safe, efficient, and effective* systems.

Movement Pattern Data

Movement pattern analyses, therefore, must be conducted so that data can be collected with respect to abrasion, absorption, elasticity, and traction. To date, most researchers have focused upon running and walking force-time analyses [1,2]. Lunging has been investigated in the context of the sport of fencing [3,4]. Stopping (planting) and jumping have been researched primarily in non-field sports, such as volleyball, field and track athletic events (long jump and high jump), and basketball [5,6]. The ten basic movement patterns have not previously been identified or compared. Such a comparison should be made to provide a basis for playing field design and evaluation of design and of playing surfaces.

In order to analyze the ten basic movement patterns, this study used one elite athlete, with a mass of 735 N, who performed a series of the ten locomotor patterns indoors using an Advanced Medical Technology, Inc. (AMTI) force platform set on a concrete base and embedded in a spring-suspension wood gymnasium floor. Three trials of each of the ten locomotor patterns were performed at moderate speed, at what were typical speeds for this person's movements during simulated field hockey and basketball play. These data provide the basic model for comparison of activities and are expressed in multiples of body weight since ratios do not change with increases in body weight. Only magnitudes of forces will change. In addition, magnitudes will change with speed of movement. The force-time characteristics of the ten basic movement patterns were investigated using the AMTI force platform and a computerized analysis package. Force-time data were plotted and are depicted in Figs. 1 through 10 and discussed in the following sections.

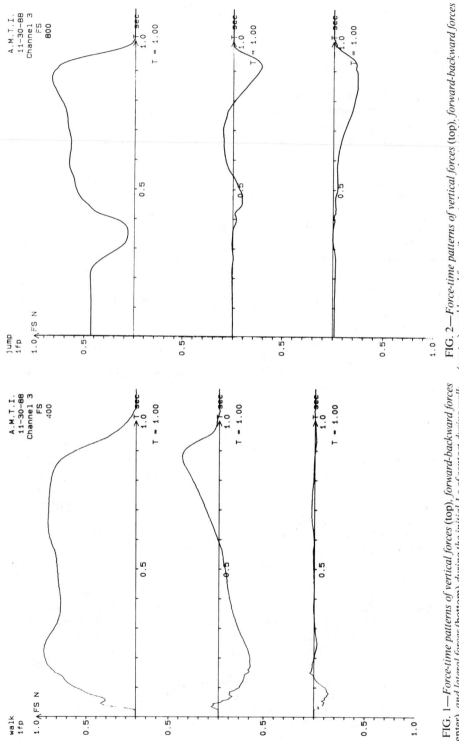

FIG. 1—*Force-time patterns of vertical forces* (top), *forward-backward forces* (center), *and lateral forces* (bottom) *during the initial 1 s of contact during walking. The first major vertical peak is impact and the last vertical peak is push-off.*

FIG. 2—*Force-time patterns of vertical forces* (top), *forward-backward forces* (center), *and lateral forces* (bottom) *during the initial 1 s of contact during jumping. The last vertical peak is push-off.*

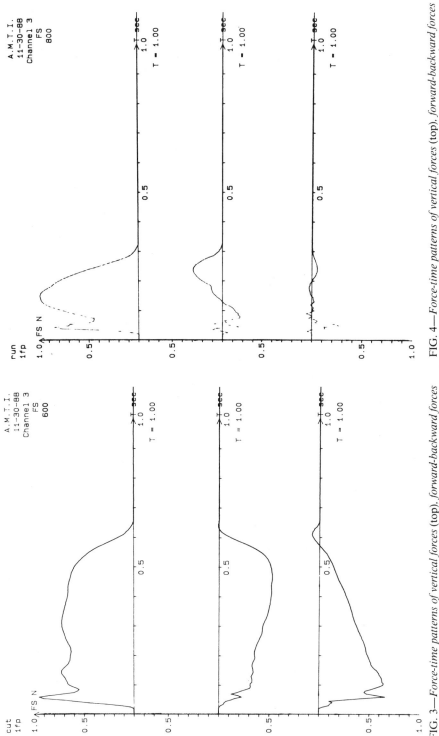

FIG. 4—*Force-time patterns of vertical forces (top), forward-backward forces (center), and lateral forces (bottom) during the initial 1 s of contact during running. The first major vertical peak is impact and the last vertical peak is push-off.*

FIG. 3—*Force-time patterns of vertical forces (top), forward-backward forces (center), and lateral forces (bottom) during the initial 1 s of contact during cutting. The first major vertical peak is impact and the last vertical peak is push-off.*

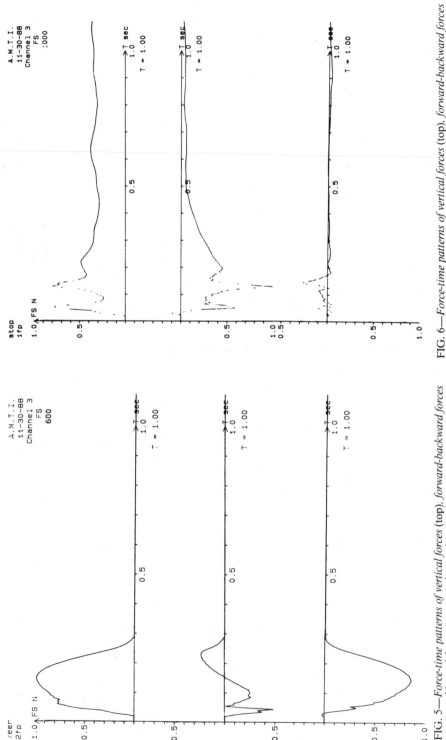

FIG. 5—*Force-time patterns of vertical forces (top), forward-backward forces (center), and lateral forces (bottom) during the initial 1 s of contact during veering. The first major vertical peak is impact and the last vertical peak is push-off.*

FIG. 6—*Force-time patterns of vertical forces (top), forward-backward forces (center), and lateral forces (bottom) during the initial 1 s of contact during stopping. The first major vertical peak is impact.*

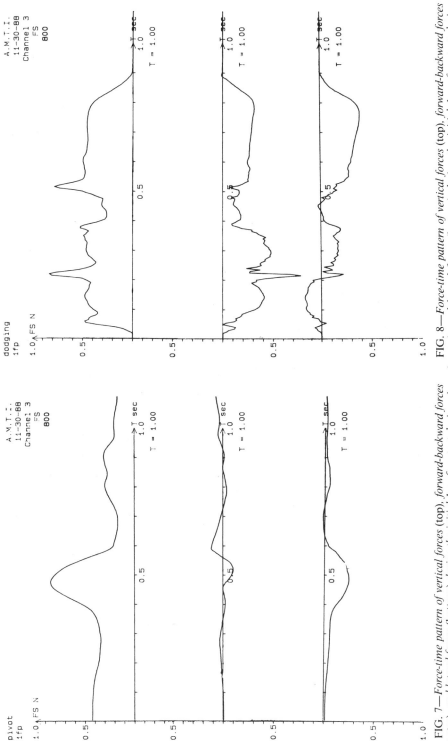

FIG. 7—Force-time pattern of vertical forces (top), forward-backward forces (center), and lateral forces (bottom) during the initial 1 s of contact during pivoting. The major vertical peak is push-off.

FIG. 8—Force-time pattern of vertical forces (top), forward-backward forces (center), and lateral forces (bottom) during the initial 1 s of contact during dodging.

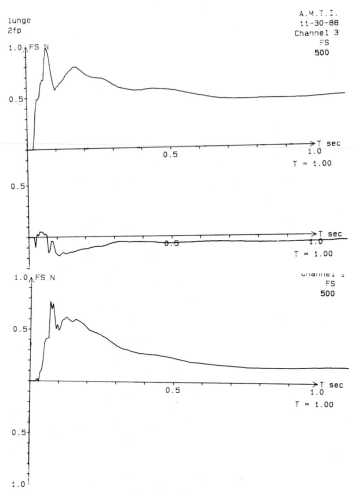

FIG. 9—*Force-time pattern of vertical forces* (top), *forward-backward forces* (center), *and lateral forces* (bottom) *during the initial 1 s of contact during lunging. The first major vertical peak is impact.*

Absorption Characteristics

The vertical force-time data from the ten movement patterns are listed in Table 1. All data are expressed in multiples of body weight (BW) since the maximum vertical forces occurring during execution of these movement patterns are influenced by the weight of the player. The speed of execution also influences the maximum forces. All recorded forces were less than 3 × BW. If one assumes that the ranges in body mass are 450 to 1350 N, the maximum forces would range from 1350 to 4050 N. The time of application or absorption of this force varied from 20 to 200 ms. The maximum g forces would be less than 10 g (4 g is the maximum produced in this set of data).

Approximately 50 ms is required to reach maximum vertical force during the pivot and veer movements. Walking has an initial rise time of 20 ms, a force of no more than ½ BW, and, then, a rise time of approximately 200 ms to a maximum force of 1¼ BW. The initial peak in running is approximately 2 × BW, occurring within 20 to 30 ms. These fast rise times are also characteristic of dodging, cutting, stopping, lunging, and landing. The application times for the vertical push-off force phase tend to be in the range of 80 to 120 ms.

It must be remembered that all these tests were conducted using a metal force platform. Thus, the loss of force to the supporting surface material was not significant; the body parts safely absorbed the forces by means of flexion at the ankle, knee, and hip joints. These vertical forces and rise times would be less when moving on commonly manufactured artificial playing fields, since deformable materials are used for these surfaces.

Traction Characteristics

None of the shearing forces were greater than 1½ BW (see Table 1). Therefore, if the player had a mass of 500 N, the maximum shearing force would be 750 N or less. The force-time patterns included two patterns in which slipping occurred. In all cases, the combined shearing force and vertical force at any given instant in time were such that no slipping occurred. This might be interpreted to mean that the coefficient of friction was sufficient for the movement patterns.

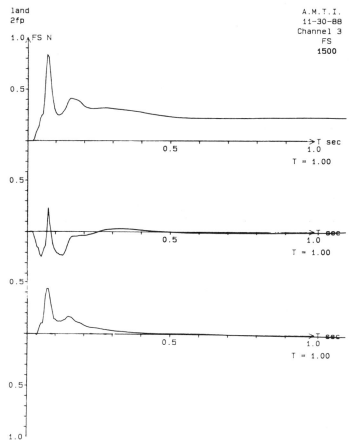

FIG. 10—*Force-time pattern of vertical forces* (top), *forward-backward forces* (center), *and lateral forces* (bottom) *during the initial 1 s of contact during landing. The first major vertical peak is impact.*

TABLE 1—*Vertical and horizontal maximum ground reaction forces during ten basic movement patterns, expressed as multiples of body weight.*

Movement Pattern	Vertical Force	BWD/FWD[a]	RT/LT[b]	Rise Time[c]
Walking	1⅓	⅙ to ¼	⅒	slow
Running	2½	⅙ to ⅓	⅓	fast
Veering	2	⅓ to ⅙	⅚	slow
Cutting	2	⅔	⅔	slow
Stopping	2⅔	. . .	. . .	fast
Dodging	2⅔	. . .	⅔	slow
Pivoting	2⅔	⅙	⅙	slow
Jumping	2	⅙ to ⅓	⅓	slow
Landing	3⅓	1	. . .	fast
Lunging	2⅔	¾	⅛	fast

[a] BWD/FWD = backward and forward shearing forces.
[b] RT/LT = right and left (medial/lateral) shearing forces.
[c] The relative rise time is given; fast equals approximately 20 ms.

The maximum shearing (horizontal) forces usually occurred coincident with the maximum vertical force at initial contact of the foot with the ground. In reference to the equation for calculating the maximum frictional force or the coefficient of friction, the greater the normal force, the greater will be the potential for application of shearing forces. One could speculate that the coefficient of friction changes in direct relationship to the required horizontal application of forces.

At other times, the maximum shearing force occurred during the descending slope of the vertical force. These latter cases usually occurred during the push-off phase. The forces were not as great and did not occur over as short a period of time as did the coincident forces.

Abrasiveness Characteristics

The speeds at which players are running, cutting, and veering can be used as the criterion for determination of abrasive limits. For example, normally, speeds will be 2.7 m/s or less during dodging, cutting, lunging, jumping, landing, and walking. During running and veering, these speeds may be as great as 8 m/s. If the person falls, slides, or otherwise has body contact with the playing field, the heat generated and the resistance to deformation of the playing surface can be experimentally determined. One method of doing so is to slide a material specimen over this surface at a predetermined speed and measure the change in the height of the specimen. ASTM Subcommittee F08.52 on Playing Surfaces and Facilities, a subcommittee of ASTM Committee F-8 on Sports Equipment and Facilities, is sponsoring work in this field.

Elasticity Characteristics

The energy return or elasticity of playing fields has not been investigated. The force platform used in this study was a rigid, virtually nondeformable supporting surface. The work of McMahon and Greene [7] can be utilized to determine the characteristics of playing fields. The movement pattern used in their field design was running on a track. Their work, however, can be used as a model for estimating the elastic requirements for the other nine basic movement patterns used in field sports. It is unlikely that the requirements would be much different for these movement patterns than those determined for running.

It appears that enough knowledge and data exist (or can be compiled) to design a safe, effective, and efficient, consistent and multidirectional, playing field. The characteristics of the field should be stated with respect to test data for absorption, deformation, abrasiveness, friction, uniformity, and durability. Are the playing fields of today so designed? Have the manufacturers adequately specified the characteristics of their playing fields in terms of player use? As "faster playing fields" are designed, the need to consider abrasiveness and friction becomes increasingly greater. The problem is a complex one, but biomechanics researchers, materials engineers, and design engineers working together can facilitate the improvement of sports playing fields. *The field can, indeed, be matched to the player!*

References

[*1*] Stewart, D., "Effects of Prolonged Running on Ground Reaction Force Patterns Wearing Shoes of Different Midsole Durometers," Ph.D. dissertation, University of Illinois at Urbana-Champaign, Urbana, IL, 1985.

[*2*] McPoil, T., "Effect of Orthotics on Forefoot Varsus and Valgus," Ph.D. dissertation, University of Illinois at Urbana-Champaign, Urbana, IL, 1987.

[*3*] Klinger, A. and Adrian, M. J., "Power Output as a Function of Fencing Technique," *International Series on Biomechanics: Biomechanics X,* B. Jonsson, Ed., Human Kinetics Publishers, Champaign, IL, 1985.

[*4*] Klinger, A., Adrian, M., and Dee, L., "Effect of Pre-Lunge Conditions on Performance of Elite Female Fencers," *Biomechanics in Sports II: Proceedings of ISBS,* J. Terauds and J. Barham, Eds., Academic Publishers, Del Mar, CA, 1985, p. 210.

[*5*] Adrian, M. J. and Cooper, J., Eds., *Biomechanics of Human Movement,* Benchmark Press, Indianapolis, IN, 1989.

[*6*] Coleman, J., Adrian, M., and Yamamoto, H. "The Teachings of Mechanics of Jump Landings," *Proceedings,* Second National Symposium on Teaching Kinesiology and Biomechanics in Sports, Colorado Springs, CO, R. Shapiro, Ed., Dekalb, 1984.

[*7*] McMahon, T. A. and Greene, P. R., "The Influence of Track Compliance on Running," *Journal of Biomechanics,* Vol. 12, 1979, pp. 893–904.

Francis A. Cosgrove[1]

Recommendations for the Operation and Safer Use of Playing Fields

REFERENCE: Cosgrove, F. A., **"Recommendations for the Operation and Safer Use of Playing Fields,"** *Natural and Artificial Playing Fields: Characteristics and Safety Features, ASTM STP 1073*, R. C. Schmidt, E. F. Hoerner, E. M. Milner, and C. A. Morehouse, Eds., American Society for Testing and Materials, Philadelphia, 1990, pp. 20–28.

ABSTRACT: Responsibility for the safe design, construction, management, and maintenance of athletic facilities clearly rests today with the owner/operators of these facilities.

Current litigation related to athletic injuries has shifted responsibility for the players "assumption of risk" to the operators "duty to provide a standard of care."

This paper addresses three important legal implications—i.e., "reasonable manner, duty to care, and the standard of reasonable care"—by providing a number of specific guidelines directed toward the safe design, management, and maintenance of softball/athletic facilities. It also identifies guidelines designed to inform the players of the types of risks they will be exposed to and the appropriate steps they can take to reduce the potential for injury while they are participating in the softball program.

This paper represents the view of an owner/operator of a major softball program.

KEY WORDS: playing fields, reasonable manner, standard of care, assumption of risk, maintenance, management, play responsibility, and contributory factors

This paper is presented from the viewpoint and experience of an owner/operator of a major municipal recreation and parks department, directly responsible for the operation of 53 softball and baseball facilities and 37 multiuse field sports facilities for soccer, football, lacrosse, field hockey, and so forth. These programs involve approximately 17 300 annual scheduled softball games, 8640 scheduled baseball games, and 3442 scheduled games for the other field sports. These scheduled games involve a total of 704 405 participation units[2] by adult men, women, and youth ranging in abilities from novice to highly skilled recreation and intercollegiate athletes [1].

For the purposes of this paper, the primary focus will be on the operations aspect of the softball program. Softball play nationwide is an enormous participation sport, involving some 40-million players and still growing [2]. Along with this incredible growth has emerged the proliferation of injuries; for example, softball, combined with baseball play, has been reported to lead all other team and individual sports in the number of injuries treated at emergency departments [2]. Add to the injuries reported to emergency rooms those not reported, but perhaps no less serious, and it becomes quite apparent that the reduction of softball-related injuries must be given significant attention by the providers of softball/baseball programs nationwide.

---

[1] Deputy Commissioner, Nassau County Department of Recreation and Parks, East Meadow, NY 11554.
[2] Participation units = number of participants × hours played.

The major contributory factors to softball related injuries, in the opinion of the author, can be attributed to:

1. the effect of the enormous proliferation in the numbers of softball players, resulting in greater exposure to injury by more players;
2. the significant differences in skill and fitness levels of the recreation softball player and players of intermediate skill levels;
3. lack of knowledge about the fundamentals of playing the game of softball by many recreation players;
4. improper design and layout of softball facilities;
5. poor seasonal and daily routine maintenance;
6. use of fixed, rigid bases;
7. inappropriate administration of softball programs including supervision, officiating, team/league organization, and scheduling; and
8. misguided priorities of softball program organizers related to the attention and resources given to the premier players as contrasted with the novices and those in between.

Identifying Softball-Related Injuries

As a consequence of its unprecedented growth, softball has achieved a unique position in that softball injuries, coupled with baseball injuries, lead all other team and individual sports in the number of injuries treated at emergency departments. Recent studies conducted in San Francisco, Michigan, Hawaii, New Jersey, and Long Island represent leading-edge work being carried on to determine the scale and nature of softball injuries. From these data have evolved valuable insight into the reasons for these injuries, thus suggesting ways in which owner/operators, planners, equipment manufacturers, and players can develop a variety of ways to reduce the potential for injury.

Responsibility

Anyone familiar with contemporary litigation knows that when an injury occurs, all associated parties are held responsible in part or whole for negligence until proven otherwise. Acknowledging this legal fact of life, it becomes essential to clearly define the roles and responsibilities of the "key players" when providing softball facilities and programs. These "key players" are the following:

(a) the architects and engineers who design and oversee the development of the facilities;
(b) the contractors who construct the facilities;
(c) the equipment manufacturers who provide the balls, bats, helmets, pads, bleachers, benches, and other equipment;
(d) the owner/operators who plan, administer, operate, and maintain softball facilities and programs;
(e) the managers and coaches who guide the team and players;
(f) the sponsors who support the events, programs, and teams;
(g) the officials who supervise and control the games;
(h) the players, men, women, youth, and seniors who participate within a wide range of skill levels, conditioning, and knowledge ranging from inadequate to superior; and
(i) the spectators who support individual players and teams.

As a "key player" in two specific areas (an owner/operator and active player), the author, for the purpose of this paper, will focus on the responsibility of the owner/operator to provide for a well-managed and safely maintained softball program. It is also important to note that owner/operators must interface regularly with all the other "key players" in order to provide for the best possible softball program. There must exist a systems approach to the management and operations of the modern softball program.

Ball Field Specifications

Owner/operators of contemporary softball programs are responsible for knowing the current state of the art for the design and layout of safe, attractive softball facilities and, where necessary, to redesign, refurbish, or abandon those facilities that do not measure up.

Because of the rapid changes in the makeup of players and the nature of the game of softball, many softball fields are now inadequate relative to their layouts and playing areas. For example, the recommended distance for outfields for men's fast-pitch softball is 68 to 76 m (225 to 250 ft). Fast-pitch softball for many areas of the country is no longer the game of choice and has been replaced with the very popular slow-pitch game. Slow-pitch outfield distances for men now require outfield depths of 83 to 91 m (275 to 300 ft) [3]. However, since many earlier fields were built around the old fast-pitch standards, and are now being used for slow-pitch, we find conditions exist that may preclude safe play by men in outfields beyond 76 m (250 ft).

Many fields today do not have the appropriate fencing to protect both the players and spectators. A review of many softball fields show that fence heights along the sidelines and outfields will range from no fencing to 91, 182, or 243 cm (3, 6, or 8 ft) or even higher. Current Amateur Softball Association (ASA) guidelines recommend that sidelines and outfield fencing should be a minimum of 2.43 m (8 ft) [4], the simple reason being that 91 to 121-cm (3 to 4-ft) fencing is too low and will not protect a player from falling over the fence nor will it protect the spectator in the seating area. Fencing that is 1.8 m (6 ft) high is still low and presents a hazard to the average 1.8 m (6-ft) player whose head could easily come in contact with the metal cross-piece. The 2.4 m (8-ft) fence appears to eliminate the potential hazards to both players and spectators that are inherent in the lower fence heights [5].

These are two simple examples of how improper design and layout will effect the safety of players and spectators, and it is therefore incumbent upon the owner/operators to be aware of these changes and to respond by upgrading their facilities to meet the new standards.

The new guidelines are readily available and widely distributed. Of particular note is the Softball Field Complex Specification Guide, published by the Amateur Softball Association of America. In the opinion of the author, this publication provides the state-of-the-art recommendations for softball facilities, and it should be in the hands of every owner/operator of softball programs.

Since there does exist reliable and reputable standards to guide owner/operators, it is incumbent upon the owner/operators to seek them out and to reasonably respond in order to provide safe and attractive softball facilities. Failure to keep pace with a change in standards, ultimately places the owner/operators in a "no-win" situation in the event of accidents and litigations.

Ball Field Maintenance

"Softball/baseball facilities when used for competitive play require a great deal of attention and care" [6]. This simple but very important statement was taken from the book, *Park and Recreation Maintenance Management*, printed in 1977.

Proper ball field maintenance, in the opinion of the author, is one of the major contributory factors in the prevention of softball related accidents in the outfield and infields of softball/baseball facilities.

Owner/operators of softball facilities may schedule as many as 30 games a week on a single field equipped with lights. The most intense use comes on Saturdays, Sundays, or holidays when a softball field will be scheduled from 8 a.m. until midnight, usually without a break. In Nassau County, New York, over 17 000 softball games were conducted during the 1988 season (October 1 to April 15).

With this intense use, the need for a comprehensive seasonal, weekly, and daily maintenance program is mandatory, if the softball field is to be kept safe and attractive. Owner/operators have a duty to provide a reasonably hazard-free playing environment that incorporates accepted maintenance practices designed to reduce the potential for injury to players and spectators.

In order to provide a reasonably well-maintained softball facility, the following elements must be in evidence.

1. The maintenance plan must define in writing the tasks to be carried out on a daily, weekly, and seasonal basis.
2. The maintenance plan must be effectively implemented by knowledgeable and sensitive ground crews.
3. Quality control of the maintenance program must be assured by the owner/operators of the softball facilities.
4. The maintenance plan must be effectively communicated to the managers, coaches, officials, and players who use the facilities. This is suggested because the best feedback comes from those who use the facility, and if there is a deviation from the maintenance plan, they should be encouraged to bring this information to the attention of the appropriate personnel.
5. The actual work performed whether daily, weekly, or seasonally must be documented in writing, reflecting the task elements defined in the maintenance plan. Written documentation is particularly important when faced with litigation. Often cases are lost on behalf of the owner/operators because they could not "document" their maintenance plans.

For the purposes of this paper, the author will identify those maintenance procedures that are basic to a daily, weekly, and seasonal maintenance plan designed with safety first in mind. The technical maintenance procedures as they relate to turf maintenance, renovations, and rehabilitation are not covered in this paper. However, the current state of the art regarding natural sports turf maintenance is quite advanced and readily available to owner/operators.

In the opinion of the author, the following procedures are required in order to provide a safe softball/baseball environment.

Daily Maintenance—In Season

1. Check and correct outfield, infield, players bench areas, and bleacher areas for glass, cans, litter, rocks, roots, and any other debris.
2. Check and correct outfields, infields, players bench (dugouts), and sidelines for holes, depressions, equipment, ruts, and so forth.
3. Check and correct outfields, sidelines, and backstop fences for protruding points, damaged or disconnected fencing fabric, and posts. Do not use snow fencing for outfield or sideline fencing.

4. Check and correct player and bleacher seating for broken seats, steps, ramps, support structures, and so forth.
5. Check and correct home plate and pitcher's rubber for raised or torn edges, protruding anchors, or spikes.
6. Check and correct lighting fixtures that are out, missing, or misdirected for lighted ball fields.
7. Check and correct bleacher seating for placement behind backstop or appropriate sideline fencing.
8. Fill in all holes and depressions around home plate, pitcher's mound, and first, second, and third bases. To properly fill holes and depressions:
    (*a*) sweep out the hole or depression to remove loose fill,
    (*b*) dampen the hole or depressed area, and
    (*c*) rake back displaced clay mixture and dampen again. Add additional clay mixture if needed to bring the hole or depression to grade. Dampen, rake out, and tamp down the area. This will provide a uniform and cohesive surface in the areas that get most of the heavy activity.
9. Periodic checks of the batter's boxes, pitcher's mound, and the base areas should take place during extended periods of play, and any holes or depressions should be corrected as required. On lighted fields used over a period of 12+ h, there should be a maintenance period integrated into the playing schedules.
10. During inclement weather, if the playing field cannot be readied for safe play, it should not be opened. If standing water or mud areas around home plate and the bases create a situation involving slick or poor footing, play should not be permitted until these conditions are corrected.
11. Irrigation heads must be checked for breakage, settling, or elevations. Also, automatic timers must be checked *not* to come on immediately prior to or during games.
12. Infields and baselines should be dragged and dampened.

Weekly Maintenance

The following are recommended on a weekly basis:

1. Mow infield and outfield turf area grass as needed. Keep grass lengths 1 to 1½ in. during the season and 2 to 3 in. off season.
2. Edge baselines to keep proper widths of skinned base paths.
3. Add additional clay mixture to areas that are starting to form low spots; keep infields uniformly graded.
4. Monitor and remove the lip-building where the outfield turf line meets the infield and the base paths.
5. Restore outfield foul lines as needed.

Seasonal Maintenance

Seasonal maintenance in order to be effective must be carried out in cooperation with the changing climatic seasons. All too often the scheduling of ball games will take priority, precluding the critical time needed to do the needed postseason and preseason maintenance.

Owner/operators must resist the year-round scheduling syndrome and allow for the appropriate preseason and postseason maintenance program.

An essential element of a seasonal maintenance program includes ball field renovation, defined as field improvement beyond routine but short of completely rebuilding the field. The best time for renovations is in the fall of the year [7].

The key elements in an effective renovation plan include the following:

1. Recrowning or reshaping the infield to enhance drainage.
2. Removal of clay mixture lip buildup usually at the point where the turf meets the infield and along baselines where turf infields are used.
3. Aeration of all turf areas to enhance surface drainage and reduce compaction.
4. Overseeding of bare and worn turf areas.
5. Resodding of badly worn or damaged areas.
6. Fill and level warning track areas.
7. Drag and level infield and base paths.
8. Fertilize to the recognized standards.
9. Check and correct bleachers, lights, and other support facilities. Winterize and ready for new season.

Maintenance, like scheduling, is absolutely essential to the success of any softball program. Owner/operators must recognize its importance to injury prevention, as well as the aesthetics, and provide the necessary resources (equipment, materials, and manpower), along with the use of recognized ball field maintenance procedures in order to reasonably provide for a safe and aesthetic playing environment. Current basic maintenance practices must be in evidence once the owner/operators' plans and schedules his softball/baseball programs. They have a "duty to provide reasonable care" in the maintenance and operations of their facilities.

Program Operations

The owner/operators' responsibility does not end with his or her maintenance of the facility. Once a commitment is made to provide for programming, other key operational factors must be implemented. Of particular importance are the following:

1. The appropriate and safe organization of softball leagues, tournaments, and special events. Players' skill levels, experience, age, etc., must be taken into account when organizing leagues. Serious mismatches not only diminishes the fun of playing softball, but significantly exposes all the players to injury.
2. Match the teams with the playing field dimensions. As indicated earlier, many older playing fields do not have sufficient outfield playing areas to accommodate the long ball hitters in slow-pitch softball. Consequently, we see other areas, i.e., playgrounds, picnic areas, parking lots, tennis courts, jogging trails, etc., literally being "bombarded by softballs." Conditions such as these expose both the softball player and the unsuspecting user of the other facilities to serious injuries. Failure to recognize and correct these hazards will expose the owner/operators to serious liability.
3. Duty to inform softball players of the "inherent risks" in playing softball and suggesting ways in which the players can take responsibility for reducing exposure to injury to themselves, their competitors, and spectators. This becomes increasingly important as inexperienced and poorly skilled players decide to play softball.

The owner/operators should provide, in writing, clearly set forth policies and procedures related to league and tournament play. However, equally important are written guidelines to the players on how to play safely. Some specific written recommendations to players include the following:

- Establish and sustain a reasonable level of cardiovascular and muscular fitness appropriate for softball play.
- Develop the levels of knowledge and skills necessary to play softball properly. Do not overestimate abilities to *play softball* at the level consistent with the players knowledge and skills.
- Avoid use of the head-first slide under any playing condition. This is a very dangerous slide, in spite of its general popularity.
- Develop proper foot first sliding skills. This will help to avoid injuries to ankles, legs, and the other ball players.
- Avoid the consumption of alcoholic beverages, and other drug substances prior to and during games.
- Use the recognized standard footwear when playing.[3]
- Use the recognized standards for protective masks, protectors,[3] etc., designated for the type of softball being played, e.g., fast-pitch, modified, slow-pitch, and youth.
- Observe your playing area for potential hazards, i.e., holes, debris, sprinkler heads, bleachers, benches, etc.
- Become familiar with the ground rules and the "out-of-bounds" areas. Be alert to potential hazards in these areas, e.g., trees, bleachers, pathways, parking lots, light poles, etc.
- Cooperate fully with the umpires and operating officials when games are called or postponed due to inclement weather.
- Cooperate fully when games are postponed or delayed due to electrical storms in the area.
- Refrain from the use of abusive language and unsportsmanlike conduct toward players and officials.

The foregoing are examples of the type of written guidelines necessary for the owner/operators to prudently inform their players on how to play softball safely.

4. Provide adequate supervision of facilities and programs. Scheduled play unsupervised by owner/operators of softball programs is unacceptable.
5. Provide appropriate first aid, along with an effective accident/incident reporting format.
6. Coordinate and standardize operating policies, rules, and regulations in cooperation with the umpires who cover the games at your facilities. Umpires must have a clear set of guidelines to work from as it relates to ground rules, safety measures, player behavior, etc. If not, then each umpire will interpret the rules as he or she sees fit.
7. Provide current training opportunities for supervisory and maintenance personnel on changing operating standards applicable to facilities maintenance, safety, supervision, etc.
8. Effectively communicate to all concerned the current written policies, procedures, guidelines, etc.
9. Provide resources equitably for all players. Unfortunately, many owner/operators are misguided when it comes to providing the best maintenance, fields, and scheduling for the "premier players" at the expense of their less accomplished players. All players must have the opportunity to play on safe, well-maintained and manicured facilities. A well-

---

[3] Refer to current Amateur Softball Association rules and regulations.

managed softball program will provide quality facilities and scheduling for all their players regardless of player abilities.

Conclusions

Perhaps the best way to summarize the salient points of this paper is to view the role and responsibility of owner/operators within the context of three very important legal implications.

1. The duty to carry out ones' responsibilities in a "reasonable manner."
2. The "duty to care" in providing facilities programs and services.
3. The duty to provide the "standard of care."

Reasonable Manner

When providing softball facilities and programs, owner/operators have a legal obligation to perform their duties in a reasonable manner. Being reasonable can be described as rational, amenable to good sense, and not exceeding the bounds of common sense [8].

When deciding what is reasonable, the owner/operators must determine what they can provide in light of the resources they must work with. A reasonable softball owner/operator is expected to be able to identify and take the appropriate measures to avoid foreseeable risks that might affect his or her players, spectators, officials, and employees [8].

Duty to Care

The law imposes upon owner/operators the obligation to take the required care to prevent injury to their players, spectators, officials, and staff. They must see to it that persons playing in their programs are reasonably safe.

Standard of Care

The standard of care or state of the art for planning, conducting, and maintaining softball facilities and programs has been addressed in part in this paper. Owner/operators have an obligation to see to it that their programs meet reasonable, recognized standards of care. Suggested elements in a standard of care program should include:

(a) written procedures for accidents/emergencies;
(b) adequate supervision;
(c) written safety rules, regulations, and guidelines;
(d) procedures for regular inspections of facilities;
(e) procedures for daily, weekly, and seasonal maintenance;
(f) appropriate planning criteria that takes into account skill levels, ages, sex, and conditioning of ball players;
(g) an updated file on the current rules, regulations, guidelines, etc., prepared and distributed by recognized softball organizations; and
(h) ongoing education and training of staff in a variety of topical areas, i.e., facility design, maintenance, scheduling, first aid, supervision, and security.

Owner/operators who diligently and professionally attempt to carry out their programs and services suggested by these legal implications can be said to be acting as reasonable men and women in providing for the safe and attractive participation of their players, spectators, officials, and staff.

References

[1] Dressler, E., "Levels of Athletic Participation," unpublished report, Nassau County Department of Recreation and Parks, East Meadow, NY, 1988.

[2] Loosli, A., Requa, R., Ross, W., and Garick, J., "Injuries in Slo-Pitch Softball," *The Physician and Sports Medicine*, Vol. 16, No. 7, July 1988, pp. 110–118.

[3] Porter D. and Hauke, E., *Softball Field and Complex Specifications Guide*, 4th ed., Amateur Softball Association, Oklahoma, 1988, p. 10.

[4] Porter, D. and Hauke, E., *Softball Field and Complex Specifications Guide*, 4th ed., Amateur Softball Association, Oklahoma, 1988, p. 19.

[5] Porter, D. and Hauke, E., *Softball Field and Complex Specifications Guide*, 4th ed., Amateur Softball Association, Oklahoma, 1988, p. 19.

[6] Sternlaff, R. and Warren R., *Park and Recreation Maintenance Management,* Holbrook Press, Boston, 1977, pp. 282–283.

[7] Taylor, D., Blake, G., and White, D., *Athletic Field Construction and Maintenance*, Minnesota Extension Service, University of Minnesota, St. Paul, MN, 1987, pp. 8–10.

[8] McPhail, R., *Recreation and Community Services Risk Management Manual*, Public Risk and Insurance Management Association, Washington, DC, 1988, pp. 5–7.

P. M. Canaway,[1] M. J. Bell,[1] G. Holmes,[1] and S. W. Baker[1]

Standards for the Playing Quality of Natural Turf for Association Football

REFERENCE: Canaway, P. M., Bell, M. J., Holmes, G., and Baker, S. W., **"Standards for the Playing Quality of Natural Turf for Association Football,"** *Natural and Artificial Playing Fields: Characteristics and Safety Features, ASTM STP 1073,* R. C. Schmidt, E. F. Hoerner, E. M. Milner, and C. A. Morehouse, Eds., American Society for Testing and Materials, Philadelphia, 1990, pp. 29–47.

ABSTRACT: For athletic fields used for soccer (association football), important components of playing quality include: ball rebound resilience, rolling resistance, traction (i.e., grip), and hardness. Other criteria related to, but not direct measures of, playing quality include surface evenness, grass cover, and water infiltration rate.

Standards of playing quality were developed on the basis of comparisons between players' perceptions of surfaces and the results of objective tests taken on the fields within 2 h of matches. Questionnaires were collected from 444 football players at 20 different fields. The fields were tested in the same locations within each field at six 5 by 5-m plots.

The results were used to formulate standards in the form of "preferred" and "acceptable" limits for each component of playing quality. The apparatus, test methods, and proposed standards for association football fields are described.

KEY WORDS: playing fields, standards, playing quality, ball rebound resilience, ball rolling resistance, traction, hardness, player evaluation

In the past, research on athletic fields was based largely on principles drawn from agronomy and ecology. These principles held good for many purposes but largely ignored the needs of the player, with certain notable exceptions. Since the purpose of athletic fields and other sports turf areas is to sustain play, the attributes that make it a good surface for sport are of primary importance and may be collectively termed "playing quality." The components of playing quality for association football (soccer) can be divided into two sets of characteristics: ball/surface properties and player/surface properties. Ball/surface properties include ball rebound resilience and ball roll. Player/surface properties include traction and friction ("grip") and hardness (or, more strictly, stiffness and resilience). In addition, there is a group of characteristics which, while not being measures of playing quality, influence it directly. These include the grass cover and species composition, surface evenness, and water infiltration rate.

Prior to 1982, the only component of playing quality measured routinely was traction, consequent on the development of suitable apparatus [1,2]. This was originally termed "shear strength" from its original German usage as "Scherfestigkeit" [3]. In the early 1980s we routinely began measuring ball rebound resilience in turfgrass trials [4], to be followed by hardness in 1984 [5]. In parallel with these developments, there was much interest in the playing quality of synthetic surfaces for sport, leading to the production of draft standards and specifications [6–9]. There were, however, no equivalent standards for natural turf, and

---

[1] The Sports Turf Research Institute, Bingley, West Yorkshire, England BD16 1AU.

the objective of the work described in this paper was to develop such standards for association football (soccer) fields. The work was part of a larger study, financed by the Sports Council for England and Wales, to develop apparatus and test methods for a number of sports, including football, field hockey, tennis, and lawn bowls, and to produce standards for soccer and bowls. In this paper, the apparatus and test methods used and the proposed standards for ball rebound resilience, ball roll, traction, hardness, and surface evenness on athletic fields for soccer are described.

Materials and Methods

Playing Quality Tests

The important characteristics of the playing quality test equipment used were that they should reproduce as accurately as possible the aspects of playing quality they were designed to represent, that they should be robust and operate in "all weathers," and that their design should be kept as simple and cheap as possible. Thus, some standard pieces of apparatus, particularly the electronic tests of severity of impact [7], surface deflection [10], and football deceleration [11] were not considered because of the operational difficulties in their use outdoors.

Wear on soccer fields follows a regular diamond-shaped pattern, with wear "radiating" out from the goal areas at each end and becoming lightest on the field edges or "wings." Therefore, the six test areas shown in Fig. 1 were chosen so as to sample areas of high (goal mouths), intermediate (center circle), and low (wings) levels of wear. The playing quality tests described in Table 1 were undertaken in each test area on each field.

Measurements of two other associated factors that affect playing quality were also made. The percentage of green vegetation on the surface (ground cover) was measured using a reflectance ratio meter, which was similar in principle to that used in weed control studies [12]. The moisture content of the root zone was measured as a percentage of the soil dry weight of 35-mm-diameter cores taken from a depth of 0 to 50 mm in each test area. The playing quality tests were made on 49 football fields of 5 different construction types: sand carpet ($n = 6$), sand/soil ameliorated ($n = 8$), slit drained ($n = 7$), pipe drained ($n = 15$), and fields sited on native soil with no inbuilt drainage system ($n = 13$). Each field was visited

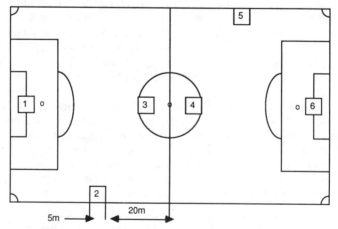

FIG. 1—*Location of the six test areas on soccer fields.*

TABLE 1—*Playing performance tests and test procedures.*

Test	Description
Football rebound resilience	A Mitre "Delta 1000" football inflated to 0.7 bar was dropped from a height of 3m and its rebound height measured as a percentage of the release height [4]. Six readings were taken within each test area.
Surface hardness	A cylindrical hammer, with a mass of 0.5kg and a diameter of 50mm was dropped down a guide tube from a height of 300mm [13]. An accelerometer attached to the hammer gave the peak deceleration in gravities (g) caused by impact with the surface. This test was undertaken ten times in each test area.
Traction	Six 15mm long and 12.5mm diameter football studs were spaced at 60° intervals at a radius of 46mm on a 150mm diameter steel disc. The disc (weighted with a mass of 45.36kg) was dropped from 50mm height so that the studs penetrated the surface. The torque required for the studs to tear the surface layer was then measured in Nm using a torque wrench [14]. Six readings were taken within each test area.
Distance rolled by a football	A Mitre "Delta 1000" football inflated to 0.7 bar was released from a height of 1m down a ramp inclined at 45° and the distance rolled by the football from the end of the ramp was measured [7]. Three observations were made in two opposing directions in each test area.
Surface evenness	Ten graduated rods set 200mm apart and free to move vertically in a frame were displaced by surface undulations. Three sets of ten measurements were taken in each test area to an accuracy of ±1mm. The evenness values are given as the average sample standard deviation of 3 x 10 measurements.

between one and five times during the two-year period of the study, and a total of 675 plots measuring 5 by 5 m was tested.

Player Questionnaires

The player questionnaire used in this study (see Appendix) was a simplified version of the one used during the Winterbottom study of artificial turf for association football [9]. The questionnaire asked for players' opinions concerning those characteristics of the playing surface that the mechanical and electronic tests sought to represent. Question 9 (see Appendix) was also included to obtain the players' opinions on the variability in playing quality within different areas of the field. Where tests of playing quality were made in conjunction with a

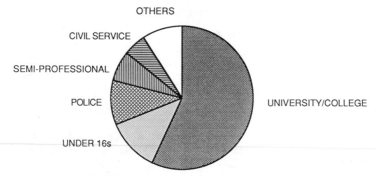

FIG. 2—*Composition of the questionnaire survey.*

player questionnaire survey, it was ensured that the tests were made within 2 h either before or after a game. A total of 444 completed questionnaires was collected from a wide range of football players. Figure 2 shows that the majority of the responses came from university/ college teams (mostly from the first and second teams) with other significant contributions being made by "under 16" and police teams.

The 444 records comprising the main data set consisted of the coded responses for each questionnaire with the average value for each of the playing quality tests for the goalmouth and center circle positions on which the respondent played. In the special case of respondents who were goalkeepers, the responses were compared with the playing quality attributes of the goalmouth plots alone. It is important to note that the analyses of the players' perceptions of the playing quality described in the results section compare the questionnaire results with the data from the test plots lying within the main playing area of the football field (that is, Positions 1, 3, 4, and 6 in Fig. 1). The reason for excluding the test plots on the wings (Positions 2 and 5 in Fig. 1) is that they receive relatively little wear and, as will be shown later, they are often quite different in their playing characteristics when compared with the central area of the field.

Results

Table 2 gives the mean, the minimum, and the maximum values, and the range of each playing quality test recorded during the study. The number of measurements for each test is also shown. The range of recorded values for all the tests was large, with the ground cover measurements reaching the maximum possible range for the test (that is, 0 to 100%). The data give some impression of the wide range of playing quality conditions provided by nat-

TABLE 2—*Summary of the test values.*

Test	Number of Test Areas	Mean	SEM[a]	Minimum	Maximum	Range
Rebound resilence, %	671	32.5	0.5	0.0	58.8	58.8
Clegg impact hardness, g	671	42.6	1.2	0.0	198.0	198.0
Traction, N·m	654	29.2	0.3	9.0	51.0	42.0
Distance rolled, m	208	6.88	0.11	3.65	12.03	8.38
Surface evenness, mm	636	5.57	0.08	1.89	14.16	12.27
Ground cover, %	651	55.4	1.3	0.0	100.0	100.0

[a] SEM = standard error of the mean.

ural turf football fields in Britain. Zero values of ball rebound and hardness were associated with severely "puddled" muddy conditions. However, deceleration could not have actually been zero but was simply not registered on the instrument which could not register <1 g.

Playing Quality Variations Within Natural Turf Fields

Table 3 shows the mean values of the tests for the three field areas: goalmouth (Positions 1 and 6 in Fig. 1), field edges or wings (Positions 2 and 5), and center circle (Positions 3 and 4). All the tests except surface evenness had similar mean values for the goalmouth and center circle areas. Some of the measures for the goalmouth and center circle areas showed considerable differences from the wings. For instance, average rebound resilience and Clegg impact values were lower on the wings (an indication of generally softer surfaces caused by less wear and compaction). Traction values and rolling distances were usually lower on the wings. This is thought to be the result of the generally higher grass cover on the wings (see below).

Table 3 also gives the players' responses to the questions regarding the quality of the goalmouths, wings, and central area of the field (see the Appendix). The percentage replies for the goalmouth and central areas were similar, but there were more "good" and "satisfactory" replies for the quality of the wings. These responses probably reflect the generally better grass cover on the wings, which may give players the impression of a better quality surface.

Statistical Analysis of the Questionnaire Survey

For the purposes of comparing the data from the questionnaires with the playing quality test results, each test was arbitrarily categorized into classes (for example, for the traction test: 10 to 19.9 N·m, 20 to 29.9 N·m, etc.) and the number of responses to each question given in the form of cells. The columns shown in the following figures are the categories for the test results, and the rows record the different responses to each question. The cells are shaded to indicate the proportion of responses within each cell expressed as a percentage of each column, e.g., what proportion of the players that played on a surface with a football rebound resilience between 40 to 49.9% thought that ball bounce was "high" or "low." The chi-square test was used to compare the distribution of responses within the cells. The null hypothesis was that there were no differences in the proportions of responses within each

TABLE 3—Variation of playing quality within pitches and players' perceptions of the quality of the different pitch areas.

	Mean Playing Quality Test Value in Each Pitch Area ($\pm$ SEM)[a]		
Test	Goalmouths	Wings	Center Circle
Rebound resilience, %	34.5 $\pm$ 0.9	29.1 $\pm$ 0.7	33.9 $\pm$ 0.9
Clegg impact hardness, g	51.7 $\pm$ 2.3	29.5 $\pm$ 1.6	46.7 $\pm$ 1.9
Traction, N·m	27.1 $\pm$ 0.5	33.0 $\pm$ 0.5	27.4 $\pm$ 0.5
Distance rolled, m	7.17 $\pm$ 0.2	6.02 $\pm$ 0.2	7.45 $\pm$ 0.2
Surface evenness, mm	5.83 $\pm$ 0.2	5.59 $\pm$ 0.1	5.28 $\pm$ 0.1
Ground cover, %	37.0 $\pm$ 2.0	85.3 $\pm$ 0.9	43.6 $\pm$ 2.0
Good responses, %	24	49	25
Satisfactory responses, %	44	42	45
Poor responses, %	32	9	30

[a] SEM = standard error of the mean.

category. For instance, a surface with a given level of traction should give equal numbers of players stating that the grip underfoot was good, poor, or satisfactory. A significance level of 1% ($P \leq 0.01$) was chosen for all the chi-square tests. The use of chi squared for this purpose is not entirely satisfactory since the experimenter is looking for a relationship between the observed player responses and the values of the playing quality tests. Thus the pattern of responses in relation to the results of the objective tests must be taken into account as well as the occurrence of a significant chi-squared value. A further problem is that the stronger the relationship between the player responses and the objective tests, the greater the likelihood of empty cells being found which inflate the chi-squared values. It should also be noted that the chi-squared value tends to increase with the number of cells; therefore, in the interpretation of the results, where fewer categories are present, the chi-squared value tends to be smaller even though the relationship between the player responses and the results of the objective tests in question may subjectively appear good. These problems arise from questionnaire data where the scope for statistical analysis is rather limited.

Football Rebound Resilience—The football players were asked to rate the degree of ball bounce on the field (see the Appendix), and a total of 369 responses to this question was received. Five categories of rebound resilience were selected, and Fig. 3 shows the number of replies received within each category. The responses to the question on ball bounce were not equally distributed (chi square = 69.6, $P < 0.001$), with 6 of the total of 25 cells having no respondents. The responses to the question on ball bounce show that 66% of the players sampled stated that the ball bounce was satisfactory with 1% stating that ball bounce was "unacceptably high" and 2% stating that ball bounce was "unacceptably low." The highest level of satisfaction was for rebound resilience values of between 20 and 29.9%, although the range 20 to 50% appeared to be acceptable to most players.

Player/Surface Impacts—The players were asked to comment on two forms of player/surface impact: (*a*) falling/diving on to the surface and (*b*) running on the surface (see Appendix).

(*a*) *Falling/diving*—A total of 416 respondents answered the question on the hardness of the field for falling or diving on to. Five arbitrary categories of Clegg impact hardness were selected, and Fig. 4 gives the distribution of responses by category. The player responses were not evenly distributed within the cells (chi square = 121.4, $P < 0.001$) but appeared to be conditioned by changes in the stiffness of the surface as measured using the Clegg impact soil tester. Of the 20 cells, 3 were empty and 2 others (20 to 39.9 g "unacceptably hard" and 80 to 99.9 g "soft") had 1 respondent each where individuals gave opposing opinions of the surface to those given by other respondents and to the measured hardness.

Overall, 49% of the 416 players stated that the surfaces tested were satisfactory to fall or dive on to, with 34% expressing the opinion that the surfaces were soft. Two percent of the sample stated that a playing surface was unacceptably hard to fall on to.

The Clegg impact hardness category giving the highest proportion of satisfactory responses was 60 to 79.9 g with 65% of the 80 responses in this subsample. The categories 20 to 39.9 g and 40 to 59.9 g both contained 51% satisfactory responses. Thus the range 20 to 80 g appeared to be ideal for falling or diving on to.

(*b*) *Running*—A total of 425 responses was received to the question relating to the hardness of the fields for running on (see Appendix), and an unequal distribution was also found in the player responses when categorized by Clegg impact test (chi square =

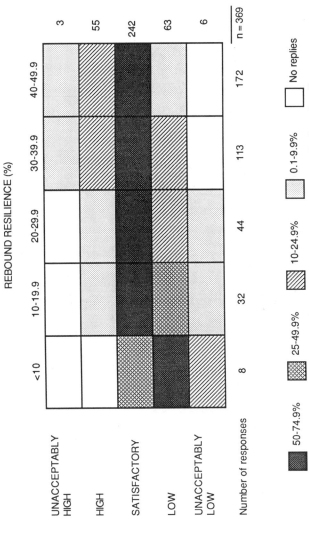

FIG. 3—*Players' perceptions of ball bounce in relation to measured rebound resilience.*

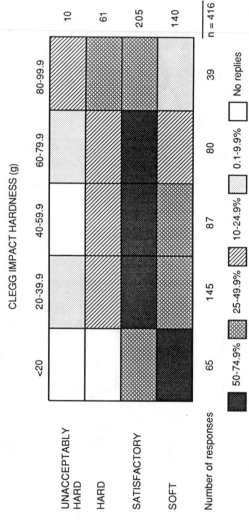

FIG. 4—*Players' perceptions of surface hardness for falling/diving on to in relation to Clegg impact hardness.*

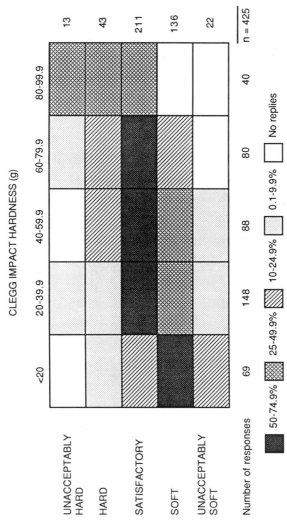

FIG. 5—*Players' perceptions of surface hardness for running on in relation to Clegg impact hardness.*

166.7, $P < 0.001$). Figure 5 shows that five of the cells were empty. Two cells had one respondent.

The highest proportion of satisfactory responses was found in the category 60 to 79.9 g with 69% of the subsample of 80 players. In the category 20 to 39.9 g, 51% said that the playing surfaces were satisfactory to run on; in the 40 to 59.9 g category, 53% of responses were satisfactory. The preferred limits of surface hardness for running on a surface therefore appeared to be 20 to 80 g.

Traction—A total of 379 players answered the question relating to the amount of grip they obtained from the surface. Figure 6 shows that there was a good relationship between the values for the test of traction and the player responses. The responses were not equally distributed within the cells (chi square = 95.7, $P < 0.001$). Of the 379 players, only 25% stated that the traction was good, most players (59%) stated that the grip underfoot was satisfactory, with the remaining 16% stating that traction was poor. The highest proportion of satisfactory responses (73%) was found in the 20 to 29.9 N·m category, and the highest proportion of good responses (71%) was in the 40 to 49.9 N·m category of traction.

Distance Rolled—Figure 7 shows that no real pattern emerged between the players' opinions of the speed of ball roll and the test of distance rolled, although the distribution of responses within the categories was not equal (chi square = 42.0, $P < 0.001$). Of the 347 responses given to the question on the speed of ball roll, 196 (56%) said that the speed of ball roll was satisfactory, and 81 (23%) said that it was "fast." The highest proportion of satisfactory responses was 64% in the distance rolled categories 6 to 6.99 m and 7 to 7.99 m.

A possible explanation for the fact that there was a poor relationship between the players' responses and the ball roll test results is that on some wet surfaces when ball roll is slow, the ball may skid across the surface when being passed along the ground. This can give the misleading impression to players that ball roll is fast.

There are other differences between a ball passed along the ground by a player and the test of rolling resistance. A pass along the ground by a player may have little spin imparted by the player, whereas the rolling resistance test almost certainly imparted excessive topspin to the football as it rolled down the ramp. Also, the initial velocity of a football in a pass is likely to be higher than that given by the distance rolled test, the latter being about 3 m·s^{-1}. It is likely that the ball also has little opportunity to roll during the early stages of a pass,

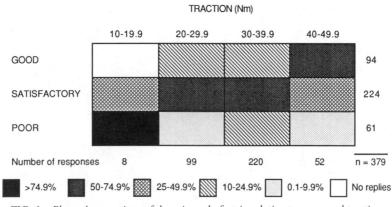

FIG. 6—*Players' perceptions of the grip underfoot in relation to measured traction.*

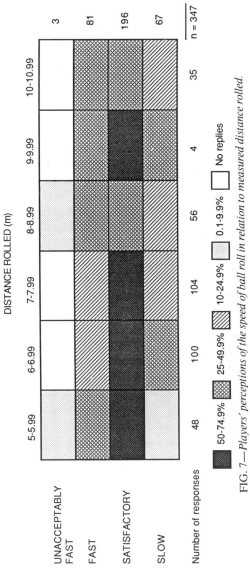

FIG. 7—Players' perceptions of the speed of ball roll in relation to measured distance rolled.

much of its progress will be in low, shallow-angle bounces, the ball gradually picking up topspin.

Surface Evenness—A total of 383 responses was given to the question of the evenness of the surface, and a good relationship was found (Fig. 8) between the players' perceptions of surface evenness and the measurements made using the profile gage with an unequal distribution in the responses (chi square = 36.8, $P < 0.001$).

Over the range of surface evenness values, most of the players (74%) stated that the surface evenness was satisfactory. In the category 2 to 3.99 mm ($n = 59$), 98% of the players stated that the surfaces were satisfactory. Conversely, in the evenness category 10 to 11.99 mm ($n = 8$), 88% of the players said that the surfaces were "unacceptably bumpy." There were 70 and 78% satisfactory responses in the 4 to 5.99-mm and 6 to 7.99-mm categories, respectively. Only two replies were received for the category 8 to 9.99 mm (one unacceptably bumpy and one satisfactory), so these responses must be treated with caution.

Spatial Variation in Field Quality—Reference has already been made to the possibility of players' assessments of the overall quality of different areas of the field being influenced by the amount of grass cover present. All measurements of ground cover on the wings were in excess of 60%, and these figures are reflected in the responses to the question regarding the quality of the wings. For the 348 cases where ground cover measurements were made on the wings, 51% of the respondents stated that the quality of the wings was good, 42% said the quality was satisfactory, and just 7% said the quality was poor.

Players' opinions ($n = 350$) of the quality of the goalmouths appeared to be influenced by the percentage ground cover. For values of ground cover greater than 80% ($n = 74$), only 5% stated that the quality was poor, and 58% stated that the quality was good. Conversely, for ground cover of less than 20% ($n = 24$), no players thought that the quality of the goalmouths was good, whereas 63% thought that the quality was poor.

The distribution of the players' opinions of the quality of the central area of the field and the ground cover measurements made in the center circle ($n = 350$) showed that for ground cover values of less than 20% ($n = 23$), 39% thought that the quality was poor, 52% thought that it was satisfactory, and 9% thought the quality was good. Where ground cover was greater than 80% ($n = 107$), 42% stated that the quality of the central area was good, 45% said it was satisfactory, and 13% said that the quality was poor.

Standards for Association Football Fields

Existing Recommendations

There have been several previous suggestions for standards of playing quality for soccer. Although these have been proposals for artificial turf surfaces, some of them take account of tests made on natural turf. In previous work [6,7,15], "acceptable" values for the playing characteristics of synthetic turf for football have been recommended. Winterbottom [9] suggested standards for artificial turf for three levels of play, based on measurements of playing quality made on a number of synthetic turf surfaces and on the natural turf fields of professional clubs. The approach made by the researchers in the Winterbottom study was similar to that made here. Professional players played and practiced on a field while the playing quality tests were carried out. The players were then asked to complete questionnaires relating to the playing quality of the field. The questionnaire responses were compared with the results of the playing quality tests, and standards were proposed based on the responses.

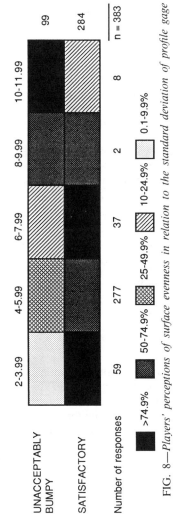

FIG. 8—*Players' perceptions of surface evenness in relation to the standard deviation of profile gage measurements.*

TABLE 4—*Existing recommendations for rebound resilience.*

Reference	Proposed Acceptable Rebound Resilience, %
Dury & Dury [15]	25 to 38
Anonymous [7]	20 to 45
Winterbottom [9]	25 to 46 (national level of play)
	20 to 50 (regional level)
	15 to 55 (local level)

Rebound Resilience

Table 4 summarizes the recommendations for rebound resilience for football proposed previously [7,9,15]. The first two publications cited in Table 4 did not include a recommendation of the type of ball that should be used or its inflation pressure. Dury & Dury [15] commented on the apparent variation in the rebound characteristics of the ball used at different inflation pressures. This observation was confirmed by Holmes & Bell [16], who found differences in rebound resilience of about 14% for 17 types of Federation of International Football Associations (FIFA) approved footballs when inflated to the same pressure and dropped on to concrete. Winterbottom [9] attempted to account for such variations by stating that a ball inflated to 0.7 bar that rebounds between 57 and 59% when dropped on to concrete should be used in rebound resilience tests.

Surface Hardness

No proposals have been suggested for acceptable surface hardness as measured by the Clegg impact soil tester, although Winterbottom [9] gave recommendations for the severity index text [7] and the surface deformation as measured using the Stuttgart artificial athlete [10].

Traction

Winterbottom [9] gave minimum and maximum limits for the traction coefficient between an "approved" shoe sole and artificial turf for football, but it is difficult to relate these figures to the torque required for a studded disc apparatus to tear through natural turf because the physical action of studs shearing through natural turf is different from that of other sole profiles moving in contact with synthetic turf.

Rolling Resistance

The only recommendations that exist for limits of rolling resistance were proposed by Winterbottom [9]. However, these were given in terms of the deceleration of a rolling football and cannot accurately be converted to a measure of distance rolled. However, Bell and Holmes [11] fitted a linear regression model of the relationship between distance rolled and deceleration and found that the equivalent distance rolled was between 3.5 and 10.1 m.

Surface Evenness

No specific recommendations for surface evenness for football have been made, although there have been two suggestions for general sports use. For synthetic turf, it is recommended that the gap underneath a 3-m straight edge should not be greater than 3 mm [7]. Gooch & Escritt [17] recommended that for natural turf sports fields the maximum gradient across the line of play should be 1:40, and along the line of play the gradient should not exceed 1:80.

Proposal of Standards

Recommended Test Procedures and Test Conditions

The recommended playing quality test methods for football are described in Table 1. For the rebound resilience and distance rolled tests, a ball inflated to 0.7 bar that rebounds between 57 and 59% on concrete shall be used. The tests shall be undertaken in six test plots, the positions of which are shown in Fig. 1. The tests shall be undertaken on the same day.

Playing Surface Conditions

Before testing can be undertaken, the condition of the playing surface must be similar to that before a match. For instance, the grass must be mown to the usual cutting height and repairs to the surface, such as replacing divots, should be carried out if required. Weather conditions can also influence test results, and we are currently working on the definition of antecedent meteorological conditions for testing.

Proposed Standards

As most of the playing quality questionnaires were completed by university first and second teams (Fig. 2), it is assumed that the responses relate mainly to a standard of play similar to the "regional" level described by Winterbottom [9]. The proposed standards are given as "preferred" and "acceptable" limits and apply to the whole field, so that none of the six areas tested should fall outside the recommended limits. The preferred limits are those identified from the questionnaire survey as corresponding to the players' opinions of a good playing surface. The acceptable limits are less restrictive and allow for the inevitable variability that natural turf displays both within a playing area and through the playing season.

Rebound Resilience

Table 5 gives the proposed standards for rebound resilience.

This study has confirmed that the limits of acceptability for rebound resilience proposed by Winterbottom [9] are indeed acceptable to the majority of players, so the figures suggested here are similar to those of Winterbottom.

Surface Hardness

Table 6 gives the proposed standards for surface hardness as measured by the Clegg impact soil tester.

TABLE 5—*Proposed standards for rebound resilience.*

	Minimum, %	Maximum, %
Preferred limits	20	50
Acceptable limits	15	55

TABLE 6—*Proposed standards for surface hardness.*

	Minimum, *g*	Maximum, *g*
Preferred limits	20	80
Acceptable limits	10	100

In the range of Clegg impact hardness of 80 to 99.9 *g*, 15% of respondents stated that the field was unacceptably hard to fall or dive on to, and 25% replied that the surface was unacceptably hard to run on. In the same category there were also large proportions of satisfactory and hard responses. Thus a Clegg impact value of 80 *g* appears to be the appropriate maximum level. At Clegg impact values less than 20 *g*, 59% thought that the surface was soft to run on, and 14% thought it was unacceptably soft. The proposed minimum level of surface hardness is therefore 20 *g*.

Traction

The proposed standards for surface traction are given in Table 7.

At traction values less than 20 N·m, none of the respondents thought that the grip underfoot was good, whereas 75% stated that it was poor. Between 20 N·m and 29.9 N·m, however, 73% said that the grip was satisfactory. Therefore, 20 N·m is clearly the appropriate cutoff point. Regarding preferred limits, it has been found that if the limit is set much above 25 N·m, otherwise satisfactory fields fail on this parameter [18]; therefore, 25 N·m is proposed as the minimum preferred limit.

It is difficult to suggest a maximum acceptable level of traction because little is known about the relationship between injuries and high traction. However, the maximum traction measured during this study was 51.0 N·m, which was not felt to be dangerous. Baker [19] has measured traction in excess of 80 N·m on trials of root zone reinforcement materials, and it is considered that such levels may be unsafe because of the possibility of injuries to knees and ankles induced by torsion.

Distance Rolled

The proposed standards for the distance rolled by a football are shown in Table 8.

There was poor agreement between the players' opinions of the pace of the ball roll and the measurements of distance rolled. Baker & Bell [20] gave distance rolled values for some

TABLE 7—*Proposed standards for traction.*

Preferred minimum, N·m	25
Acceptable minimum, N·m	20

TABLE 8—*Proposed standards for distance rolled.*

	Minimum, m	Maximum, m
Preferred limits	3	12
Acceptable limits	2	14

TABLE 9—*Proposed standards for surface evenness.*

Preferred maximum standard deviation, mm	8
Acceptable maximum standard deviation, mm	10

football league fields (i.e., corresponding to the "national" standard of play of Winterbottom [9]). The maximum rolling distance was 11.9 m, under very dry conditions, and the minimum was 5.3 m. The shortest and longest distance rolled measurements in this study were 3.65 and 12.03 m, respectively. The proposals given in Table 8 are therefore calculated from actual measurements on football fields of a wide range of quality, rather than from the responses of players; however, there is reasonable agreement with previous recommendations [9].

Surface Evenness

Table 9 gives the proposed standards for surface evenness as measured using the profile gage.

The questionnaire replies showed that there was an increase in the proportion of responses stating that the surface was unacceptably bumpy at a profile gage standard deviation of 8 mm. This is therefore the figure proposed for the maximum preferred value for surface evenness.

There is no requirement for a minimum level of surface evenness because a football field cannot be "too flat." However, this statement does not preclude the need for an overall gradient or crown to assist drainage.

Ground Cover

It would be impractical to propose minimum standards for the percentage ground cover on a field. It was noted earlier that it is the density of rooting that probably controls the tractional properties of a surface and not the ground cover itself. Once the ground cover is lost, however, it is likely that the roots will gradually lose their effectiveness in providing traction, and smearing by mud will reduce their effectiveness still further. However, it should be emphasized that the best conditions of playing quality were found in areas where a good ground cover was combined with a firm surface. The questionnaire responses suggest that players prefer grass cover to bare soil and base their opinions of the overall quality of a field on the amount of grass cover present, although other factors such as traction and surface firmness will influence these opinions.

Acknowledgments

The authors wish to thank the Sports Council for funding this four-year study of standards of playing quality for natural turf. They particularly wish to acknowledge the overall supervision of the project given by Mr. A. L. Dye (senior research officer, Sports Council).

Finally, the success of this part of the work was in great part due to the efforts of individual football players, club secretaries, and grounds men who are too numerous to mention individually. Their help is gratefully acknowledged as is the cooperation of governing bodies, football clubs, universities, local authorities, and many other organizations.

APPENDIX

Football Players' Questionnaire

SPORTS COUNCIL/STRI SURVEY OF   Date . . . .
THE PLAYING QUALITY OF FOOTBALL   Location . . . .
PITCHES   Questionnaire No . . . .

1.   Name of team . . . .
2.   What was your main playing position during the game?

   ☐ Goalkeeper
   ☐ Defence
   ☐ Midfield
   ☐ Attack

3.   Overall how did the pitch feel for running on?

   ☐ Unacceptably hard
   ☐ Hard
   ☐ Satisfactory
   ☐ Soft
   ☐ Unacceptably soft

4.   How would you describe the grip underfoot given by the pitch?

   ☐ Good
   ☐ Satisfactory
   ☐ Poor

5.   Overall how would you rate the bounce of the ball on this pitch?

   ☐ Unacceptably high
   ☐ High
   ☐ Satisfactory
   ☐ Low
   ☐ Unacceptably low

6.   Overall how would you rate the speed of the ball rolling along the ground?

   ☐ Unacceptably fast
   ☐ Fast
   ☐ Satisfactory
   ☐ Slow
   ☐ Unacceptably slow

7.   Overall would you consider the surface of the pitch to be:

   ☐ Unacceptably bumpy
   ☐ Satisfactory

8.   Overall how did the pitch feel for falling or diving on?

   ☐ Unacceptably hard
   ☐ Hard
   ☐ Satisfactory
   ☐ Soft

9.   Please tick the appropriate boxes to indicate the quality of the wings, goalmouths
   and central area of the pitch.

	Good	Satisfactory	Poor
Wings	☐	☐	☐
Goalmouths	☐	☐	☐
Central area	☐	☐	☐

References

[1] Canaway, P. M., "Fundamental Techniques in the Study of Turfgrass Wear: An Advance Report on Research," *Journal of the Sports Turf Research Institute,* Vol. 51, 1975, pp. 104–115.

[2] Liesecke, H. J. and Schmidt, U., "Scherfestigkeit und Scherfestigkeitsmessungen an Rasentragschichten," *Das Gartenamt,* Vol. 27, 1978, pp. 70–80.

[3] Stuurman, F. J., "Ein Gerät zur Messung der Scherfestigkeit der Narbe," *Rasen und Rasengräser,* Vol. 6, 1969, pp. 32–37.

[4] Canaway, P. M., "The Effect of Rootzone Construction on the Wear Tolerance and Playability of Eight Turfgrass Species Subjected to Football Type Wear," *Journal of the Sports Turf Research Institute,* Vol. 59, 1983, pp. 107–123.

[5] Canaway, P. M., *Proceedings,* Fifth International Turfgrass Research Conference, INRA Publications, Versailles, France, 1985, pp. 45–56.

[6] "Specification for Artificial Sports Surfaces: Part 1—General Principles and Classification," Sports Council, London, 1984a.

[7] Anonymous, "Specification for Artificial Sports Surfaces: Part 2—Surfaces for General Sports Use," Sports Council, London, 1984b.

[8] Anonymous, "Specification for Artificial Sports Surfaces: Part 3—Surfaces for Individual Sports, Section 1—Cricket," Sports Council, London, 1984c.

[9] Winterbottom, W., "Artificial Grass Surfaces for Association Football," Sports Council, London, 1985.

[10] "Sports Grounds—Synthetic Surfacings (Requirements, Test, Maintenance)," DIN 18035 Part 6, Beuth-Verlag, Berlin, Germany, 1978.

[11] Bell, M. J. and Holmes, G., "The Playing Quality of Association Football Pitches," *Journal of the Sports Turf Research Institute,* Vol. 64, 1988, pp. 19–47.

[12] Haggar, R. J., Stent, C. J., and Isaac, S., "A Prototype Hand-Held Patch Sprayer for Killing Weeds, Activated by Spectral Differences in Crop/Weed Canopies," *Journal of Agricultural Engineering Research,* Vol. 28, 1983, pp. 349–358.

[13] Clegg, B., "An Impact Testing Device for *in situ* Base Course Evaluation," *Australian Road Research Bureau Proceedings,* Vol. 8, 1976, pp. 1–6.

[14] Canaway, P. M. and Bell, M. J., "Technical Note: An Apparatus for Measuring Traction and Friction on Natural and Artificial Playing Surfaces," *Journal of the Sports Turf Research Institute,* Vol. 62, 1986, pp. 211–214.

[15] Dury, P. and Dury, P. L. K., "A Study of Natural Materials (Dynamic/Particulate) in the Provision of Synthetic Non-Turf Sports Facilities, Particularly for Soccer and Other Winter Games," Nottinghamshire County Council Education Department, Playing Fields Service, Nottingham, England, 1983.

[16] Holmes, G. and Bell, M. J., "Technical Note: The Effect of Football Type and Inflation Pressure on Rebound Resilience," *Journal of the Sports Turf Research Institute,* Vol. 61, 1984, pp. 132–135.

[17] Gooch, R. B. and Escritt, J. R., *Sports Ground Construction—Specifications,* 2nd ed., National Playing Fields Association, London, 1975.

[18] Baker, S. W., Cole, A. R., and Thornton, S. L., "Performance Standards and the Interpretation of Playing Quality for Soccer in Relation to Rootzone Composition," *Journal of the Sports Turf Research Institute,* Vol. 64, 1988, pp. 120–132.

[19] Baker, S. W., Isaac, S. P., and Isaac, B. J., "An Assessment of Five Reinforcement Materials for Sports Turf: II—Playing Quality," *Zeitschrift für Vegetationstechnik im Landschafts- und Sportstättenbau,* Vol. 11, 1988, pp. 12–15.

[20] Baker, S. W. and Bell, M. J., "The Playing Characteristics of Natural Turf and Synthetic Turf Surfaces for Association Football," *Journal of the Sports Turf Research Institute,* Vol. 62, 1986, pp. 9–35.

S. W. Baker[1]

Standards for the Playing Quality of Artificial Turf for Association Football

REFERENCE: Baker, S. W., **"Standards for the Playing Quality of Artificial Turf for Association Football,"** *Natural and Artificial Playing Fields: Characteristics and Safety Features, ASTM STP 1073,* R. C. Schmidt, E. F. Hoerner, E. M. Milner, and C. A. Morehouse, Eds., American Society for Testing and Materials, Philadelphia, 1990, pp. 48–57.

ABSTRACT: In Britain, over 100 full-sized artificial playing surfaces have been installed for association football (soccer). Performance standards for the playing quality of artificial turf pitches (athletic fields) are required, and the development of different test methods is reviewed. For surfaces for soccer, it is necessary to consider both ball/surface and player/surface interaction. The principal techniques for testing surfaces used in Britain are ball rebound resilience, rolling resistance, traction/friction, sliding resistance, surface hardness (using Stuttgart and Berlin Artificial Athlete instrumentation), and the impact characteristics of a 5.5-kg head striking the turf.

Playing quality standards for soccer on artificial turf surfaces published in 1985 gave performance requirements for three levels of play. Classification to a national standard required ball rebound resilience in the range of 25 to 46%, ball deceleration of 0.45 to 1.5 m/s^2, and a traction coefficient of 1.5 to 2.2. These limits are compared with data obtained from six natural turf pitches used by professional clubs covering a wide range of weather and pitch conditions. For ball rebound resilience and traction there was a reasonable comparability of the specified performance limits and the data for natural turf: the interquartile ranges were 31.7 to 44.4% for ball rebound resilience and 1.38 to 1.96 for traction. Some slight modifications to these performance limits are, however, proposed. For natural turf pitches, almost 90% of deceleration values were in the range 0.45 to 1.5 m/s^2, but it was evident that values on artificial pitches, after the pile had been compacted by play, were not satisfying the threshold of 0.45 m/s^2. Peak deceleration of a 5.5 kg headform after it had been dropped from 1.5 m was lower on natural turf surfaces than on artificial pitches. However, the values on the artificial pitches were comparable with those of safety tiles used as a playground surfacing.

KEY WORDS: playing fields, playing quality, football, artificial turf, ball rebound resilience, rolling resistance, traction, sliding resistance, player/surface impact

Artificial turf pitches provide a valuable recreational facility in that they can sustain very high intensities of play, and the playing quality of the surface is rarely affected by weather conditions. From a commercial point of view they can also be used for a wide range of activities, for example, pop concerts and boxing. In consequence, over 100 full-sized artificial pitches have been installed in Great Britain, including a number which are used for professional soccer matches.

The need for performance standards for the construction of artificial turf has been recognized. The British Sports Council [1,2] has produced a specification for artificial sports surfaces detailing test methods for factors such as wear resistance, seam strength, and playing

---

[1] The Sports Turf Research Institute, Bingley, West Yorkshire, England BD16 1AU.

quality. A subcommittee of the British Standards Institution (BSI) has been meeting since October 1985 to develop the Sport Council's specification into a formal British Standard.

One of the most important aspects of the work on performance standards for artificial sports surfaces has been to characterize their playing quality. For soccer, a detailed study of the playing quality and safety of artificial turf surfaces has been completed [3,4] with the objective of developing performance standards for three grades of play, that is: national standard/international competitions; national league and cup competitions; regional standard/senior competitions at county and regional level; and local standard/local competitions, recreation, and training.

The rationale behind the work was to develop a series of mechanical and electronic tests to characterize the playing quality of sports surfaces. Comparative data were collected from 10 natural turf pitches, 13 full-sized artificial turf pitches, and test beds of 18 different artificial grass systems. Nine of the natural turf and eight of the synthetic turf pitches were also visited by a squad of professional soccer players. This research led to recommendations for six aspects of playing quality performance: ball rebound resilience, ball deceleration, traction, sliding distance, surface deflection, and impact severity.

The purpose of this paper is to review test methods for assessing the playing quality of artificial turf surfaces that are used in Britain and to consider how closely the performance standards outlined by Winterbottom [3] accord with the playing performance of natural turf pitches used for professional soccer matches.

Test Procedures for Evaluating the Playing Quality of Artificial Turf

In Britain, a number of test methods have been used to characterize the playing quality of artificial turf soccer pitches. The main developments are summarized below and, for convenience, are divided into ball/surface and player/surface interactions.

Ball/Surface Interaction

Ball Rebound Resilience—The standard method for assessing the bounce of the ball on the surface has been a vertical drop test in which the ball is released from a height of 3 m and the percent rebound recorded [2,3]. Ball type and pressure have a significant effect on rebound resilience [5], and this effect is standardized by using a ball which has a rebound resilience on concrete of 57 to 59% when the ball is inflated to 70 kPa. This method has now been produced as a draft British Standard.

Rolling Resistance—A number of techniques have been used for assessing the pace of the ball over the surface. These being (*a*) distance rolled, (*b*) deceleration, and (*c*) velocity change.

For the distance rolled and deceleration tests, the ball is released from a height of 1 m down a standard ramp inclined at 45° [2]. The simplest index of rolling resistance is to record the distance rolled before the ball stops [2]. However, on outdoor sites, the movement of relatively light soccer balls can be influenced by the force of the wind and, in addition, it is more realistic to measure the effects of deceleration at a high velocity [3]. Using the standard ramp (above), the ball is initially rolling at approximately 3.15 m/s [6], and its deceleration can be measured using a series of infrared beams connected to a timing mechanism. Winterbottom [3] used three light gates at intervals of 1 m, our current version uses four infrared beams. The ball is released from the ramp and allowed to roll a distance of 1 m to eliminate any top spin generated by the ramp. Deceleration is then measured over a 2 m distance with the initial, u, and final velocities, v, being calculated as the ball crosses two pairs of beams, each set being 0.3 m apart. Assuming the deceleration is uniform, it can be calculated using the relationship

$$a = \frac{v^2 - u^2}{2s}$$ (1)

where

a = acceleration, m/s², and
s = distance (= 2 m).

To avoid the necessity of squaring the velocities in Eq 1 and hence doubling the error term, a third index of rolling resistance has been proposed. For velocity change, ΔV, measurements for soccer, the timing gate apparatus with four infrared light beams is also used, but instead of using a constant release height from the ramp, the ball is released from varying heights to give a range of initial velocities. The relationship between the initial and final velocities can be fitted by either a linear regression model ($v = a + bu$) or a power curve ($v = au^b$) to obtain the value, v, when $u = 2.5$ m/s. Velocity change is calculated as

$$\Delta V = 2.5 - v$$ (2)

in metres per second. Of the measurements of the ball roll properties, rolling distance and velocity change have been included as draft British Standards.

Player/Surface Interaction

Surface Grip—The grip provided by a surface is an important component of playing quality: if there is too little grip, the players will slip and fall, while if the grip is excessive, there is danger of players suffering knee and ankle injuries as their feet become locked during turns and maneuvers [7]. In Britain, two main tests have been used to assess this property:

(a) a traction test which measures the rotational force required to initiate movement of a sole plate in contact with the sports surface, and
(b) a sliding resistance test which measures the stopping distance of a moving test foot after it makes contact with the turf. Both tests have been accepted by the British Standards Subcommittee as test methods for artificial turf.

The traction test was developed from a method originally used for natural turf [8,9]. For artificial turf the apparatus consists of a test foot (150 ± 2 mm diameter) with an appropriate sole for artificial turf. This is weighted to give a total mass of 46 ± 2 kg, and a double-handled dial-indicating torque wrench is used to measure the rotational force required to initiate movement. The traction coefficient is calculated as

$$\text{traction coefficient} = \frac{3T}{2WR}$$ (3)

where

T = torque, N·m,
W = applied force, N, and
R = radius of the disc (0.075 m).

The sliding distance test is based on a trolley of total mass 45 $\pm$ 2 kg with a steel plate foot assembly (60 by 85 mm) onto which is bonded a 60 by 75 mm piece of sports shoe material [3]. The trolley is released down a standard ramp and when the trolley wheels leave the ramp, the foot assembly makes contact with the turf and the distance before stopping is measured. Winterbottom [3] recommended a release velocity of 1.15 m/s, but this has been modified to 2.0 m/s by the British Standards Subcommittee for Artificial Turf Surfaces.

Traction results are not only dependent on the physical properties of artificial turf but also on the nature of sole material [4,7,10]. A standard multistudded sole consisting of 55 studs (6 mm in length, 12 mm basal diameter tapering to 9 mm diameter) has therefore been designed for the traction apparatus, and a sole with 13 similar studs has been used for the sliding distance apparatus. The sole configuration has intermediate traction properties, over a range of surfaces, to those given by Baker & Bell [4].

Player/Surface Impacts

Player/surface impacts can be divided into those involving a player running, jumping, and falling on to the surface. In particular, test methods are required to assess the players' comfort while running on a surface and also to assess injury potential particularly related to a player falling.

Winterbottom [3] used a Stuttgart Artificial Athlete [11] to measure surface deflection. This was considered to be appropriate for detecting hard surfaces which may lead to possible stress injuries and soft surfaces which may cause excessive fatigue or injury due to twisting.

The validity of the Stuttgart Artificial Athlete as a test for artificial turf surfaces has subsequently been questioned, and the method has been rejected by the BSI Subcommittee. The Stuttgart Artificial Athlete was developed primarily as a test for elastomeric surfaces showing no permanent deformation during the course of the test. On artificial turf surfaces, deformation of the pile occurs before the loading pattern of the foot is influenced by any shockpads or underlying layers. The results may, therefore, be unrealistically influenced by the length of the pile. In response, the Berlin Artificial Athlete [12] which measures force reduction relative to a concrete surface is currently being evaluated as a test method for this type of impact for soccer surfaces.

For the safety of a surface in relation to falls, Winterbottom [3] used an impact severity test [2]. This measured the deceleration of a 5.5-kg, 220-mm-diameter head form during impact with the ground. The deceleration was integrated over time to give a measure of severity index (SI), i.e.

$$SI = \int_{t_1}^{t_2} a^{2.5} \, dt \tag{4}$$

where

a = acceleration, in gravities,
t_1 = the time of first contact with the surface, and
t_2 = the time of the first break of contact.

The concept of impact severity was developed specifically in relation to head injuries [13]. There is, therefore, little basis for relating this index to other types of high-energy impacts, e.g., falls involving injuries to limbs. As a consequence, the results of this impact test are now usually given as the peak deceleration (g-max) rather than by using the severity index.

Comparison of Existing Performance Criteria for Artificial Turf Soccer Pitches with Values Obtained from Natural Turf Surfaces

Artificial turf pitches initially meeting the criteria outlined by Winterbottom [3] have been installed at a number of sites. However, there have been comments that their playing characteristics are still different from traditional natural turf pitches. The objective of this section is to compare performance limits of ball rebounce resilience, deceleration, and traction given by Winterbottom [3] with data from natural turf pitches used for professional soccer matches. In addition, some comparative data on peak forces during impacts are given.

Materials and Methods

Six natural turf pitches, all used for professional soccer, were selected with the intention of obtaining a representative set of playing quality data. In construction, the pitches ranged from those where the drainage capabilities were substantially upgraded using heavy sand amelioration or slit drainage to sites with only rudimentary pipe drainage systems. Each pitch was visited five times during the course of the playing season (18 Sept. 1987 to 27 April 1988) to ensure that a range of weather and pitch conditions were encountered during monitoring. Three artificial turf pitches used for professional and semiprofessional soccer were also monitored. Three areas on each pitch were monitored, i.e., goal, center circle, and wing. The measurement techniques were discussed in the introductory section but are briefly summarized in Table 1.

Results

Ball Rebound Resilience—A histogram of ball rebound resilience showing the frequency distribution of values from natural turf in relation to the limits given by Winterbottom [3] is given in Fig. 1. On the natural turf surfaces, there was a pronounced spatial variation in rebound resilience, mean values being 37.8% for the goal area, 40.6% for the center circle,

TABLE 1—*Measurement techniques.*

Ball rebound resilience	A Mitre Delta 1000 ball inflated to 70 kPa was dropped from a height of 3 m, and its rebound height measured as a percentage of the drop height [2]. Eight readings were taken per test area.
Distance rolled	A Mitre Delta 1000 ball was released from a height of 1 m down a standard ramp [2] and the distance rolled in metres was measured. Four readings were taken in each direction per test area.
Ball deceleration	Infrared timing gates were used to measure the deceleration of the ball after its release from the ramp (above) situated 1.0 m from the first timing gate. The initial and final velocities were determined from sets of gates 0.3 m apart, and there was a distance of 2.0 m between the central points of the two sets of gates. The calculation of deceleration is given in Eq 1.
Traction	The torque, T, required to tear the grass was measured using a studded disc apparatus with six 15-mm-long studs [9]. Torque values were converted to a traction coefficient, μ, using $\mu = T/WR$, where $W =$ total applied vertical force in newtons and $R =$ radius of stud setting in metres. Eight readings were taken per test area.
Peak deceleration	A 5.5-kg sphere containing an accelerometer [2] was dropped vertically from a height of 1.5 m. The peak deceleration (g-max) was recorded. Six readings were taken per test area.

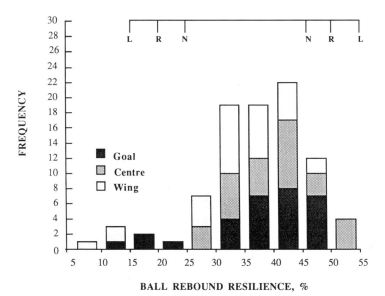

BALL REBOUND RESILIENCE, %

FIG. 1—*Frequency distribution for ball rebound resilience on natural turf in relation to limits for artificial turf given by Winterbottom (1985) (L, R, and N are the limits for the local, regional, and national standards, respectively).*

and 33.5% for the wing area. The recommended limits for artificial turf to the national standard are 25 to 46%, and 75.6% of the measured values for natural turf fell within this limit.

Ball Roll—Figure 2 shows the relationship between distance rolled and deceleration for both natural turf and artificial turf pitches. The existing performance standard for synthetic turf is also given. The national standard for artificial turf of a deceleration of 0.45 to 1.5 m/s^2 initially appears well founded, as 89.6% of values for natural turf fall into this range. However, it appears that artificial turf surfaces at best just satisfy the threshold of 0.45 m/s^2 with only two values greater than 0.45 m/s^2. The remaining deceleration values for artificial turf in Fig. 2 range from 0.21 to 0.41 m/s^2.

Traction—Traction coefficients for natural turf are given in Fig. 3 and are shown in relation to the limits for artificial turf given by Winterbottom [3]. Considerable care is needed in comparing traction values from natural and artificial turf pitches as the action of studs tearing through natural turf is different from the process of a sole moving in contact with artificial turf. Furthermore, the player can exert a major control on traction properties by subtle changes in the contact area between his footwear and the surface and on the load applied on the sole area. Additionally, the player may change his type of footwear to achieve the level of grip which he requires.

With natural turf surfaces, spatial variation of values within the pitch is again evident. On the wing areas, where a high density of shoot and root material is retained throughout the season, the mean traction coefficient was 1.74. On the high wear areas in the goal and center circle, the mean values were 1.40 and 1.50, respectively.

The range of traction coefficients recorded on the natural turf pitches is generally lower than the limits proposed for artificial turf, and indeed the mean values for the goal and center circle areas fall at or below the minimum traction coefficient at the national standard for artificial turf.

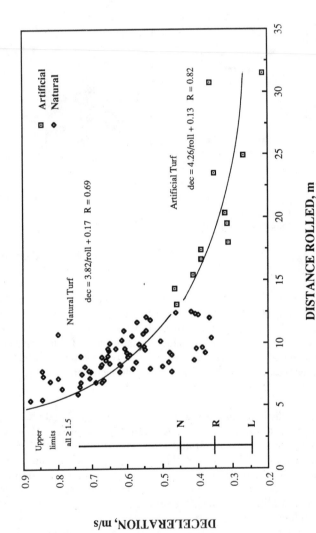

DISTANCE ROLLED, m

FIG. 2—*Deceleration and distance rolled for natural and artificial turf in relation to limits for artificial turf given by Winterbottom (1985) (L, R, and N are the limits for the local, regional, and national standards, respectively).*

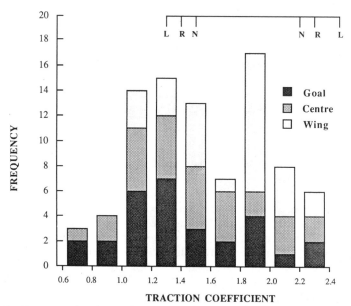

FIG. 3—*Frequency distribution for traction values on natural turf in relation to limits for artificial turf given by Winterbottom (1985) (L, R, and N are the limits for the local, regional, and national standards, respectively).*

Peak Deceleration During High-Energy Impacts—Winterbottom [*3*] gives limits for high-energy impacts in terms of severity index (Eq 3). In the current study, peak deceleration (g-max) was used to characterize such impacts, and therefore direct comparisons with the Winterbottom [*3*] limits cannot be made. Figure 4, however, shows values obtained from a range of natural turf pitches with those from two artificial turf pitches used for professional soccer.

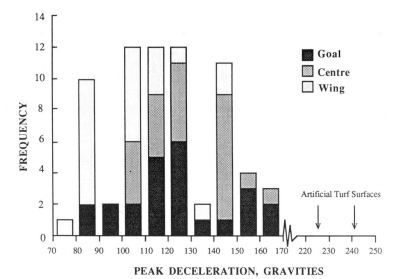

FIG. 4—*Frequency distribution for peak deceleration for natural turf in relation to values from artificial turf pitches (arrowed).*

Peak deceleration values on natural turf ranged from 70 g on a wing area under wet conditions in February 1988 to 165 g in the center circle in April 1988 under much drier conditions. The one incidence of moderate frost in March 1988 gave figures in the range of 146 to 159 g. On the artificial turf surfaces, the values were higher, the average figures at two sites ranging from 225 to 241 g. There was no overlap of values between the natural turf and artificial turf surfaces.

Discussion

Four components of playing quality have been considered, and while values obtained from natural turf pitches accord closely with published performance limits for ball rebound resilience and traction on artificial turf, there are pronounced differences in the ball roll and high-energy impact data. The natural turf data were collected from a range of pitches under varying weather conditions, and some pitches were inevitably too soft and slippery for satisfactory play, while others were too hard. The interquartile range for each data set (i.e., excluding the top and bottom 25% of values) does, however, give some indication as to what might be considered to be typical conditions. By excluding extreme values, the interquartile range is also a useful guide to what might be considered to be good playing conditions for soccer, but the extent to which specifications for artificial turf should accord to this range inevitably must vary for the different components of playing quality.

For ball rebound resilience, the interquartile range was 31.7 to 44.4%. The current performance standards for the national level of play (i.e., appropriate for professional soccer) of 25 to 46% are slightly wider than this, but it was interesting to note that mean rebound resilience for one of the newer sand-filled synthetic surfaces was 37.4% compared wtih an overall mean of 37.3% for the natural turf pitches. This suggests that a more rigorous standard for rebound resilience can be satisfied.

For the traction coefficient, the interquartile range on natural turf was 1.38 to 1.96. This is in broad agreement with the limits proposed by Winterbottom [3], although the lower limit of 1.5 could be reduced. Bell and Holmes [14], after conducting player evaluation tests on natural turf, suggested a preferred lower limit for traction of 30 N·m. This would equate to a traction coefficient on artificial turf of 1.37.

The interquartile range for ball deceleration on natural turf was 0.53 to 0.71 m/s². However, deceleration figures were only available for the second half of the season, and the data may not therefore be entirely representative. The correlation between ground cover and distance rolled was high ($r = 0.75$, $p < 0.01$), and if values for the first part of the season were included, the proportion of values with a higher deceleration would increase. Distance rolled was measured throughout the season, and the interquartile range was 6.34 to 8.94 m. Using a negative exponential model for rolling distance and deceleration [15], this would correspond to deceleration limits of 0.54 to 0.83 m/s². From the data presented in Fig. 2, the majority of ball roll values on artificial surfaces do not meet the existing limit of 0.45 m/s², let alone a more stringent limit such as this.

High-energy impact tests are not a direct measure of playing quality in the same sense as tests for ball motion and traction. They do, however, indicate the safety of the surface. The g-max values for the two artificial turf pitches were considerably higher than for natural grass, but they should be put into the context that resin-bound rubber shred playground safety tiles give values in the range 195 to 203 g when subjected to this impact test.

The adequacy of published performance standards for soccer played at a senior level within Britain have been discussed. On the basis of comparisons with natural turf surfaces, some modifications to the limits are required if they are to be accepted for professional soccer. Further work is being carried out on artificial turf surfaces before suitable performance standards can be finalized.

Acknowledgments

The author wishes to thank M. J. Bell, J. P. Murphy, C. D. Pye, P. Smithies, and D. Yaffey for technical assistance. The contributions of the Rubber and Plastic Research Association and the Centre for Sports Technology in developing test methods are also acknowledged.

References

[*1*] Sports Council, "Specification for Artificial Sports Surfaces: Part 1—General Principles and Classification," Sports Council, London, England, 1984.
[*2*] Sports Council, "Specification for Artificial Sports Surfaces: Part 2—Surfaces for General Sport Use," Sports Council, London, England, 1984.
[*3*] Winterbottom, W., *Artificial Grass Surfaces for Association Football,* Sports Council, London, England, 1985.
[*4*] Baker, S. W. and Bell, M. J., "The Playing Characteristics of Natural Turf and Synthetic Turf Surfaces for Association Football," *Journal of the Sports Turf Research Institute,* Vol. 62, 1986, pp. 9–35.
[*5*] Holmes, G. and Bell, M.J., "The Effect of Football Type and Inflation Pressure on Rebound Resilience," *Journal of the Sports Turf Research Institute,* Vol. 61, 1985, pp. 132–135.
[*6*] Baker, S. W., Isaac, S. P., and Isaac, B. J., "An Assessment of Five Reinforcement Materials for Sports Turf II—Playing Quality," *Zeitschrift für Vegetationstechnik,* Vol. 11, 1988, pp. 12–15.
[*7*] Torg, J. S., Quedenfeld, T., and Landau, S., "The Shoe-Surface Interface and Its Relationship to Football Knee Injuries," *Journal of Sports Medicine,* Vol. 2, No. 5, 1974, pp. 261–269.
[*8*] Canaway, P. M., "Fundamental Techniques in the Study of Turfgrass Wear: An Advance Report on Research," *Journal of the Sports Turf Research Institute,* Vol. 51, 1975, pp. 104–115.
[*9*] Canaway, P. M. and Bell, M. J., "Technical Note: An Apparatus for Measuring Traction and Friction on Natural and Artificial Playing Surfaces," *Journal of the Sports Turf Research Institute,* Vol. 62, 1986, pp. 211–214.
[*10*] Stanitski, C. L., McMaster, J. H. and Ferguson, R. J., "Synthetic Turf and Grass—a Comparative Study," *Journal of Sports Medicine,* Vol. 2, No. 1, 1974, pp. 22–26.
[*11*] "Sports Grounds—Synthetic Surfacings—Requirements, Test, Maintenance," DIN 18 035, Part 6, Beuth-Verlag, Berlin, Germany, 1978.
[*12*] Kolitzus, H. J., "Functional Standards for Playing Surfaces," *Sports Shoes and Playing Surfaces,* E. C. Fredricks, Ed., Human Kinetics Publishers, Champaign, IL, 1984, pp. 98–118.
[*13*] Gadd, C. W., "Use of a Weighted Impulse Criterion for Estimating Injury Hazard," *Proceedings,* 10th Stapp Car Crash Conference, Society of Automotive Engineers, 8–9 Nov. 1966.
[*14*] Bell, M. J. and Holmes, M. J., "The Playing Quality of Association Football Pitches," *Journal of the Sports Turf Research Institute,* Vol. 64, 1988, pp. 19–47.
[*15*] Holmes, G. and Bell, M. J., "A Pilot Study of the Playing Quality of Football Pitches," *Journal of the Sports Turf Research Institute,* Vol. 62, 1986, pp. 74–91.

Surface Traction

Gordon A. Valiant[1]

Traction Characteristics of Outsoles for Use on Artificial Playing Surfaces

REFERENCE: Valiant, G. A., **"Traction Characteristics of Outsoles for Use on Artificial Playing Surfaces,"** *Natural and Artificial Playing Fields: Characteristics and Safety Features, ASTM STP 1073*, R. C. Schmidt, E. F. Hoerner, E. M. Milner, and C. A. Morehouse, Eds., American Society for Testing and Materials, Philadelphia, 1990, pp. 61–68.

ABSTRACT: This report summarizes a series of studies which address the compromise between high translational and low rotational traction in the development of cleated shoe outsoles. In translation, a soccer shoe outsole must possess a coefficient of friction greater than 0.8 when forces are exerted in an anterior direction in order for the frictional forces to counter the high shear forces developed by a rapidly stopping foot. This can be achieved by molding outsoles from compounds such as styrene-butadiene rubber or by adding cleats as short as 2.6 mm to the outsole. If peak moments resisting rotation of a soccer shoe outsole could be reduced to values less than 30 N·m, the incidences of skeletal injuries may be reduced. It was also found that the classical laws of Coulomb friction do not apply to conventional soccer shoe outsoles. Coefficients of friction decrease with increases in normal pressure. This relation can possibly be exploited in future designs to reduce the compromise between translational and rotational traction.

KEY WORDS: playing fields, translational traction, rotational traction, artificial turf, ground reaction forces, coefficient of friction, cleat length

Football, according to DeHaven and Lintner [1], has one of the highest injury rates of any sport. Aside from the player collisions that occur during tackling and blocking, many other factors have been implicated in the cause of football injuries. One factor that is related to severe injuries of the knee joint in football and other field sports is foot fixation due to excessive traction between the playing surface and the shoe outsole. Torg and Quedenfeld [2] observed that when compared with a conventional football shoe outsole containing seven 19.05-mm (¾ in.)-long screw-in cleats, use of a multicleated football shoe outsole was related to a decrease of approximately 50% in the total number of knee injuries, and a 75 to 80% decrease in the number of severe or very severe knee injuries.

Specifically, it is excessive resistance to rotation, rather than simply excessive foot fixation, which is related to traumatic knee injury during a twisting motion. Many shoe outsole concepts have been proposed to minimize resistance to rotation.

Cameron and Davis [3] tested a football shoe that had an outsole combining a cleatless heel with a cleated, swiveling turntable in the forefoot. Their results showed that of 466 high school football players wearing the swivel shoe, only 2.1 and 3.0% sustained injuries to the knee and ankle, respectively, during one football season. These percentages are considerably less than the 7.5 and 8.1% of the 2373 control athletes wearing conventional cleated outsoles that sustained knee and ankle injuries, respectively. Although the swivel shoe appears to have protected the athlete to some extent from the serious knee injuries that occur as a result of

[1] Biomechanics researcher, NIKE Sport Research Laboratory, Beaverton, OR 97005.

foot fixation, the athletic footwear industry has not embraced this concept. Perhaps this is because of the difficulties and the high cost of manufacturing a shoe with moving mechanical parts.

Another concept developed to reduce resistance to rotation has been recently patented and marketed by the Tanel Corp. [4]. Different outsole designs with an annular cleat arrangement are proposed for use on natural and artificial turfs. The starting and stopping traction of the artificial turf outsole due to the penetration of the annular projections into the playing surface is claimed to be very good. It is also claimed that the annular projections of this outsole greatly enhance the pivotability of the foot on the playing surface, hence, minimizing the risk of sustaining knee and ankle injuries. However, this concept has not been subjected to empirical tests in a scientific study.

Many other athletic footwear manufacturers design cleated outsoles with cleats arranged in concentrically circular patterns with the intent to reduce resistance to rotation between shoe outsole and playing surface. Simply arranging cleats in a concentrically circular pattern does not ensure that resistance to rotation will always be reduced, as evidenced by tests of basketball shoe outsoles molded in concentrically circular patterns [5]. Generally, a shoe outsole that develops high translational traction forces also develops high rotational traction forces [6]. On the other hand, concepts that are developed to reduce resistance to rotation, may not always possess the high translational traction characteristics necessary for aiding athletes in performing some of the skills of their particular sport. High traction characteristics are a necessary feature of shoe outsoles because they enhance the athlete's ability to successfully run fast, make quick starts and stops, and make rapid changes in running direction. This creates a compromise between protection and performance in the design of shoe outsoles that are developed for use in field sports.

This report summarizes a series of studies which address the compromise between high translational and low rotational traction needs for cleated shoe outsoles. The minimum translational traction requirements for shoe outsoles were determined, using soccer as a model. Aspects of outsole material and design that could significantly affect translational traction were then investigated. Finally, the interaction between translational and rotational traction characteristics of different outsoles were examined through empirical measures with a physical test of friction forces.

Description of Studies

Measurement of Translational Traction Requirements

The translational traction needs of shoes for use in field sports were determined by measuring ground reaction forces (GRF) developed during lateral movements [7]. Testing was conducted on an artificial playing surface with a separate section firmly fastened to a six degree-of-freedom force measuring platform. Eight subjects performed five trials each of (*a*) straight-line running, (*b*) stopping rapidly with the right foot and quickly making a 90° cut to the left, and (*c*) stopping rapidly with the right foot followed by pivoting 180° medially and pushing off. All subjects wore the same pair of indoor soccer shoes, the outsole of which contained 56 molded rubber cleats that were 5 mm in length.

The foot was filmed with a high-speed camera and a frame-by-frame analysis located the foot with respect to the force platform. This allowed the horizontal forces, or frictional forces, as well as the center of pressure of the resultant ground reaction force vector, to be expressed with respect to the foot.

The friction forces that were developed on artificial turf by the soccer shoes were sufficiently high since every trial was successfully performed by each subject without slipping.

Thus, the ratio obtained by dividing horizontal by vertical GRF components is a dimensionless measure of the minimum traction needs of a cleated shoe for playing soccer on artificial surfaces. This ratio, which is equivalent to a dimensionless coefficient of friction (COF), is termed a minimum translational traction coefficient. Two coefficients were calculated. The longitudinal translational traction coefficient was calculated by dividing anteriorly directed shear forces by the vertical GRF. Laterally directed GRF were used in the calculation of the transverse translational traction coefficient.

The maximum value of the translational traction coefficients occurred when subjects completely stopped their forward progression to make either the 180° pivot or the 90° cut. This is demonstrated by the plots in Fig. 1, which show, for the cutting movement, the mean vertical GRF component (FZ) and the mean GRF component (F A/P) resolved along the anteroposterior shoe axis, both normalized to subject body weight. The longitudinal translational traction coefficient (MU A/P) equals the ratio of (F A/P)/(FZ). The mean peak anteriorly directed shear force equaled 1.9 ± 0.5 body weights (BW), and the maximum value of the longitudinal translational traction coefficient averaged 0.80 ± 0.15. Since averaging curves whose peaks do not occur at exactly the same time results in an attenuation of the mean peak value, reported means are averages of individual trials, not peaks from average curves. These peak values occurred during the first 25% of the support phase. At this time, the center of pressure of the resultant ground reaction force vector was located beneath the center of the foot along the midline, as shown by the circled region in Fig. 2. These findings imply that shoe outsoles must possess a COF of 0.8 or greater when forces are exerted in an anterior direction.

It can be seen from the mean mediolateral component of the GRF for the cutting movement, which is plotted in Fig. 3, that relatively high shear forces were also developed in the lateral direction. The mean peak mediolateral force component (F M/L) equaled -1.5 ± 0.4 BW. This force component remained high from about 10 to 60% of the support time. The transverse translational traction coefficient (MU M/L), which is the ratio of F M/L divided by FZ (from Fig. 1), had a maximum value of 0.6. This coefficient remained fairly constant at this value from 11% of the support time to a time as late as 95%. Thus, when

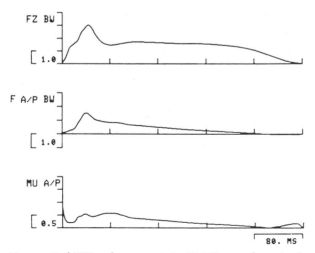

FIG. 1—*Mean vertical (FZ) and anteroposterior (F A/P) ground reaction force components and mean longitudinal translational traction coefficient (MU A/P) developed during a 90° cutting movement. Forces are normalized with respect to body weight. (n = 38 trials).*

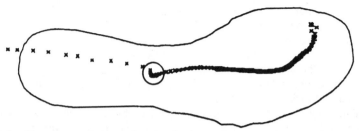

FIG. 2—*Mean center of pressure location for the resultant ground reaction force vector during a 90° cutting movement. Spacing between crosses equals 2 ms.*

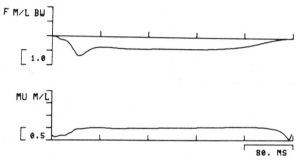

FIG. 3—*Mean mediolateral (F M/L) ground reaction force component and mean transverse translational traction coefficient (MU M/L) developed during a 90° cutting movement. (n = 38 trials.)*

horizontal forces are exerted in a lateral direction, the COF of the shoe outsole need only be greater than 0.6 on the playing surface for which the shoe is designed.

Friction Characteristics of Cleated Outsole Material

The effects that different outsole materials had on the translational traction characteristics on artificial turf were determined. Empirical determinations of COF were made. An artificial playing surface was securely fastened to a six degree-of-freedom force measuring platform. Molded specimens were placed on the artificial surface under vertical forces that equaled or exceeded typical body weights (mean vertical force = 829 N). The specimens had a rectangular geometry, measuring 83 mm by 107 mm. They were pulled a distance of 0.35 m across the test surface at a mean sliding velocity of 0.53 m/s. These loading conditions were selected to approximate the loading conditions that typically occur when athletes perform in the shoes. Force components were sampled at 500 Hz, and COF were determined by dividing the horizontal force component by the vertical force component.

The material out of which a flat plate is composed was found to have a very large effect on the COF of that material on artificial turf. COF ranged from 0.32 for nylon to 1.00 for styrene-butadiene rubber. Even different rubber compounds were found to exhibit different COF on artificial turf. For example, the static COF of nitrile rubber specimens were 26% lower than the static COF of styrene-butadiene rubber specimens.

Also tested on a physical friction measuring device were flat rubber plates with cleats having a truncated conical shape [8]. The cleats were symmetrically oriented in an array of six rows of five cleats. Adjacent cleats had a center-to-center spacing of 18.7 mm. Outside

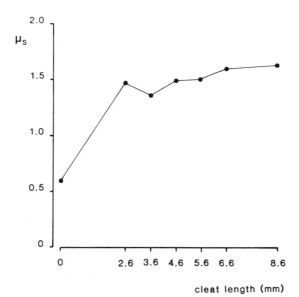

FIG. 4—*Static coefficient of friction of different styrene-butadiene rubber specimens on an artificial playing surface.*

dimensions of the specimens measured 102 mm by 114 mm. The COF of flat rubber plates increased over 100% with the addition of cleats 2.6 mm in length. Increases in cleat length from 2.6 mm to 8.6 mm resulted in further but smaller increases in COF. The relationship between cleat length and COF is shown in Fig. 4.

It was also found that COF of the cleated specimens decreased with increases in normal load and with decreases in surface area. These results were combined to reveal an approximate 55% decrease in COF with a 568% increase in normal pressure in the range 19 to 129 kPa.

Rotational Traction Characteristics of Cleated Shoes

The transducer in the physical traction testing device that was used to measure translational traction characteristics is a six degree-of-freedom force measuring platform. Therefore, this device can also be used to quantify the rotational traction characteristics of shoe outsoles. The amount of resistance developed by a shoe outsole when it is rotated about a vertical axis can be expressed by the free moment component measured by the force platform.

When rotated medially at an average velocity of 7.4 rad/s under an average vertical force of 750 N, the peak magnitude of the moment resisting rotation on artificial turf ranged from a high of 53 to 72 N·m for a conventional rubber basketball shoe outsole to a low of 48 to 55 N·m for a 56-cleat rubber indoor soccer shoe outsole. These moments plus peak moments resisting rotation developed by other outsoles commonly used on artificial turf are plotted in Fig. 5. A sport sock, which is an example of low traction, developed only half the resistance (22 to 30 N·m).

Discussion

The translational traction needs of soccer shoe outsoles are greatest when subjects exert high shear forces in an anterior direction during rapid stopping. The peak value of the lon-

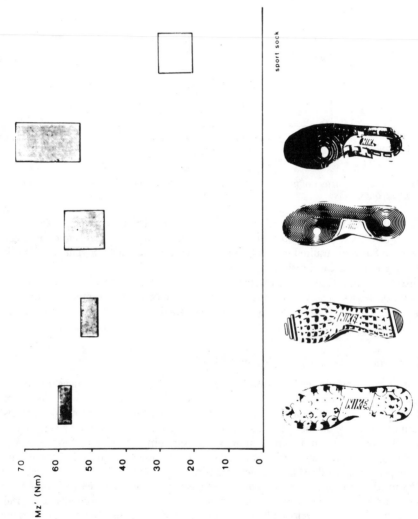

FIG. 5—*Ranges of the peak moment developed during rotation of different shoe outsoles on an artificial playing surface. Only the anterior half of the outsole was in contact with the playing surface. The unshaded box represents the peak moments developed by a sport sock.*

gitudinal translational traction coefficients, 0.8, were the same regardless of whether the subjects were stopping their forward progression to make a cut or to make a pivot. Thus, in order for soccer players to perform in their shoes without slipping, the shoe outsole must possess a COF of 0.8 or greater. Only with a coefficient this great will the outsole develop frictional forces that can counter the high shear forces developed by the stopping foot.

It is worth noting that the maximum value of the translational traction coefficient occurred early in the support period during the braking phase. The calculated coefficient was greatest at this time in spite of a very large force, the vertical force, in the denominator of the calculation. During the braking phase, peak vertical forces averaged 3.35 BW for the cutting movement and 3.02 BW for the pivoting movement.

Results have also indicated that several approaches can be undertaken to develop shoe outsoles that have a COF of 0.8 on artificial turf. For example, employing cleats in an outsole design is a method of achieving sufficiently high values of COF. A dense array of cleats only 2.6 mm in length will increase COF of flat rubber outsoles by more than 100%. Traction of a cleated outsole can be further increased, if needed, by increasing the length of the cleats. One of the easiest approaches used to ensure sufficiently high translational traction characteristics is to simply construct the outsole from materials that are known to possess high COF on the playing surface for which the shoe outsole is intended. Outsoles molded in a flat patternless geometry from styrene-butadiene will possess COF greater than 0.8 on a dry artificial turf surface.

The results further indicate that when horizontal forces are exerted in a lateral direction, such as when cutting sharply to one side, the translational traction needs are not as great as they are during stopping. For laterally directed shear forces, the shoe will still meet the translational traction needs for playing soccer if the COF of the outsole are greater than 0.6 on the playing surface for which the shoe was designed.

It may thus be possible to design shoe outsoles with frictional characteristics that are directional. The present results suggest that outsole designs for soccer shoes that possess a COF greater than 0.8 in an anterior direction and a COF greater than 0.6 in a lateral direction would not slip when subjected to the loads that are typically developed while playing soccer. In general then, there is a potential advantage in developing outsoles that have a lower COF along some axes. This approach could be a means of reducing resistance to rotation without jeopardizing the translational traction characteristics of an outsole.

Simply designing cleated shoe outsoles with as high a COF as possible to ensure that the minimum translational traction requirements are always met is not the proper approach. Several researchers who have quantified both translational and rotational traction characteristics of shoe outsoles have shown that, in general, shoes which have a high COF on a particular surface, and hence develop high translational friction forces, also develop high rotational traction forces [6]. However, increased resistance to rotation is often implicated in serious knee injuries, especially in the sport of football [2]. Therefore, low resistance to rotation about a normal axis is desired in order to protect an athlete's knee joint from high rotary forces that can be transmitted to the leg if the shoe is not free to rotate on the playing surface.

Ideally, the smallest rotational traction attainable is desired for cleated outsoles. However, if peak moments developed by outsoles about a vertical axis passing through the forefoot could be decreased to values approaching 30 N·m, the incidences of injuries due to foot fixation may be reduced. Moments of this peak magnitude are similar to those developed when soccer players wear sport socks, which presumably is a very slippery situation, and one where foot fixation is not likely to occur.

It was found that COF was dependent on normal force and on surface area. This indicates that the concepts of Coulomb friction do not always apply to shoe outsole materials and designs or to artificial playing surfaces. These findings are in agreement with findings from other investigators [6,9]. The COF of materials commonly used in the construction of shoe outsoles decreases with increases in normal pressures. Therefore, designs that lend themselves to the creation of high localized pressures during rotation but lower more distributed pressures during translation would possibly develop lower frictional forces during rotation and higher frictional forces during translation. Future cleated outsole designs should address the compromise between performance and protection by reducing rotational traction for the purposes of decreasing injury while still preserving sufficiently high translational friction.

At the time of occurrence of the maximum translational traction coefficient, the center of pressure of the resultant ground reaction force vector was located beneath the center of the outsole along the midline. Thus, the normal load is distributed both behind this center of pressure location and in front of it. This implies that the design of both the rear part of the outsole and the fore part of the outsole contribute to the outsole's translational traction characteristics. However, COF is directly related to normal force. Therefore, in future studies, measurement of the distribution of the normal loading as opposed to simply measurement of the center of pressure will be more helpful when developing outsoles with either translational traction characteristics that are directional or with low resistance to rotation.

All tests described in this paper were performed on an artificial surface. Although the results are specific to artificial turf, the principles can be applied to natural turf fields or other playing surfaces. One objective in the design of shoe outsoles is to achieve both high translational traction and low rotational traction. The high translational traction is necessary to successfully perform the many lateral movements in field sports. The low rotational traction is necessary to decrease the incidence of injury by preventing the transmission of high rotary forces to the vulnerable knee joint if the foot inadvertently becomes fixed to the ground during rotary movements. The specified coefficients of friction and minimum peak moments during rotation should be applicable to all playing surfaces. This thus means that outsole designs that achieve the desired results would be specific to the playing surface for which the outsole is intended. Also, outsole designs would be specific to the condition of a playing surface (dry or wet, worn or new, and so forth).

References

[1] DeHaven, K. E. and Lintner, D. M., *American Journal of Sports Medicine*, Vol. 14, 1986, pp. 218–224.
[2] Torg, J. S. and Quedenfeld, T., *Research Quarterly*, Vol. 42, 1971, pp. 203–211.
[3] Cameron, B. M. and Davis, O., *Journal of Sports Medicine*, January 1973, pp. 16–27.
[4] Tanel, M. L., U.S. Patent No. 4,653,206, 31 March 1987.
[5] Valiant, G. A. in *Biomechanics of Sport III and IV*, J. Terauds, B. A. Gowitzke, and L. E. Holt, Eds., Academic Publishers, Del Mar, CA, 1987, pp. 29–37.
[6] van Gheluwe, B., Deporte, E., and Hebbelinck, M. in *Biomechanical Aspects of Sport Shoes and Playing Surfaces*, B. M. Nigg and B. A. Kerr, Eds., University of Calgary, Calgary, 1983, pp. 161–168.
[7] Valiant, G. A. in *Science and Football*, T. Reilly, A. Lees, K. Davids, and W. J. Murphy, Eds., E. & F. N. Spon, London, 1988, pp. 406–415.
[8] Valiant, G. A., McGuirk, T., McMahon, T. A., and Frederick, E. C., *Medicine and Science in Sport and Exercise*, Vol. 17, 1985, pp. 222–223.
[9] Schlaepfer, F., Unold, E., and Nigg, B. in *Biomechanical Aspects of Sport Shoes and Playing Surfaces*, B. M. Nigg and B. A. Kerr, Eds., University of Calgary, Calgary, 1983, pp. 153–160.

C. J. Abraham,[1] M. Newman,[1] J. Pugh,[1] and L. S. Shulman[1]

Design Criteria for Footwear and Functional Testing on Artificial and Natural Surfaces

REFERENCE: Abraham, C. J., Newman, M., Pugh, J., and Shulman, L. S., **"Design Criteria for Footwear and Functional Testing on Artificial and Natural Surfaces,"** *Natural and Artificial Playing Fields: Characteristics and Safety Features, ASTM STP 1073*, R. C. Schmidt, E. F. Hoerner, E. M. Milner, and C. A. Morehouse, Eds., American Society for Testing and Materials, Philadelphia, 1990, pp. 69–73.

ABSTRACT: Twisting and cutting sports such as football, baseball, and soccer involve torsional forces placed on the knee which can result in traumatic injuries. In many cases, these injuries relate directly to the sport shoe design and the nature of the playing surface. Although there are many tests performed on shoes involved in various sports, most are performed in the laboratory. There is a distinct difference between the variables in those tests and the ones encountered in the field environment. Laboratory tests that do not take into account the actual motions demonstrated in the field cannot yield meaningful results. A relationship between the loading, surface, and performance aspect of the athlete's movements must be used in order to properly design the sole and heel of any sports shoe. By using a mechanical testing device which consists of a direct readout torque wrench and a detachable foot, one can quantitatively and qualitatively predict whether the forces created during a twisting motion on artificial and natural surfaces could result in injuries. Such measurements are valuable as design criteria for footwear in sports.

KEY WORDS: playing fields, sport shoes, natural surfaces, grass, synthetic surfaces, leg injuries, knee injuries, frictional testing, warnings and instructions

In the late 1960s, when synthetic surfaces were initially being used for track and field sports, there was a reported increase in injuries and pain felt by the athletes running on such tracks as compared with those running on cinder tracks. However, although the injuries were described as painful, they required limited medical treatment. Since that time, some clinicians working in conjunction with industry have improved the synthetic surfaces of both track and field sports to a point where there is now little difference between the performance and characteristics of either surface.

Natural Grass

Even if natural grass is used as a playing surface, problems will arise as a result of improper installation or a lack of budget commitment to its maintenance. Such maintenance includes adequate fertilization, mowing, seeding, proper drainage, and irrigation. Obviously, more attention must be given to an athletic field than a residential lawn because of the frequency of use and abuse an athletic field receives. Natural turf cannot be used following a watering

[1] Associate director, director, director of biomedical engineering and materials science, director of sports, recreation, and athletics division, respectively, Inter-city Testing and Consulting Corp., Mineola, NY 11023.

or after it has just rained, as the grass and subsurface will become damaged, and, ultimately, the turf would deteriorate to a point where it would become unsafe as a playing surface.

Synthetic Turf

In contrast to natural turf, synthetic surfaces are constructed to withstand not only harsh environmental conditions, but continuous usage. Where natural turf fields would be showing damage shortly after the start of the football season, artificial turf fields not only remain consistent throughout, but they increase the length of time that an individual field can be used.

The synthetic surface used on football fields has been developed to a point where its properties are largely isotropic. Therefore, runners should have the same traction regardless of which direction they run. The shock absorbency of the surface results from a porous pad underneath the synthetic carpet. There are synthetic surfaces which do not have porous pads. However, such properties are not affected by temperature extremes to the extent of earlier formulations and, unlike natural turf, the artificial surface retains its cushioning properties in freezing weather. The 0.016-m (⅝-in.) pad under the turf's surface is reported to exceed the shock absorbency capabilities of natural grass in good condition.

The more advanced synthetic turf is produced by a new process which crimps the synthetic turf blades, bunches them up, and forms a denser carpet. The fiber used for strength in the backing is a polyester tire cord. Since the bulkier blades of the turf cannot pack together, they resist the flattening out which was common to the older, straight synthetic blades. As a result, we have a softer, thicker-looking and feeling, nondirectional playing surface which can be utilized in all types of weather.

The subbase is designed to allow water to run off the surface, away from the field itself, into collecting pipes. The design of this drain system eliminates the formation of puddles on the surface, thereby eliminating the need for heavy water-removal machines which, prior to this time, were required for use on baseball fields. This drainage system also permits reducing the 0.30-m (12-in.) crown at the center of the field to approximately 0.15 m (6 in.), and ultimately to the flat field.

Sports Shoes and Mechanisms of Leg Injuries

Since the studies performed by the National Football League, and the National Collegiate Athletic Association (NCAA), and the Consumer Products Safety Commission [1,2] have shown no significant difference between artificial and grass turf with regard to the frequency or severity of injuries, the issue of shoe selection becomes important. There are literally hundreds of shoes on the market which are claimed, by their manufacturers, to be both natural-grass and artificial-turf shoes.

Since there is no regulation as to what a shoe manufacturer may represent with regard to his product, there have been many horror stories about athletes who have worn poorly constructed athletic shoes believing them to be "fast." Too often, players desire the best promotional contract and disregard their own safety.

There are two basic types of accidents that occur in field sports: collisions and falls. Collisions can be caused by an unlimited number of factors which result in a wide variety of injuries to any part of the body. Falls, on the other hand, can be definitely related to the design of the shoe and the surface of play. During the fall, the potential for lower limb injury exists, resulting in sprains and fractures of the legs.

When the frictional rotation between the shoe and the surface is too high, the mechanisms that produce the injuries to the legs involve two factors: fixation and enhancement. In addition, there are three types of forces acting: (1) external rotation, (2) forward fall, and (3) internal rotation. Injury results when both factors occur in conjunction with at least one of the three factors.

Fixation alone, which results from cessation of motion of the shoes relative to the playing surfaces, does not usually cause injury since individuals can fall without injury. The additional factor responsible for injury is *enhancement*. This is where the kinetic energy which is present during the running or movement of the individual is converted into strain energy. If the person continues to rotate clockwise or counterclockwise, and the frictional forces (fixation) between the shoe and the surface do not release, injury will result. However, if the frictional forces between the shoe and the surface release before an injury threshold level is released, any forces previously exerted on the leg will be relieved, and injury to the lower limb will be eliminated. In other words, if the forces are not sustained, they are enhanced and converted into strain energy greater than the physiological tolerance, resulting in injury to various parts of the lower limb.

As stated previously, there are three basic forces that can produce injury when the frictional forces between the shoe and surface become extreme: external rotation, forward fall, and internal rotation. Each force produces injuries that are unique and characteristic for those specific forces. Injuries due to frictional rotational failures involve the lower limb at three sites: the ankle, the lower leg, and the knee.

Extensive studies relating to the mechanical properties of locomotor organs and tissues have been performed and reported on [3]. The known values allow the design of shoes with the frictional force between the shoe and the playing surface sufficient to allow the wearer to maintain sufficient frictional forces necessary to accomplish a task without reaching the threshold value, which would result in injury to any part of the leg. By applying the principles set forth in the sport of skiing, one can design footgear for the athlete involved in field sports which can be worn on both artificial and natural surfaces without being the cause of a leg injury.

Proposed Testing of Frictional Forces (Measurements)

For many years, the ski industry, with the use of a testing device, has measured the release torque between the ski/boot/binding system. The primary function of the testing is to adjust the ski/boot/binding system to a point where the binding releases below the threshold of injury to any part of the wearer's leg, in any type of fall. The guidelines created by the ski industry, in accordance with ASTM recommendations, take into account an individual's capability (experience), weight, and height. Application of these principles would provide a useful guide to shoe manufacturers in the design of the sole for each specific sport and surface.

Andréasson et al. [4] studied the torque developed between a variety of sports shoes and artificial turf. They found that a heavy person was exposed to a larger torque than a lighter person, and the torque was 70% larger in the foot stance position (whole foot in contact with the surface) than in the toe stance position (toe part in contact with the surface). Noncleated shoes gave a smaller torque than cleated shoes on both artificial turf and natural grass.

An extension of the testing performed by Andréasson in conjunction with the release torque evaluation of ski/boot/binding systems can yield data allowing for proper and safe sole design. Weights could be added to the system to yield fairly accurate data relating to the behavior between the sole of the shoe and the surfaces on which the shoe is intended to be used. Knowing the injury threshold values of load for various parts of the leg, the shoe manufacturers would be placed on notice as to the limitations of the design of the sole by meeting the minimum recommendations (guidelines) that would be created for that industry.

Although their work has not been updated, Torg et al. proposed an alternative test protocol in the early 1970s [5].

Warnings and Instructions

With reference to the elimination of product liability or mitigation of liability, failure to warn or instruct (inadequate warnings) becomes an issue of significant importance to the manufacturer. The warnings or instructions accompanying a product should place the consumer on notice as to the proper use and application of that product so that the user will be able to protect himself and others. The warnings, if properly designed and interpreted, should fulfill the applicable legal requirements and have an effect in the reduction of injuries.

When the shoes worn for field sports are examined, the conclusion is easily reached that there are no satisfactory warnings or instructions designed or used for this particular industry. Misuse of shoes, for example, when a shoe is designed specifically for a particular sport and is inappropriately worn for another sport, can result in injuries to the wearer. If an individual is hurt due to misuse, the manufacturer could be held responsible for part or all of the injury sustained. Therefore, it is essential for the industry to devise standards placing the consumer on notice as to the proper use and application of the product. The industry should also set forth the limitations and restrictions to be placed on each product.

General Conclusion

There are no available data that sufficiently demonstrates, with regard to participant safety, the superiority of an artificial playing surface over a natural surface. There is a noticeable increase of player speed on synthetic playing surfaces, which creates an increased probability for higher collision forces between players, resulting in increased severity of injuries of this type. Stanitski et al. [6] reported these findings using AstroTurf, Tartan Turf, Poly Turf, and natural grass surfaces. The studies included the effects of those surfaces on player speed, impact energy, and shoe traction.

While properly designed sport shoes are most important for good foot function, there is no replacement for proper training programs which include strength and flexibility exercises. Once the athlete achieves the proper conditioning, the incidence of injury should be reduced. In addition, the art of falling and protecting oneself from injury on impact with the ground must also be a part of the training program. Romick-Allen and Schultz [7] investigated whole-body responses to unexpected disturbances. No other comprehensive study of fall response for whole-body biomechanics had ever been reported prior to their paper. This study indicates that if an individual is properly conditioned, through training, to prepare his body during a fall for contact with the ground, the extent of any injury could be significantly diminished.

In conclusion, the interrelationship among playing surface, training program, and the nature of the sports shoe is a complex one. Although there is no evidence as to whether an artificial surface is superior to a natural one or vice versa, the manufacturers of sport shoes have a responsibility to the public to further aid in reducing injuries by creating a set of standards for testing frictional parameters between the sole and the surfaces on which the shoe is intended to be used. Precautionary warnings and instructions should be affixed to the shoe, placing the wearer on notice as to any restrictions or limitations in its use, and informing the wearer that the shoe design has been tested in a meaningful, realistic way and has passed minimum requirements set forth by the sports shoe industry.

References

[1] Walsh, U. and Petr, A., "Football Injuries on Natural Turf," 1987, unpublished.
[2] *The NCAA News*, Vol. 25, No. 5, 3 Feb. 1988.
[3] Vaughan, C. L., "Biomechanics of Sport," CRC Press, Inc., 1989.
[4] Andréasson, G., Lindenberger, P. R. and Peterson, L., *The American Journal of Sports Medicine*, Vol. 14, No. 3, 1986, pp. 225–230.
[5] Torg, J. S., "Football Shoes and Playing Surfaces: From Safe to Unsafe," *The Physician and Sports Medicine*, November 1973.
[6] Stanitski, C. L., McMaster, J. H., and Ferguson, R. J., *Journal of Sports Medicine*, Vol. 2, No. 1, January/February 1974, pp. 22–26.
[7] Romick-Allen, R. and Schultz, A. B., *Journal of Biomechanics*, Vol. 21, No. 7, 1988, pp. 591–600.

Testing and Correlation to Actual Field Experience

R. Bruce Martin[1]

Problems Associated with Testing the Impact Absorption Properties of Artificial Playing Surfaces

REFERENCE: Martin, R. B., "**Problems Associated with Testing the Impact Absorption Properties of Artificial Playing Surfaces,**" *Natural and Artificial Playing Fields: Characteristics and Safety Features, ASTM STP 1073,* R. C. Schmidt, E. F. Hoerner, E. M. Milner, and C. A. Morehouse, Eds., American Society for Testing and Materials, Philadelphia, 1990, pp. 77–84.

ABSTRACT: The problem of the safety of synthetic playing surfaces, as well as natural playing fields, is multifaceted. An important factor is the force generated when an athlete strikes the surface. Since this force is directly related to the total deformation of the surface-athlete system during the impact, the compressibility of the surface is a key factor to be considered in surface design and in testing of both new and old surfaces. Using a mathematical model, these concepts are developed in this study. The results show that the accelerations produced during an impact are greater for smaller masses, and equations are derived which indicate the appropriate scaling of the drop height needed to make impacts with small test masses that are equivalent to those of human body weights. The author suggests that testing of playing surfaces should not be limited to measurement of force impulses at a fixed impact momentum, which may be significantly less than the extremes encountered during use, but should include values revealing the total compressibility of the surface.

KEY WORDS: playing fields, sports biomechanics, impact absorption, injury, safety testing

The relative safety of natural and synthetic playing surfaces is much debated. It is difficult to draw conclusions, partly because conditions vary widely, depending on the type of surface, the climate, the sport being played, the ages of the athletes, and coaching decisions (e.g., style of play, cleat choice). Some studies show that the incidence of injuries is greater on synthetic surfaces than on grass, and others maintain that it is not, or that it decreases [1–5].

There are basically two characteristics of a playing surface which affect safety (and also performance)—friction and impact absorption. This paper is concerned with the latter. Impact absorption is used here to mean the ability of a surface to diminish the forces that occur when an object strikes it. This quality depends on both the thickness of the playing surface and its mechanical properties. Surfaces with grass-like upper layers tend to suffer changes in both thickness and mechanical properties as the "grass" fibers are damaged by exposure to sun, the weather, and use. At least in some cases, these reduce the surface's impact absorption ability [6].

For many years the impact absorption properties of playing surfaces have been assessed using methods that typically involve dropping a mass onto the surface and determining the resulting impact force or acceleration (or deceleration, as some may prefer to think of it). As a matter of convenience, the mass of the impacting object is usually much less than that of

---

[1] Professor, Orthopaedic Research Laboratory, University of California at Davis, Davis, CA 95616.

an adult human, or even a child. One may postulate that larger masses or impact energies would increase the acceleration in a nonlinear manner, and that eventually the playing surface would become totally compressed before the kinetic energy could be absorbed by deformation. In order to interpret properly the results of such standard tests as the ASTM Test for Shock-Absorbing Properties of Playing Surface Systems and Materials (F 355-86), the mechanics of this problem need to be explored.

The purpose of this paper is to present a theoretical analysis of the impact absorption problem. This analysis indicates which aspects of the problem may be more important when designing a surface system or predicting the behavior of an existing system. The results also suggest some modifications to the ASTM standard for testing such surfaces (ASTM Test F 355-86).

Theory

Analysis of Impact Absorption

When a body of mass, m, falls from a height, H, and impacts on a surface, there is a simple relationship between the weight of the object (mg) and the *average* reaction force during the impact (F_{av}). Let T be the duration of the impact and z be the distance that the object's center of gravity moves during the impact. If v is the impact velocity and a_{av} is the *average* acceleration during T, from kinematics one has

$$z = \frac{a_{av}T^2}{2} \tag{1}$$

$$v = a_{av}T \tag{2}$$

Combining Eqs 1 and 2 produces

$$a_{av} = \frac{v^2}{2z} \tag{3}$$

The average impact force is

$$F_{av} = \frac{mv^2}{2z} \tag{4}$$

From conservation of energy, one has $v^2 = 2\,gH$; therefore

$$F_{av} = \frac{mgH}{z} \tag{5}$$

(An alternative way of deriving this relationship is to equate the potential energy of the mass when it is at height H to the work done during the impact, $F_{av}z$.) Of course, athletes usually arrange for z to be large by flexing their joints during an impact and using eccentric muscle contractions to reduce a_{av}, and thus F_{av}. However, in an accidental landing, the head or some other body part may strike the surface passively. In that case, z is just the combined deformation of the body (z_o) and the surface (d) during T. Clearly it is advantageous for z_o to be nearly zero; thus, d must be as large as possible. Assuming the playing surface lies on a rigid substrate, the maximum possible value of z is the surface layer thickness, h. Since the average acceleration (in units of gravity, g) during the impact is $a_{av} = F_{av}/mg$

$$a_{av} > \frac{H}{h} \qquad (6)$$

For example, if a player falls from an effective height of 1 m and the surface layer is 2 cm thick, $a_{av} > 50$ g.

Consider now the effect of the mechanical properties of the surface layer on the impact. Most materials used for playing surfaces have nonlinear load-deformation curves when loaded in compression [7]. The stiffness of such surfaces increases as they are deformed. It is convenient to represent the stress-strain behavior of such materials by an exponential relationship

$$S = qs^p \qquad (7)$$

where S is stress, s is strain, and p and q are constants. As a first approximation, an impact on the surface (e.g., the Procedure A test described in ASTM Standard F 355-86) may be regarded as simple compression. If A is the contact area and h is the surface layer thickness, the force, F, at any instant during the impact is related to the deformation of the surface, d, at that instant by the formula

$$F = \left(\frac{Aq}{h^p}\right) d^p \qquad (8)$$

It will be assumed that, as the impact proceeds, the kinetic energy of the falling object is transferred to the surface in the form of elastic energy. Energy loss through plastic deformation and hysteresis will be ignored, since these effects usually involve less than 15% of the total energy [7]. The total kinetic energy must then equal the area under the load-deformation curve up to the point of maximal deformation, when the velocity of the object is zero. Letting $k = Aq/h^p$ and $c = p + 1$, one has by integration of Eq 8 with respect to d

$$E_d = \left(\frac{k}{c}\right) d^c_{max} \qquad (9)$$

By substituting this expression for z in Eq 5, and dividing through by mg, the average acceleration, in gravity units, during the impact can be calculated

$$d_{max} = \left(\frac{cmgH}{k}\right)^{1/c} \qquad (10)$$

By substituting this expression for z in Eq 5, and dividing through by mg, the average acceleration, in gravity units, during the impact can be calculated

$$a_{av} = \frac{H}{d_{max}} = \left[H^{c-1}\left(\frac{k}{cm}\right)\right]^{1/c} \qquad (11)$$

In many cases, the acceleration-time curve may be approximated by the expression

$$a = a_{max} \sin\left(\frac{\pi t}{T}\right) \qquad (12)$$

where a_{max} is the peak acceleration and T is the duration of the impact. With this assumption, the average and peak accelerations are related by $\pi/2$, and one has

$$a_{max} = \frac{\pi}{2}\left[H^{c-1}\left(\frac{k}{cm}\right)\right]^{1/c} \tag{13}$$

Here, a_{max} is expressed in gravity units.

In addition to a_{av} and a_{max}, the severity of the impact may be quantified by the Gadd severity index (G) [8]

$$G = \int_0^T a^{2.5}dt \tag{14}$$

When Eqs 12 and 13 are substituted into this integral, a simple solution does not follow. However, by interpolating between integrals of $\sin^2 \pi t/T$ and $\sin^3 \pi t/T$, one obtains

$$G = 0.462Ta_{max}^{2.5} \tag{15}$$

Recalling Eq 2, the duration of the impact is

$$T = \left(\frac{2d}{a_{av}}\right)^{1/2} = 1.41\left(\frac{cm}{k}\right)^{1/c}H^{(2-c)/2c} \tag{16}$$

(Here, a_{av} must be expressed in metres per second squared rather than in gravity units.) Substituting this and the expressions for k and a_{max} into Eq 15, one has

$$G = 2.02\left(\frac{Aq}{cmh^{c-1}}\right)^{3/2c}H^{(4c-3)/2c} \tag{17}$$

This equation reveals several important things about the nature of impacts on a playing surface. Using typical values for playing surface material properties and the other variables, the sensitivity of G to various components of the equation was explored. Unless otherwise specified, the values of the variables are as follows:

$q = 3 \times 10^8$ Pa,
$p = 3$ ($c = 4$),
$h = 15$ mm,
$m = 70$ kg,
$H = 1$ m,
$g = 9.8$ m/s, and
$A = 100$ cm^2.

These values were chosen as typical of playing surfaces [7] and approximately representative of a human body (70 kg) falling from a reasonable height (1 m) and landing on the head, shoulder, or some other portion of the body which is of relatively small area (<100 cm^2) and unable to absorb energy by eccentric muscle contraction. Figure 1 shows the sensitivity of the Gadd severity index [8] to h, the thickness of the surface layer. The G values shown here and in the subsequent graphs are for the sake of comparison only, and cannot be assigned direct biological significance; however, in experiments using biological subjects, G values

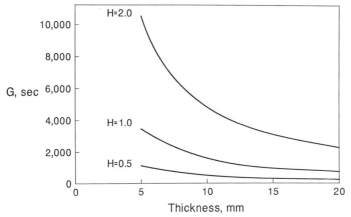

FIG. 1—*Graph of the Gadd severity index (G) versus the thickness of the surface layer.* H *denotes the drop height.*

greater than 1000 are considered unsafe. A reduction in h causes a proportional increase in the severity index. While playing surfaces having grass-like upper layers are not as simple as this model, the results show how diminishment of the overall thickness of the system by deterioration and matting of the "grass" could substantially increase the severity of impacts. Figures 2 and 3 show how G values depend on the mechanical property parameters p and q. Clearly, both the stiffness of the surface and the nonlinearity in its stress-strain curve are very important factors in determining its impact responses. In particular, surfaces with highly nonlinear deformation characteristics are desirable.

Finally, Fig. 4 shows that G *increases* as the mass of the falling object *decreases*. This result is contrary to intuition, but results from the fact that the amount of deformation of the surface increases with the mass of the object. That, in turn, increases T and decreases the acceleration and the severity index. However, very large masses (or drop heights) will cause d_{max} to approach the thickness of the surface layer, and the impact severity will then rapidly

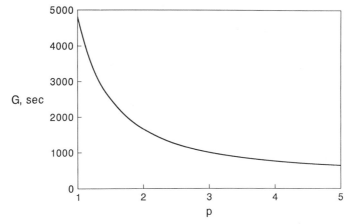

FIG. 2—*Graph of the Gadd severity index versus* p, *the exponent in the constitutive equation of the surface.*

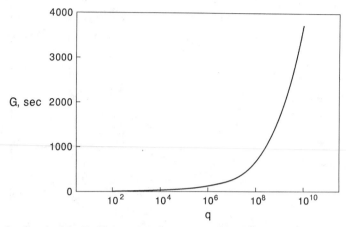

FIG. 3—*Graph of the Gadd severity index versus* q, *the coefficient in the constitutive equation of the surface.*

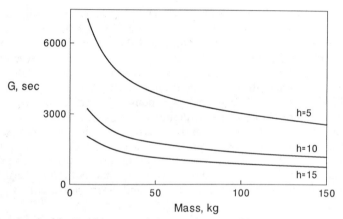

FIG. 4—*Graph of the Gadd severity index versus the mass of the impacting object.* h *denotes the thickness of the surface layer.*

increase with m or H. By setting d_{max} equal to h in Eq 10, one finds that "bottoming out" is a linear function of m and H. When using the above demonstration values, this problem would not occur until a 150-kg mass were dropped from a height of 16 m.

Discussion

Clearly, the analysis of impact absorption presented above has a number of limitations: e.g., the surface consists of a single, elastic material on a rigid substrate being deformed in simple compression by a rigid body. An approximate approach, using energy considerations to calculate the average acceleration during the impact, was used in order to obtain a closed-form solution, since the exact solution involved a nonlinear differential equation. The results shown here were confirmed by modeling the exact differential equation on a computer, but experimental work is needed to determine the parameters of actual playing surfaces and to test the predictions of this model. Nevertheless, the principles it illuminates should apply to

TABLE 1—*Gadd severity index, in seconds, for various combinations of drop height and mass.*[a]

Mass, kg	Drop Height, m			Equivalent Drop Height for 9 kg, m
	0.6	1.0	2.0	
9 (test)	1040	2380	7340	...
20 (child)	770	1760	5440	0.83
70 (adult)	480	1100	3400	1.24

[a] The contact area $= 129$ cm^2.

some degree to many playing surfaces, both synthetic and natural. Perhaps the most important of these is the effect of the object mass on the impact dynamics. The fact that lighter objects experience more severe landings in terms of acceleration is important for two reasons. First, the probability of injury from falling on a surface may be greater for children than for adults. Of course, injuries depend on many factors not considered here, but this implication of the analysis should be considered. Second, this result suggests that impact testing of surfaces using ASTM Test F 355-86 (or similar protocols) may produce accelerations and G values which need to be carefully interpreted, because the mass used is usually less than 10 kg. By increasing H, smaller masses can be made to impact like larger ones, but Eqs 13 and 17 indicate that this adjustment is not a simple one. Procedure A of the ASTM standard (F 355-86) recommends dropping a 9-kg mass with a 129-cm^2 flat face from a height of 0.6 m. Table 1 shows how the resulting G value (about 1040 s) compares with those that would be obtained if the mass of a child (20 kg) or an adult (70 kg) were dropped from 0.6 m, or if any of these masses were dropped from 1 or 2 m. The present model predicts that the Procedure A result (ASTM Test F 355-86) would be quite similar to that for an adult mass falling from 1 m, but significantly less than G for a child's mass dropped from 1 m. The right side of the table shows the 9-kg drop heights which the model predicts would yield the G values for adult and child masses dropped from 1 m.

Because of these problems, the author recommends that modification of the ASTM standard (F 355-86) be considered so that the testing more closely simulates the masses of both an adult and a child striking the surface with body height as the drop height. In each case, the test mass, area, and drop height should be adjusted to give appropriate scaling for G, a_{max}, d_{max}, or some other variable. Ideally, testing should determine the combinations of mass and drop height required to "bottom out" the surface layer or determine that these critical values are outside an envelope of "usage values." In addition, testing should determine the material properties p and q for the surface in question. Clearly, before these modifications can be made, experimental work is necessary to confirm and perhaps refine the theoretical model presented here.

References

[1] Buckley, W. E., "Concussions in College Football: A Multivariant Analysis," *American Journal of Sports Medicine*, Vol. 16, 1988, pp. 51–56.

[2] Halpern, B., Thompson, N., Curl, W. W., Andrews, J. R., Hunter, S. C., and Boring, J. R., "High School Football Injuries: Identifying the Risk Factors," *American Journal of Sports Medicine*, Vol. 15, 1987, pp. S113–S117.

[3] Nigg, B. M., "Biomechanics, Load Analysis and Sports Injuries in the Lower Extremities," *Sports Medicine*, Vol. 2, 1985, pp. 367–379.

[4] Nigg, B. M. and Segesser, B., "The Influence of Playing Surfaces on the Load on the Locomotor System and on Football and Tennis Injuries," *Sports Medicine*, Vol. 5, 1988, pp. 375–385.

[5] Nigg, B. M. and Yeadon, M. R., "Biomechanical Aspects of Playing Surfaces," *Journal of Sports Sciences,* Vol. 5, 1987, pp. 117–145.
[6] Bowers, K. D. and Martin, R. B., "Impact Absorption: New and Old Astroturf at West Virginia University," *Medicine and Science in Sports,* Vol. 6, 1974, pp. 217–221.
[7] McCullagh, P. J. J. and Graham, I. D., "A Preliminary Investigation into the Nature of Shock Absorbency in Synthetic Sports Materials," *Journal of Sports Sciences* Vol. 3, 1985, pp. 103–114.
[8] Gadd, C. W., "Use of the Weighted Impulse Criterion for Estimating Injury Hazard," Paper 660793, *Proceedings,* Tenth Stapp Car Crash Conference, Society of Automotive Engineers, New York, 1966.

Stephen T. Cockerham,[1] Victor A. Gibeault,[1] John Van Dam,[2] and Matthew K. Leonard[1]

Tolerance of Several Cool-Season Turfgrasses to Simulated Sports Traffic

REFERENCE: Cockerham, S. T., Gibeault, V. A., Van Dam, J., and Leonard, M. K., "**Tolerance of Several Cool-Season Turfgrasses to Simulated Sports Traffic,**" *Natural and Artificial Playing Fields: Charateristics and Safety Features, ASTM STP 1073,* R. C. Schmidt, E. F. Hoerner, E. M. Milner, and C. A. Morehouse, Eds., American Society for Testing and Materials, Philadelphia, 1990, pp. 85–95.

ABSTRACT: Cool-season turfgrasses have potential for use on sports fields in the Southwestern United States. Fifty-three cultivars were planted in the National Perennial Ryegrass Evaluation Trial at the University of California at Riverside in 1984. After four years, Palmer, HR-1, Tara, Citation II, M-382, Gator, Blazer, Prelude, and SWRC-1 rated highest in quality with no statistically significant difference among them. A Brinkman traffic simulator (BTS) treatment, equivalent to one professional football game per week, was applied in 1988, over an eight-week period, to the perennial ryegrass cultivars. All of the ryegrasses tolerated the traffic, with Citation II performing the best.

Common Bermuda grass [*Cynodon dactylon* (L.) Pers.] was overseeded with several cool-season species. Under moderate BTS traffic, roughstalk bluegrass (*Poa trivialis* L.) disappeared almost immediately. Annual ryegrass (*Lolium multiflorum* Lam.), Flyer creeping red fescue (*Festuca rubra* L.), and Shadow Chewing's fescue (*Festuca rubra* var. *commutata* Gaud.) tolerated more traffic. Rebel II tall fescue (*Festuca arundinacea* Schreb.) withstood a moderate amount of traffic. Caliente and Elka perennial ryegrass (*Lolium perenne* L.) cultivars were traffic tolerant with the Caliente rating higher. Under the traffic and competition of the more persistent overseeded grasses (perennial ryegrass and tall fescue), the common Bermuda grass did not transition.

Established Mojave tall fescue was submitted to BTS traffic over a nine-month period. The grass tolerated moderate traffic, but it did not perform well under a once a week football game equivalent. Penetrometer measurements were significant among the treatments, indicating the heavy traffic reduced the impact absorption capability of the turf and increased the soil compaction.

The perennial ryegrasses are durable enough for consideration as sports turf for some sports in the Southwest.

KEY WORDS: playing fields, traffic tolerance, wear tolerance, sports turf, overseeding

Sports fields are high traffic turf areas that are subject to demands, not only for use and playability, but for safety and aesthetics. Sports fields include: parks; youth baseball, football, and soccer fields; high school and college fields; and stadiums. Many are used seven days per week and 16 h per day including night play under lights. The turfgrasses are expected to withstand the stress of this intense use plus the pressure of people traffic.

---

[1] Superintendent of agricultural operations, extension turfgrass specialist, and staff research associate, respectively, University of California, Riverside, CA 92507.
[2] Turfgrass advisor, San Bernardino County, University of California, Cooperative Extension, Riverside, CA 92507.

Sports turf has become an important segment of the turfgrass industry. Televised sports events have increased public awareness of sports fields; in addition, player safety and liability issues are beginning to focus attention on community turf facilities. In the United States in 1984, there were 98 473 football injuries treated in hospital emergency rooms [1], some of which were caused by unsafe football fields [2].

Traffic Tolerance

Managing a sports field is a unique task. Many of the accepted fundamentals of turfgrass culture seem to fail under the stress of heavy traffic. Traffic on a sports field subject to use by athletes wearing cleated shoes has three components: (1) wear from friction and scuffing, (2) compaction from the shoe sole and the concentrated weight distribution of the cleat, and (3) shear injury to the grass plant from the twisting of the embedded cleats of the shoe. Turfgrass cultural practices can have as much influence on wear tolerance as varieties within a species [3]. Even mowing height and frequency affect the wear resistance of turf [4]. Nitrogen can be used to increase the quality of a turf sward before wear, but when it is applied at high levels, root mass deteriorates [5] and the entire turfgrass plant deteriorates with traffic [6].

The most important single factor in relation to the shear strength, resilience, and wear tolerance of a turf is the above ground biomass [7]. Turfgrasses vary widely in the ability to tolerate wear. Perennial ryegrass (*Lolium perenne* L.) is more tolerant than Kentucky bluegrass (*Poa pratensis* L.), tall fescue (*Festuca arundinacea* Schreb.), annual ryegrass (*Lolium multiflorum* Lam.), and red fescue (*Festuca rubra* L.) [8]. This wear tolerance is dependent upon the composition of tissue in the verdure [9].

Traffic Simulator

To conduct research for sports fields, it is necessary to use a device to simulate traffic imposed by sports that use a cleated shoe. Criteria for such a traffic simulator are (*a*) to cause a shearing action, (*b*) create compaction, (*c*) impose wear, (*d*) to be of simple construction to minimize maintenance, (*e*) to be sufficiently large to cover a large number of plots, and (*f*) to be easy to use [10,11]. Canaway [12] built a differential slip wear machine (DS1) that used two cleated rollers turning at different speeds to impose simulated traffic to research plots.

Materials and Methods

Brinkman Traffic Simulator

The Brinkman traffic simulator (BTS), shown in Fig. 1, was developed at the University of California, Riverside, based upon previous information. The BTS consists of two cleated rollers (Fig. 2), connected by chain and sprockets, in a frame, which is pulled by a small tractor.

The front sprocket has 21 teeth (12 cm), and the rear has 26 teeth (14.3 cm), which causes the rollers to turn at different speeds creating a shearing action by the cleats along with compaction and wear. The cleats are hex nuts, 1.4 cm outside width by 1.25 cm deep, in a spiral with five cleats of each roller on the ground at any one time. Each roller has a 25.3 cm diameter and is 1.2 m wide. Transport wheels can be raised and lowered hydraulically, using remote ports on the towing vehicle.

The BTS was calibrated by comparing the turf injury created by the BTS to that of actual football play. A model Santa Ana Bermuda grass sports field of sand basin construction

FIG. 1—*The Brinkman traffic simulator (BTS) consists of a pair of steel rollers with welded cleats connected by a drive chain to unmatched sprockets. The rollers revolve at different speeds as the BTS is pulled across the turfgrass plots.*

FIG. 2—*The Brinkman traffic simulator chain and sprockets.*

received the BTS treatments. The Los Angeles Memorial Coliseum, also a Santa Ana Bermuda grass field of sand basin construction, was evaluated after Los Angeles Raiders and University of Southern California football games. The traffic injury occurring in the center of the football field, defined as the area between the 30-yard lines and the professional hash marks, was approximately equal to 16 passes with the BTS.

Perennial Ryegrass Cultivars

Fifty-three cultivars were planted in the National Perennial Ryegrass Evaluation Trial in October 1984 at the University of California Agricultural Experiment Station in Riverside. The grasses were rated regularly for turfgrass quality (given as turf scores on a one to nine rating scale with nine being superior), color, and leaf rust (*Puccinia* spp.) susceptibility. From mid-May to mid-July 1988, the grasses were rated for 4 weeks of moderate BTS traffic of 8 passes 1 day per week and 4 weeks of BTS game traffic of 16 passes 1 day per week. Prior to BTS treatments, four plugs per plot were removed and the thatch measured for later correlation to traffic tolerance.

Tall Fescue Traffic Tolerance

Established Mojave tall fescue was submitted to BTS traffic of 0, 7, and 14 passes 1 day per week in March through December 1987. Subplots consisted of 1 nitrogen fertilizer application at 0, 0.49, 0.98, and 1.95 kg nitrogen per are (0, 1, 2, and 4 lb nitrogen per 1000 ft^2).

The tall fescue plots were rated weekly for turf quality. At the termination of the trial, the hardness of the turf plus soil compaction was measured with a penetrometer as a simple technique to estimate the reduction in impact absorption capability. The thatch was measured in each plot during the cycle of BTS treatment.

Overseeding Traffic Study

Common Bermuda grass was overseeded with several cool-season grasses in October 1986 (Fig. 3). Roughstalk blugrass (*Poa trivialis* L.) was seeded at 1.46 kg/are (3 lb/1000 ft^2), and all of the rest were seeded at 4.88 kg/are (10 lb/1000 ft^2). Ten passes of BTS traffic one day per week was applied for a year beginning February 1987.

The plots were rated weekly for turf quality. At the termination of the trial, the plots were treated with pronamide to selectively eliminate the remaining cool-season species. The percent Bermuda grass cover was estimated after the cool-season grasses were gone.

Experimental Results

Perennial Ryegrass Cultivars

Most of the perennial ryegrasses provided acceptable quality throughout the trial (Table 1). Palmer, HR-1, Tara, Citation II, M-382, Gator, Blazer, Prelude, and SWRC-1 rated highest, but the results were not significantly different.

In the color ratings, the highest numerical rating was for the darkest green. Nearly half of the cultivars were not significantly different from each other. Out of 53 cultivars, Gator, HR-1, Tara, Palmer, Manhattan II, MOM LP 702, Birdie II, Cowboy, Ranger, Yorktown II, MOM LP 210, M-382, NK 80389, HE-168, Citation II, SWRC-1, Acclaim, Barry, Ovation, MOM LP 792, Elka, Cigil, and Pippin were all relatively free of rust, but none was significantly better than the others.

Most of the perennial ryegrasses tolerated BTS traffic much better than expected. Pippin

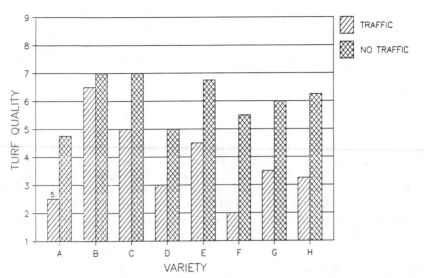

FIG. 3—*Overseeding traffic study: turf quality:* a, *control;* b, *Caliente perennial ryegrass;* c, *Elka perennial ryegrass;* d, *annual ryegrass;* e, *Rebel II tall fescue;* f, *roughstalk bluegrass;* g, *Shadow Chewing's fescue; and* h, *Flyer creeping red fescue.*

and Linn performed the poorest, weakening significantly under traffic. The highest performer was Citation II, although it was not significantly different from the remaining varieties.

Thatch thickness of each cultivar was measured prior to applying the traffic and compared with the traffic tolerance ratings. The correlation was significant ($r = -0.251$, $p = 0.001$), indicating a trend that increased thatch accumulation may enhance perennial ryegrass tolerance to BTS traffic.

Tall Fescue Traffic Tolerance

The highest turf quality rating for all Mojave tall fescue traffic treatments was in the highest nitrogen treatment (Fig. 4). As the traffic level increased, the overall turf quality decreased. The tall fescue subjected to the heaviest traffic with no fertilizer treatment was significantly below acceptable quality for a safe sports field. A sports field that has uniform turfgrass coverage and density, provides footing for the athletes, has no separate clumps of grass, some thatch, no bare spots, and has a soil surface with minimum compaction would be considered of safe quality. One nitrogen fertilizer application significantly improved the turf quality of tall fescue under traffic. At the heaviest traffic level, one game per week equivalent, and the highest nitrogen application, the tall fescue was still of acceptable quality.

The penetrometer comparison of the hardness of the field in each of the traffic treatments showed that with an increase in traffic, field hardness increased significantly (Fig. 5). The increase in hardness indicates a possible reduction of the impact absorption capability of the turf. There was no significant difference in penetrometer readings between the fertilizer subtreatments, suggesting that one application of nitrogen fertilizer did not affect impact absorption.

The thatch thickness of the tall fescue was measured in each of the traffic treatments (Fig. 6). As the level of traffic increased, there was a significant reduction in the thickness of the thatch. This also indicates the reduced impact absorption capability of the turf.

TABLE 1—*Mean turfgrass ratings for perennial ryegrass at University of California, Riverside.*

CULTIVAR	TRAFFIC TOLERANCE* LSD (0.6)	COLOR** LSD (0.5)	LEAF RUST*** LSD (1.8)	QUALITY**** LSD (0.5)
CITATION II	1.7	6.7	6.7	6.9
PALMER	2.0	7.0	7.7	7.2
M-382	2.0	7.0	7.0	6.8
GATOR	2.0	7.0	8.3	6.8
BLAZER	2.0	7.0	6.0	6.8
PRELUDE	2.0	7.0	6.0	6.8
SWRC-1	2.0	7.0	6.7	6.7
MANHATTAN II	2.0	6.7	7.7	6.6
MOM LP 702	2.0	6.7	7.7	6.6
NK 80389	2.0	6.3	7.0	6.6
RANGER	2.0	6.3	7.3	6.4
YORKTOWN II	2.0	6.3	7.3	6.4
ACCLAIM	2.0	6.7	6.7	6.4
BARRY	2.0	6.7	6.7	6.4
PREMIER	2.0	7.0	3.3	6.3
DERBY	2.0	6.0	3.3	6.3
HE-168	2.0	5.7	7.0	6.3
MOM LP 792	2.0	6.7	6.7	6.3
HE 178	2.0	6.0	6.0	6.2
FIESTA	2.0	6.7	3.0	6.2
DIPLOMAT	2.0	5.7	4.7	6.2
OMEGA	2.0	6.7	4.0	6.2
CROWN	2.0	6.3	6.0	6.1
COWBOY (2EE)	2.0	6.0	7.7	6.1
MANHATTAN	2.0	5.7	4.7	6.1
DELRAY	2.0	6.0	3.7	6.0
MOM LP 210	2.0	5.3	7.3	5.7
PENNFINE	2.0	6.3	2.7	5.6
REGAL	2.0	6.3	2.7	5.6
NK 79309	2.0	6.3	2.3	5.3
WWE 19	2.0	5.0	4.7	5.2
TARA (BT-I)	2.3	6.7	8.0	7.0
PENNANT	2.3	6.7	6.3	6.4
DASHER	2.3	6.3	4.7	6.3
ALL*STAR (IA 728)	2.3	6.3	6.0	6.2
ELKA	2.3	5.7	6.7	6.0
CITATION	2.3	6.7	2.7	6.0
COCKADE	2.3	6.0	4.7	5.9
CUPIDO	2.3	5.0	4.3	5.8
NK 79307	2.3	7.0	2.3	5.5
HR-1	2.7	6.7	8.0	7.1
BIRDIE II	2.7	7.0	7.7	6.6
OVATION (MOM LP 736)	2.7	6.3	6.7	6.3
CIGIL	2.7	6.0	6.7	5.5
PIPPIN	3.0	4.7	6.7	4.9
LINN	3.3	4.7	5.7	4.4

* TRAFFIC TOLERANCE 1=0%; 3=25%; 5=50%; 9=100% INJURY
** COLOR 1-9; 9 = DARK GREEN
*** LEAF RUST 1-9; 9 = NO DISEASE
**** QUALITY 1-9; 9 = IDEAL TURF
TO DETERMINE STATISTICAL DIFFERENCES AMONG ENTRIES, SUBTRACT ONE
ENTRY'S MEAN FROM ANOTHER ENTRY'S MEAN. STATISTICAL DIFFERENCES
OCCUR WHEN THIS VALUE IS LARGER THAN THE CORRESPONDING LSD
(LEAST SIGNIFICANT DIFFERENCE) VALUE

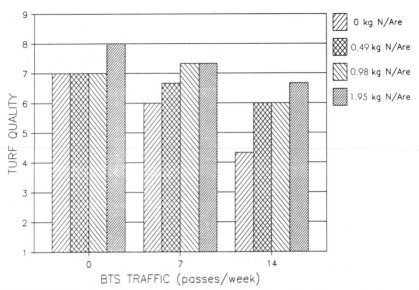

FIG. 4—*Tall fescue traffic study: nitrogen application. The turf quality generally decreased with traffic. Nitrogen application did improve the quality on some treatment plots.*

Overseeding Traffic Study

The highest quality overseeded Bermuda grass turf without traffic was seen with the two perennial ryegrasses followed closely by the three fescues. Roughstalk bluegrass and annual ryegrass were acceptable, but significantly lower in quality.

Roughstalk bluegrass did not tolerate traffic. Annual ryegrass and the two fine fescues—Shadow Chewing's fescue (*Festuca rubra* var. *commutata* Gaud.) and Flyer red fescue (*Fes-*

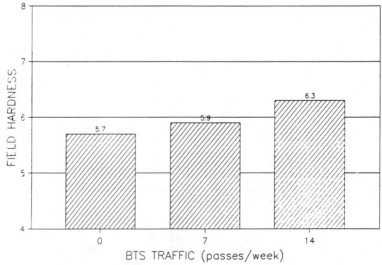

FIG. 5—*Tall fescue traffic study: penetrometer survey. As applied traffic increased, the hardness of the soil under the turf increased.*

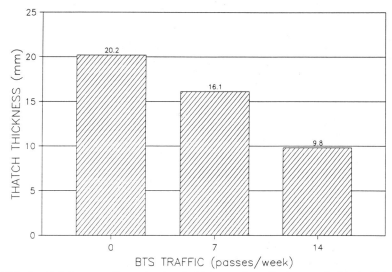

FIG. 6—*Tall fescue traffic study: thatch thickness. As traffic increased, thatch thickness decreased.*

tuca rubra L.)—performed little better. The Rebel II tall fescue was significantly better under traffic than all but the perennial ryegrasses.

The two perennial ryegrasses as overseeded grasses performed remarkably well under traffic through a wide range of temperatures. Caliente perennial ryegrass was significantly better under traffic than Elka. With no traffic there was no difference between them. There was very little observable difference between the Caliente with traffic and without.

In the spring of 1988, the plot area was treated with pronamide herbicide to eradicate the remaining cool-season grasses. Figure 7 shows the percent common Bermuda grass cover in the plots after the cool-season grasses had been eliminated. The grasses that were weak under traffic as overseeded turf were better for the spring transition from cool-season grass to Bermuda grass. The tall fescue did not allow a good transition to Bermuda grass, but it was better as a result of the traffic eliminating some of the fescue. The perennial ryegrasses allowed a poor transition without traffic and significantly reduced the Bermuda grass stand with traffic.

Discussion

In the southwest, warm-season grasses, especially the Bermuda grasses, are most often chosen for sports turf. These grasses have long been considered to provide the most durable natural turf sports fields. An accepted cultural practice to provide winter color for dormant Bermuda grass is to overseed with a cool-season grass. The intent is for the cool-season species to die out in the late spring or early summer, facilitating a turf transition back to Bermuda grass.

Perennial ryegrass has been the most commonly used species for overseeding Bermuda grasses for several years. Because of plant improvement, the perennial ryegrasses are durable, attractive, and pest-free turfgrasses; however, failures in the spring transition to Bermuda grass have become major issues with perennial ryegrasses because of their persistence. Where the spring transition is important, the use of highly traffic-resistant ryegrasses should be avoided for the overseeding of Bermuda grass. In some southwestern climates, perennial ryegrass may be used as the permanent, primary turfgrass species.

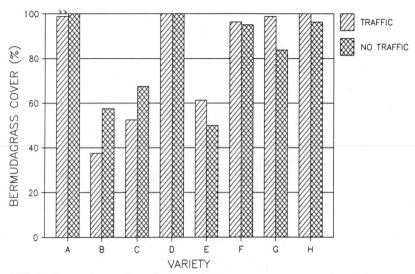

FIG. 7—*Overseeding traffic study: Bermuda Grass transition:* a, *Control;* b, *Caliente perennial ryegrass;* c, *Elka perennial ryegrass;* d, *annual ryegrass;* e, *Rebel II tall fescue;* f, *roughstalk bluegrass;* g, *Shadow Chewing's fescue; and* h, *Flyer creeping red fescue.*

Newer perennial ryegrasses have been shown to be very durable in the Mediterranean climate of Southern California. As many as 31 new cultivars showed excellent traffic tolerance in a large monostand experimental trial. Caliente perennial ryegrass vigorously resisted the affects of a long period of moderate traffic in a study of cool-season grasses used to overseed common Bermuda grass. There is reason to believe that any of these cultivars would make very good turfgrass surfaces for sports fields, especially for winter sports such as football.

In the place of hybrid Bermuda grasses on sports fields, the perennial ryegrasses would make reseeding a possible option for repairing injured turf. This could provide a very useful tool, especially on fields used primarily for football.

One serious concern about converting sports fields from Bermuda grass, especially hybrid Bermuda grass, to perennial ryegrass is the change in mowing height. As an overseeded species, the ryegrass is mowed as low as 0.24 cm (³⁄₃₂ in.) on golf greens. As a primary turf surface, the ryegrass will have to be mowed to around 3 cm. This can change the playing characteristics of closer mowed baseball infields and football fields. The objections of coaches and players are very real and may preclude a conversion from hybrid Bermuda grass to perennial ryegrass in some circumstances. The taller grass will cause a ball to roll slower and runners can be slowed. Field goal kickers tend to prefer very low mowed turf, feeling that taller turf can interfere with the kick.

The improvements in tall fescue cultivars have been rapid and significant. The old "pasture type" cultivars did not tolerate traffic well without clumping and were very poor as an overseeded species. The newest generations do not tolerate traffic as well as the perennial ryegrasses, but they are durable, and clumpy growth is not a problem. As overseed species they have acceptable turfgrass quality and cause fewer transition problems than the perennial ryegrasses. The coarse texture can be objectionable either as a primary turf surface or an overseed.

The newest generations of cool-season grasses are rapidly becoming important species for sports turf in the Southwest. As the improvements continue, the nature of sports field management can be expected to change dramatically just to keep pace with changing facility needs and available technology.

References

[1] "Most Frequent Football Injuries," *National Electronic Injury Surveillance System*, Sports Features Syndicate, Riverside, CA, 1985.

[2] Harper, J. C., Morehouse, C. A., Waddington, D. V., and Buckley, W. E., "Turf Management, Athletic Field Conditions, and Injuries in High School Football," Progress Report 384, The Pennsylvania State University, Agricultural Experiment Station, University Park, PA, 1984.

[3] Youngner, V. B., "Accelerated Wear Tests on Turfgrasses," *Agronomy Journal*, Vol. 53, 1961, pp. 217–218.

[4] Youngner, V. B., "Wear Resistance of Cool-Season Turfgrasses: Effects of Previous Mowing Practices," *Agronomy Journal*, Vol. 54, 1962, pp. 198–199.

[5] Canaway, P. M., "The Response of *Lolium perenne* (Perennial Ryegrass) Turf Grown on Sand and Soil to Fertilizer Nitrogen—II: Aboveground Biomass, Tiller Numbers, and Root Biomass," *Journal of the Sports Turf Research Institute*, Vol. 60, 1984, pp. 18–26.

[6] Canaway, P. M. and Hacker, J. W., "The Response of *Lolium perenne* L. Grown on a Prunty-Mulqueen Sand Carpet Root Zone to Fertilizer Nitrogen—I: Ground Cover Response as Affected by Football-Type Wear," *Journal of the Sports Turf Research Institute*, Vol. 64, 1988, pp. 63–74.

[7] Canaway, P. M., "The Effect of Root Zone Construction on the Wear Tolerance and Playability of Eight Turfgrass Species Subjected to Football-Type Wear," *Journal of the Sports Turf Research Institute*, Vol. 59, 1983, pp. 107–123.

[8] Shearman, R. C. and Beard, J. B., "Turfgrass Wear Tolerance Mechanisms—I: Wear Tolerance of Seven Turfgrass Species and Quantitative Methods for Determining Turfgrass Wear Injury," *Agronomy Journal*, Vol. 67, 1975, pp. 208–211.

[9] Shearman, R. C. and Beard, J. B., "Turfgrass Wear Tolerance Mechanisms—III: Physiological, Morphological, and Anatomical Characteristics Associated with Turfgrass Wear Tolerance," *Agronomy Journal*, Vol. 67, 1975, pp. 215–218.

[10] Meyer, W. A., personal communication, 1985.

[11] Murray, J., U.S. Department of Agriculture, Beltsville, MD, personal communication, 1985.

[12] Canaway, P. M., "A Differential Slip Wear Machine (DS1) for the Artificial Simulation of Turfgrass Wear," *Journal of the Sports Turf Research Institute*, Vol. 52, 1976, pp. 92–99.

John N. Rogers III[1] and Donald V. Waddington[2]

Portable Apparatus for Assessing Impact Characteristics of Athletic Field Surfaces

REFERENCE: Rogers, J. N. III and Waddington, D. V., "**Portable Apparatus for Assessing Impact Characteristics of Athletic Field Surfaces,**" *Natural and Artificial Playing Fields: Characteristics and Safety Features, ASTM STP 1073*, R. C. Schmidt, E. F. Hoerner, E. M. Milner, and C. A. Morehouse, Eds., American Society for Testing and Materials, Philadelphia, 1990, pp. 96–110.

ABSTRACT: This paper presents a method for quantitative assessment of the quality of athletic fields. Impact absorption characteristics were measured using the Clegg impact soil tester, the Bruel and Kjaer 2515 vibration analyzer, and three impact hammers (0.5, 2.25, and 4.5 kg). This apparatus was evaluated on sports fields and on research plots to obtain deceleration-time curves. The impact characteristics obtained from the curves were the maximum deceleration, time to maximum deceleration, duration of impact, rate of change of deceleration, surface deformation, severity index, and rebound ratio. After a series of experiments that evaluated the effects of turfgrass management practices on impact absorption characteristics, correlation coefficients between impact characteristics and between impact hammers were determined. The correlation between the impact characteristics was higher when the evaluations were on one type of surface (turf) instead of multiple surface types (turf and soil). The weakest correlation was between the heaviest and lightest hammers.

KEY WORDS: playing fields, Clegg impact soil tester, Bruel and Kjaer vibration analyzer, impact hammer, impact absorption, shock absorption, athletic fields, turfgrass

An athletic field surface should be a smooth, well-drained surface covered with a dense, wear-tolerant grass. Certainly, the soil type and grass species best suited for specific areas will vary widely; however, the basic requirements for maintaining a high-quality turf are similar.

The wide range of surface conditions on athletic fields is caused by factors such as construction methods, maintenance input, and use levels. Surface variation can lead to different effects on player performance in all sports and on the behavior of balls in sports such as baseball and soccer.

The effect a field has on player safety and player performance, as well as on ball performance, can be termed the playing quality of a field. Fields that are hard can be dangerous to players, while a soft, spongy field can create early fatigue in the leg muscles of a player. Similarly, uneven, bumpy, sparsely covered playing surfaces can cause the ball bounce and roll to be unpredictable and can also adversely affect footing.

Bell et al. [1] reported that playing quality of athletic fields involves three different but related interactions: (a) the effects a field has on a ball, (b) the effect the surface has on absorbing impact energy created by a player (this effect is also referred to as hardness), and (c) the

---

[1] Assistant professor, Department of Crop and Soil Science, Michigan State University, East Lansing, MI 48824.

[2] Professor of soil science, Department of Agronomy, The Pennsylvania State University, University Park, PA 16802.

type of footing a playing surface provides (traction). While the description of these interactions seems both logical and simplistic, characterization of these interactions on different surfaces depends on the number of extrinsic and intrinsic factors associated with the particular athletic field. In order to compare surfaces, quantitative means for measuring these characteristics are necessary.

While the demand for top playing quality in athletic fields is prevalent, the means for assessing this quality are not widely available. Soil and plant conditions can be rated; however, the importance of such agronomic factors is more clearly recognized when they are related to quantitative measurements of impact and traction characteristics. Researchers have investigated several methods for evaluation of athletic fields which have included both qualitative and quantitative tests.

One method for evaluating athletic surfaces has been to compare the numbers of injuries received on various surfaces [2–6]. The majority of this research has been done comparing football injuries on artificial turf with those on natural grass, and results from these studies are quite varied. Bramwell et al. [2] reported that injury rates for games played on synthetic surfaces were significantly higher than those for grass. Adkinson et al. [3] reported significant differences in injury numbers between natural and synthetic surfaces and also between different synthetic surfaces. Macik [4] indicated that, at the professional level, there was a higher probability of injury occurring on an artificial than on a natural grass field, while Keene et al. [5] reported no significant difference between natural and synthetic turf in the number of intercollegiate football injuries.

There are problems associated with comparisons of surfaces using injury data. In terms of the surface, the question of characterization of the field must be considered. The surface type will vary depending on several factors. For synthetic surfaces, the variation will increase with age, the shock-absorbing padding underneath the surface [6], and the surface fabric itself [3]. Natural surfaces can differ in many ways also. Kretzler [7] recognized this in a rebuttal to some of the early injury/surface comparison work. He questioned the use of the term "natural turf." The meaning of this term could encompass any field that was not covered by synthetic fabric, and this could range from a well-constructed and well-maintained field to a stone-laden field that was void of grass. Characterization of natural fields in relation to the soil type, moisture, and bulk density, as well as the grass species and density, is imperative when making comparisons between surfaces.

Another problem with using the number of injuries in comparing surfaces is classifying the type or nature of the injury itself. It is important to evaluate injuries that may be related to the field surfaces, which vary in characteristics because of construction methods, maintenance practices, intensity of use, or a combination of these factors. In a report on injuries in twelve Pennsylvania high schools, Harper et al. [8] stated that 20.9% of all injuries reported were either definitely or possibly field related. In this study, each school's athletic trainer was asked his opinion on the cause of the injury. Before comparisons of surface types are made using injury rates or types, methods of characterizing fields are necessary.

Another means for characterizing surfaces is through a procedure that quantitatively measures the impact absorption properties. The ability of a surface to absorb the impact energy of an object hitting that surface is known as the shock-absorbing or attenuating ability of that surface. The measurement of this shock-absorbing ability is a measure of the impact absorption or hardness of the field.

Several methods using falling objects of known weight or "missiles" have been developed to evaluate athletic field surfaces. A piezoelectric accelerometer mounted on a free-falling missile (object) senses the change in velocity (deceleration) caused by the impact and sends a signal (voltages or charges generated in the disks or crystals) corresponding to the applied acceleration [9]. Upon impact the accelerometer measures the negative acceleration (deceleration, g) of the object. The harder the surface, the faster the object decelerates and the higher the peak deceleration (g_{max}). The energy created during the fall is in part absorbed by the surface and in part returned to the missile. The more the energy is returned to the missile, the greater is the deceleration and the higher the voltage signal from the accelerometer.

Research on the impact absorption of surfaces has been mainly conducted in the late 1970s and 1980s. However, the earliest work involving impact energy for determining the playing quality of athletic surfaces was reported in 1968 by Gramckow [10]. Impact absorption was measured using an accelerometer attached to a 3.64-kg (8-lb) weight dropped from a height of 183 cm. An impact curve was measured using an oscilloscope, and pictures of the curve were recorded with a camera. The effects of the grass species, soil type, soil moisture, soil amendment, and height of the cut grass on impact absorption were evaluated. Bermuda grass [*Cynodon dactylon* (L.) Pers.] absorbed more energy than either tall fescue (*Festuca arundinancea* Schreb.) or Kentucky bluegrass (*Poa pratensis* L.). Sand mixed with 50% sawdust (by volume) had the lowest peak deceleration or g_{max} values, while the loam soil treatment had the highest readings. Increasing soil moisture caused a decrease in peak deceleration values.

The utilization of synthetic materials for playing surfaces generated comparisons between synthetic and natural surfaces. A study designed to evaluate the impact energy absorbed by old and new AstroTurf, Kentucky bluegrass, and asphalt surfaces was conducted by Bowers and Martin [6] in 1974. A 7.3-kg (16-lb) weight was dropped from a 31.8-cm height. A signal from an accelerometer was recorded on an oscilloscope. Results showed that the Kentucky bluegrass had superior impact-absorbing qualities, followed closely by new AstroTurf. Five-year-old AstroTurf had much poorer shock-absorbing characteristics.

Zebarth and Sheard [11] conducted impact-absorption research on racing surfaces for thoroughbred horses. The impact absorption (referred to as impact resistance by the authors) was measured by vertically mounting an accelerometer to a simulated hoof. They concluded that the performance of racehorses showed a strong negative correlation with impact absorption measurements. Longer race times were associated with lower impact absorption measurements.

A standard test method of ASTM is the ANSI/ASTM Test for Shock-Absorbing Properties of Playing Surface Systems and Materials (F 355-86). The procedure involves attaching an accelerometer to a circular, flat or rounded, metal-impacting missile with a specified mass, geometry, and impact velocity. The acceleration-time history of the impact is recorded with the aid of an oscilloscope or other recording device. This method suggests calculating the severity index as well as other parameters. The severity index is equal to the integral of acceleration to the 2.5 power over the total duration of impact. The severity index was developed by Gadd [12] to predict the probability of cerebral concussions due to head impacts. Henderson [13] used the ASTM method to evaluate effects of different soil types, depths of soil, and turf types on impact absorption. A 9.1-kg (20-lb) cylindrical missile was dropped from a height of 61 cm onto the different surfaces prepared in wooden boxes which could be carried into the laboratory for testing.

Another device used for measuring impact absorption is the Clegg impact soil tester (CIT) [14,15], which was developed by Baden Clegg in Western Australia for testing dirt road base surfaces. Unlike previously described apparatuses, which are bulky and cumbersome, the CIT is lightweight (11.8 kg) and portable. The readout box provides only the peak deceleration (g_{max}) as a liquid crystal display (LCD) readout. As purchased, the CIT gives a readout to the nearest 10 g. It can be modified to indicate the nearest 1 g.[3] Such modification may be important for research studies, because Henderson [13] reported statistically significant

---

[3] G. Holmes, personal communication.

differences <10 g in his studies. With the CIT, an accelerometer is mounted on a missile (4.5 kg, and several lighter missiles), which is dropped from a set height through a guide tube. Lush [16] stated that the CIT can be operated by one person, and up to 100 measurements can be made in 15 min. Among the surfaces that have been evaluated (using a 0.5-kg hammer dropped from a 30-cm height) are cricket pitches [16], tennis courts [17], bowling greens [18], and soccer fields [19,20]. The effect of root zone composition on player performance was examined using the CIT on soccer fields [21].

Standards of playing quality for natural turf have been proposed by Holmes and Bell [22,23], researchers in the United Kingdom. Their reports linked together quantitative data obtained with the CIT (related to field hardness) and subjective data obtained from players on their perceptions of the surface. The proportion of players rating a field "hard" or "unacceptably hard" increased with increasing impact values. They concluded that the preferred limits of surface hardness for running on a surface are between 20 and 80 g, as determined with a 0.5-kg hammer dropped from 30 cm. The same range was found to be acceptable for falling or diving onto the surface.

Since there are many different parameters to be considered when measuring the hardness of natural surfaces, Bell et al. [1] outlined the following factors that must be measured simultaneously in order to fully determine the impact absorbing capabilities of a surface:

(a) the total duration of impacts,
(b) the time to reach maximum deceleration,
(c) the peak deceleration,
(d) the average deceleration,
(e) the rate of change of deceleration,
(f) the area under the curve of deceleration versus time,
(g) the peak force,
(h) the deformation of the surface, and
(i) the time for the surface to return to its original state.

Holmes and Bell [22] noted that no research program has measured all these factors together.

Apparatuses that are bulky or heavy, or require an external source of electricity are inconvenient for use under many field conditions. There is a need for portable equipment with self-contained power supplies that can be used on research plots as well as on actual athletic fields. The CIT meets this need, but provides data on peak deceleration only. The correlations between the various impact characteristics need to be established under a range of soil and turf conditions to determine the most useful criteria for assessing surfaces. To date, peak deceleration has been the criterion used most often. Also, a variety of missile or hammer weights and drop heights have been used to test surfaces; thus, results have been obtained with different impact energies. There is a need to determine the relationship between data collected using different impact energies.

The objectives of this research were (a) to develop and test a method for measuring impact absorption characteristics with portable equipment, (b) to determine the correlation between various impact characteristics, and (c) to determine the correlation of results obtained with three hammer weights.

Procedure

Equipment

Previous workers had shown that the Clegg impact tester (CIT) was a reliable portable apparatus for indicating peak deceleration; however, if the criteria set forth by Bell et al. [1]

are to be met, additional equipment will be required to obtain the deceleration-time curve. Therefore, impact measurements were made using a combination of the CIT (Lafayette Instrument Co., Lafayette, Indiana) and a Bruel and Kjaer 2515 vibration analyzer (Bruel and Kjaer Instruments, Marlborough, Massachusetts) (Fig. 1). The signals from the impacts were directed to the 2515 instead of the CIT readout box. The 2515 is a portable, battery operated analyzer that weighs 16.2 kg. It displays the deceleration-time curve, has averaging capability, can store up to 50 curves in memory, and can interface with a computer for data storage and analysis.

Three hammer weights (4.5, 2.25, and 0.5 kg) were used for the impact measurements. The heavier hammers were made from cold-rolled steel and had metal pipe "T" handles, while the 0.5-kg hammer was solid polyvinyl chloride (PVC) with a plastic tubing handle. All hammers were 5.0 cm in diameter and had an accelerometer mounted at the top. To facilitate measurements in a number of areas without moving the analyzer, a 15-m accelerometer cable was used to connect the accelerometers and the analyzer. In initial use of this system, it became apparent that kinking of the cable was a problem. More convenient handling and storage of the cable was made possible by mounting the cable on a "Martin 24" fly fishing reel. The reel is attached to a 70-cm length of PVC pipe, in which the hammer can be stored when not in use.

All impact measurements were made using a drop height of 45.7 cm. In most instances, six successive drops on different spots of the test area were averaged and then stored. The stored data were transferred to a microcomputer via an Institute of Electronic and Electrical Engineers (IEEE) 488 bus cable, a multiwire cable providing for byte-serial, bit-parallel communication. The interface board was a National Instruments Model GPIB-PC IIA.

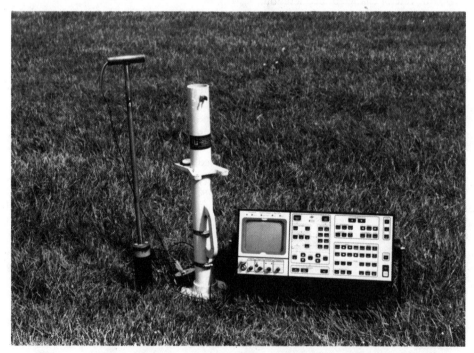

FIG. 1—*Apparatus used in the assessment of impact characteristics:* (left to right) *impacting hammer, guide tube from Clegg impact soil tester, and Bruel and Kjaer 2515 vibration analyzer.*

The hammer velocity at impact was determined by two methods. A Bruel and Kjaer photoelectric tachometer probe MM0012 was used in conjunction with the vibration analyzer to determine the time for a reflective tape of known width to pass the eye of the probe, which was mounted on the guide tube. Each hammer was dropped 20 times, and the average velocity of the three hammers was 2.91 m/s. Dropping at a height of 45.1 instead of 45.7 cm did not result in a detectable difference in velocity. High-speed motion picture film (1000 frames/s with a shutter speed of 0.0002 s) was used to measure the hammer velocity as it exited the guide tube. Two photographed drops with each hammer showed no difference due to hammer weight, and the velocity was found to be 2.79 m/s. The average velocity (2.85 m/s) determined by these methods was used in the calculation of impact energy, surface deformation, and rebound ratio.

Clegg [14] suggested that, when appropriate, 2.49-kg and 0.5-kg hammers could be used as well as the 4.5-kg hammer. For our work, the 2.25-kg hammer was constructed to obtain an energy per unit area similar to that obtained by Henderson [13] using ANSI/ASTM Test F 355-86 method (9.09-kg hammer, with an impacting surface of 129 cm^2, and dropped from a 61-cm height). Using an impact velocity of 3.39 m/s,[4] the energy per unit area (0.5 mv^2/A, where m = mass, v = impact velocity, and A = surface area) for the 9.09-kg hammer was 4049 N/m^2. The 0.5, 2.25, and 4.5 kg-hammers used in this work had impacting surface areas of 20.25 cm^2 and were dropped from 45.7 cm; the impact energies were 1003, 4512, and 9025 N/m^2, respectively. From this specific drop height, the light weight would relate more to the action of a ball impacting a surface and the heavier weights would simulate running or falling impacts of players.

The computer program used to analyze the deceleration-time curves was written by Bregar and Moyer [24]. The impact analysis program was written in BASICA to carry out analysis of data recorded during the impact of an instrument of known mass from a set height. The continuous signal generated by the accelerometer was sampled by the 2515 and stored in the memory of the analyzer. A threshold value of one-tenth peak deceleration was used to define the beginning and end of the deceleration-time impact value. The microcomputer had high-resolution graphics capability. The program provided the following information:

maximum deceleration, g_{max},
time to maximum deceleration, ms,
total duration of impact, ms,
first rate of change (threshold to point of maximum deceleration), g/ms,
second rate of change (threshold to 0.5 point of maximum deceleration), g/ms,
third rate of change (0.5 to point of maximum deceleration), g/ms,
surface deformation [integral of the velocity (v) curve, which is the integral of the
    deceleration curve, from v at impact to v = 0], cm,
severity index (the integral of $g^{2.5} \, dt$ over the total duration of impact), s, and
rebound ratio (the area under the deceleration curve after v = 0, divided by the area
    prior to v = 0).

Evaluation of Apparatus

The equipment was used to evaluate field hardness (peak deceleration) on game and practice football fields at twelve high schools in central Pennsylvania [25]. The fields were evaluated five times over a 13-month period.

---

[4] C. A. Morehouse, personal communication.

The equipment was also used to collect data from four field experiments designed to determine the effects of various management practices and agronomic factors on the following impact absorption characteristics: (*a*) cutting height, compaction, and vegetation study on Kentucky bluegrass; (*b*) compaction and aeration study on Kentucky bluegrass; (*c*) compaction and aeration study on tall fescue; and (*d*) cutting height and vegetation study on tall fescue. To determine the relationships between hammer weights and between impact characteristics, correlation coefficients were calculated. The numbers of comparisons used for correlations in the above experiments were 216, 48, 48, and 63, respectively, and represented data collected at various times during the growing season.

Results and Discussion

This portable system proved to be a convenient and efficient method for obtaining impact absorption characteristics on fields and research plots. Although one person could collect data, the procedure was much more efficient with two: one to drop the hammer and the second, stationed at the vibration analyzer, to begin the averaging function, observe the deceleration-time curve of each drop (checking for overload and resetting analyzer as appropriate), enter the average curve into memory, and reset the analyzer for the next area to be tested. After 50 curves had been stored, the analyzer was brought into the office for unloading into a microcomputer. Thus, careful scheduling of visits to athletic fields was required for

TABLE 1—*Correlation coefficients between hammers for impact absorption characteristics measured on the effects of cutting height, compaction, and surface type in Kentucky bluegrass turf, 1987.*

Peak decel. (g-max)	2.25 kg	4.5 kg	Total time (ms)	2.25 kg	4.5 kg
0.5 kg hammer	0.94	0.91	0.5 kg hammer	0.91	0.61
2.25 kg hammer		0.96	2.25 kg hammer		0.79

Peak time (ms)	2.25 kg	4.5 kg	Deformation (cm)	2.25 kg	4.5 kg
0.5 kg hammer	0.93	0.79	0.5 kg hammer	0.91	0.80
2.25 kg hammer		0.90	2.25 kg hammer		0.92

Severity index (sec)	2.25 kg	4.5 kg	Rate of change 1 (g/ms)	2.25 kg	4.5 kg
0.5 kg hammer	0.93	0.85	0.5 kg hammer	0.91	0.87
2.25 kg hammer		0.90	2.25 kg hammer		0.96

Rate of change 2 (g/ms)	2.25 kg	4.5 kg	Rate of change 3 (g/ms)	2.25 kg	4.5 kg
0.5 kg hammer	0.89	0.85	0.5 kg hammer	0.71	0.55
2.25 kg hammer		0.97	2.25 kg hammer		0.57

TABLE 2—*Correlation coefficients between hammers for impact absorption characteristics measured on the effects of aeration and compaction in Kentucky bluegrass turf, 1987.*

Peak decel. (g-$_{max}$)	2.25 kg	4.5 kg	Total time (ms)	2.25 kg	4.5 kg
0.5 kg hammer	0.98	0.96	0.5 kg hammer	0.98	0.98
2.25 kg hammer		0.98	2.25 kg hammer		0.98

Peak time (ms)	2.25 kg	4.5 kg	Deformation (cm)	2.25 kg	4.5 kg
0.5 kg hammer	0.96	0.98	0.5 kg hammer	0.96	NS[a]
2.25 kg hammer		0.97	2.25 kg hammer		NS

Severity index (sec)	2.25 kg	4.5 kg	Rate of change 1 (g/ms)	2.25 kg	4.5 kg
0.5 kg hammer	0.98	0.96	0.5 kg hammer	0.98	0.95
2.25 kg hammer		0.97	2.25 kg hammer		0.98

Rate of change 2 (g/ms)	2.25 kg	4.5 kg	Rate of change 3 (g/ms)	2.25 kg	4.5 kg
0.5 kg hammer	0.98	0.97	0.5 kg hammer	0.95	0.97
2.25 kg hammer		0.98	2.25 kg hammer		0.97

[a]NS-not significant at the 0.05 level.

maximum utilization of the storage feature. Should a return for unloading be inconvenient, a portable computer could be utilized to store data.

In general, the correlation between hammers was good for all impact characteristics (Tables 1 through 4) except for rebound ratio, where significant correlation (0.05) never occurred. The poorest correlation was between the 0.5 and 4.5-kg hammers. The impact characteristics of the 2.25-kg hammer were strongly correlated to those of the 0.5-kg hammer.

The cutting height and vegetation experiment on tall fescue had the weakest correlations among hammers (Table 4). An explanation for these results stems from the nature of the hammers and the plot area. Under the conditions present in this study for 1987, only the impact characteristics of the 0.5-kg hammer were affected by the cutting height and presence of vegetation treatments. It stands to reason that if impact characteristics fluctuate with treatments with one hammer but not with another, then the correlation coefficients between these hammers will be lower.

Correlation between impact characteristics, except those involving the rebound ratio, were high for each of the experiments. Only data from the bluegrass tests are shown (Tables 5 and 6). Because of the high correlation coefficients among impact characteristics, a conclusion that only one parameter need be measured to characterize the field would seem appropriate. However, the correlation coefficients among impact characteristics for the cutting height, compaction, and vegetation study on Kentucky bluegrass increased when the results were

TABLE 3—*Correlation coefficients between hammers for impact absorption characteristics measured on the effects of aeration and compaction in tall fescue turf, 1987.*

Peak decel. (g-max)	2.25 kg	4.5 kg	Total time (ms)	2.25 kg	4.5 kg
0.5 kg hammer	0.89	0.90	0.5 kg hammer	0.88	0.86
2.25 kg hammer		0.98	2.25 kg hammer		0.96

Peak time (ms)	2.25 kg	4.5 kg	Deformation (cm)	2.25 kg	4.5 kg
0.5 kg hammer	0.90	0.63	0.5 kg hammer	0.91	0.82
2.25 kg hammer		0.85	2.25 kg hammer		0.94

Severity index (sec)	2.25 kg	4.5 kg	Rate of change 1 (g/ms)	2.25 kg	4.5 kg
0.5 kg hammer	0.87	0.86	0.5 kg hammer	0.84	0.84
2.25 kg hammer		0.98	2.25 kg hammer		0.98

Rate of change 2 (g/ms)	2.25 kg	4.5 kg	Rate of change 3 (g/ms)	2.25 kg	4.5 kg
0.5 kg hammer	0.89	0.91	0.5 kg hammer	0.79	0.74
2.25 kg hammer		0.98	2.25 kg hammer		0.93

TABLE 4—*Correlation coefficients between hammers for impact absorption characteristics measured on the effects of cutting height and verdure in tall fescue turf, 1987.*

Peak decel. (g_{-max})	2.25 kg	4.5 kg	Total time (ms)	2.25 kg	4.5 kg
0.5 kg hammer	0.67	0.58	0.5 kg hammer	0.62	NS[a]
2.25 kg hammer		0.92	2.25 kg hammer		0.51

Peak time (ms)	2.25 kg	4.5 kg	Deformation (cm)	2.25 kg	4.5 kg
0.5 kg hammer	NS	NS	0.5 kg hammer	0.59	0.54
2.25 kg hammer		NS	2.25 kg hammer		0.72

Severity index (sec)	2.25 kg	4.5 kg	Rate of change 1 (g/ms)	2.25 kg	4.5 kg
0.5 kg hammer	0.65	0.58	0.5 kg hammer	0.53	0.45
2.25 kg hammer		0.93	2.25 kg hammer		0.89

Rate of change 2 (g/ms)	2.25 kg	4.5 kg	Rate of change 3 (g/ms)	2.25 kg	4.5 kg
0.5 kg hammer	0.53	0.45	0.5 kg hammer	0.70	NS
2.25 kg hammer		0.81	2.25 kg hammer		NS

[a]NS-not significant at the 0.05 level.

TABLE 5—*Correlation coefficients between impact absorption characteristics measured with the 0.5 and 2.25-kg hammers on the aeration and compaction study on Kentucky bluegrass turf, 1987.*

Characteristic	Total Time	Peak Time	Rate of Change 1	Rate of Change 2	Rate of Change 3	Deform Ind	Sev	Reb Ratio
0.5 kg Hammer								
Peak Decel., g-max	-0.98	-0.99	0.98	0.98	0.96	-0.99	0.99	NS[a]
Total Time, ms		0.98	-0.96	-0.97	-0.94	0.97	-0.96	NS
Peak Time, ms			-0.98	-0.98	-0.97	0.99	-0.98	NS
Rate of Change 1, g/ms				0.99	0.99	-0.96	0.98	NS
Rate of Change 2, g/ms					0.97	-0.95	0.97	NS
Rate of Change 3, g/ms						-0.95	0.97	NS
Deformation, cm							-0.99	NS
Severity Index, s								NS
2.25 kg Hammer								
Peak Decel., g-max	-0.97	-0.99	0.99	0.98	0.99	-0.98	0.99	NS
Total Time, ms		0.99	-0.96	-0.96	-0.95	0.97	-0.95	NS
Peak Time, ms			-0.97	-0.96	-0.96	0.99	-0.97	NS
Rate of Change 1, g/ms				0.99	0.99	-0.94	0.99	NS
Rate of Change 2, g/ms					0.98	-0.93	0.97	NS
Rate of Change 3, g/ms						-0.95	0.99	NS
Deformation, cm							-0.97	-0.54
Severity Index, s								NS

[a]NS-not significant at the 0.05 level.

TABLE 6—*Correlation coefficients between impact absorption characteristics measured with the 0.5 and 2.25-kg hammers on the cutting height, compaction, and vegetation study in Kentucky bluegrass turf, 1987.*

Characteristic	Total Time	Peak Time	Rate of Change 1	Rate of Change 2	Rate of Change 3	Deform	Sev Ind	Reb Ratio
0.5 kg Hammer								
Peak Decel., g-$_{max}$	-0.85	-0.83	0.90	0.92	0.76	-0.84	0.97	NS[a]
Total Time, ms		0.95	-0.65	-0.66	-0.62	0.96	-0.76	0.33
Peak Time, ms			-0.67	-0.66	-0.65	0.99	-0.78	NS
Rate of Change 1, g/ms				0.99	0.85	-0.67	0.95	NS
Rate of Change 2, g/ms					0.82	-0.66	0.95	NS
Rate of Change 3, g/ms						-0.65	0.78	NS
Deformation, cm							-0.79	NS
Severity Index, s								NS
2.25 kg Hammer								
Peak Decel., g-$_{max}$	-0.89	-0.86	0.98	0.99	0.77	-0.90	0.99	NS
Total Time, ms		0.92	-0.92	-0.82	-0.69	0.96	-0.84	0.37
Peak Time, ms			-0.85	-0.83	-0.73	0.99	-0.85	NS
Rate of Change 1, g/ms				0.99	0.83	-0.86	0.99	NS
Rate of Change 2, g/ms					0.79	-0.85	0.99	NS
Rate of Change 3, g/ms						-0.73	0.79	NS
Deformation, cm							-0.88	NS
Severity Index, s								NS

[a]NS-not significant at the 0.05 level.

TABLE 7—*Correlation coefficients between impact absorption characteristics measured with the 0.5 and 2.25-kg hammers on the cutting height, compaction, and vegetation study without bare soil treatments in Kentucky bluegrass turf, 1987.*

Characteristic	Total Time	Peak Time	Rate of Change 1	Rate of Change 2	Rate of Change 3	Deform	Sev Ind	Reb Ratio
0.5 kg Hammer								
Peak Decel., g-max	-0.96	-0.97	0.99	0.99	0.99	-0.97	0.99	NS[a]
Total Time, ms		0.96	-0.93	-0.93	-0.93	0.97	-0.93	NS
Peak Time, ms			-0.96	-0.96	-0.96	0.99	-0.97	NS
Rate of Change 1, g/ms				0.99	0.99	-0.95	0.99	NS
Rate of Change 2, g/ms					0.99	-0.95	0.99	NS
Rate of Change 3, g/ms						-0.95	0.99	NS
Deformation, cm							-0.96	NS
Severity Index, s								NS
2.25 kg Hammer								
Peak Decel., g-max	-0.91	-0.98	0.99	0.99	0.99	-0.98	0.99	NS
Total Time, ms		0.96	-0.86	-0.87	-0.86	0.95	-0.87	0.53
Peak Time, ms			-0.96	-0.96	-0.95	0.99	-0.96	NS
Rate of Change 1, g/ms				0.99	0.99	-0.95	0.99	NS
Rate of Change 2, g/ms					0.99	-0.95	0.99	NS
Rate of Change 3, g/ms						-0.95	0.99	NS
Deformation, cm							-0.96	NS
Severity Index, s								NS

[a]NS–not significant at the 0.05 level.

analyzed without the bare soil treatments (Table 7). This result suggested that grass and soil surfaces may differ somewhat in their relative effects on impact characteristics. Because the impact measurements are calculated from the measured peak deceleration values and the time periods, it seems important to measure both of the parameters when comparisons are made between turf and soil areas. If just one of these areas is being measured, one of these parameters may be sufficient to characterize the impact absorption of the field. Many athletic fields will have bare as well as turf-covered areas, so the ability to measure the time periods is essential to characterizing the entire field.

The reason for lack of significant correlation involving the calculated rebound ratio was not ascertained and needs future study. This effect may have resulted from differences in the resiliency or elasticity of surfaces. An elastic collision conserves kinetic energy, while total kinetic energy decreases in an inelastic collision. It would be of interest to characterize impacts according to the degree of elasticity.

Future research can follow several avenues. Certainly there is a need to standardize both equipment and methodology. Models predicting impact characteristics for soil type, soil moisture, and soil bulk density should be developed. Cooperation with the medical profession in research to determine limits of acceptability is necessary in order to develop standards of playing field quality that are acceptable in terms of both performance and safety.

Acknowledgment

This contribution is Journal Paper No. 8017 from the Pennsylvania Agricultural Experiment Station, University Park, Pennsylvania.

References

[*1*] Bell, M. J., Baker, S. W., and Canaway, P. M., "Playing Quality of Sports Surfaces: A Review," *Journal of the Sports Turf Research Institute,* Vol. 61, 1985, pp. 26–45.
[*2*] Bramwell, S. T., Requa, R. K., and Garrick, J. E., "High School Football Injuries: A Pilot Comparison of Playing Surfaces," *Medicine and Science in Sports,* Vol. 4, No. 3, 1972, pp. 166–169.
[*3*] Adkinson, J. W., Requa, R. K., and Garrick, J. G., "Injury Rates in High School Football," *Clinical Orthopedics,* Vol. 99, 1974, pp. 131–136.
[*4*] Macik, J., "Sports Turf Injuries—Are They Avoidable?" *Sports Turf Manager,* Vol. 3, No. 2, 1987, pp. 12–13.
[*5*] Keene, J. S., Narechania, R. E., Sachtjen, K. M., and Claney, W. G., "Tartan Turf on Trial," *American Journal of Sports Medicine,* Vol. 8, No. 1, 1980, pp. 43–47.
[*6*] Bowers, K. D., Jr., and Martin, R. B., "Impact Absorption, New and Old AstroTurf at West Virginia University," *Medicine and Science in Sports,* Vol. 6, No. 3, 1974, pp. 217–221.
[*7*] Kretzler, H. H., Jr., "Artificial Turf and Football Injuries," *Annual Safety Education Review,* 1972, pp. 61–70.
[*8*] Harper, J. C., Morehouse, C. A., Waddington, D. V., and Buckley, W. E., "Turf Management, Athletic-field Conditions, and Injuries in High School Football," Progress Report No. 384, Pennsylvania State University, College of Agriculture, Agriculture Experiment Station, University Park, PA, 1984.
[*9*] Allocca, J. A. and Stuart, A., *Transducers, Theory and Application,* Reston Publishing Co., 1984, Chapters 5 and 17.
[*10*] Gramckow, J., "Athletic Field Quality Studies," Cal-Turf Inc., Camarillo, CA, 1968.
[*11*] Zebarth, B. J. and Sheard, R. W., "Impact and Shear Resistance of Turfgrass Racing Surfaces for Thoroughbreds," *American Journal of Veterinary Research,* Vol. 46, No. 4, 1985, pp. 778–784.
[*12*] Gadd, C. W., "Tolerable Severity Index in Whole-head Non-mechanical Impact," *Proceedings,* 15th Stapp Car Crash Conference, Society of Automotive Engineers, New York, NY, 1971, pp. 809–816.
[*13*] Henderson, R. L., "Impact Absorption Characteristics and Other Properties of Turf and Soil Surfaces," Department of Agronomy, Pennsylvania State University, University Park, PA, 1986, p. 131.
[*14*] Clegg, B., "An Impact Testing Device for In Situ Base Course Evaluation," *Australia Road Research Bureau Proceedings,* Vol. 8, 1976, pp. 1–5.
[*15*] Clegg, B., "An Impact Soil Test for Low Cost Roads," *Proceedings,* Second Conference of Road Engineers Association of Asia and Australia, Manila, The Philippines, 1978, pp. 58–65.
[*16*] Lush, W. M., "Objective Assessment of Turf Cricket Pitches Using an Impact Hammer," *Journal of the Sports Turf Research Institute,* Vol. 61, 1985, pp. 71–79.
[*17*] Holmes, G. and Bell, M. J., "Technical Note: Playing Surface Hardness and Tennis Ball Rebound Resilience," *Journal of the Sports Turf Research Institute,* Vol. 62, 1986, pp. 207–210.
[*18*] Holmes, G. and Bell, M. J., "The Playing Quality of Bowling Greens: A Survey," *Journal of the Sports Turf Research Institute,* Vol. 62, 1986, pp. 50–66.
[*19*] Holmes, G. and Bell, M. J., "A Pilot Study of the Playing Quality of Football Pitches," *Journal of the Sports Turf Research Institute,* Vol. 62, 1986, pp. 74–91.

[*20*] Baker, S. W., "Technical Note: Playing Quality of Some Soccer Pitches in Saudi Arabia," *Journal of the Sports Turf Research Institute,* Vol. 63, 1987, pp. 145–148.
[*21*] Baker, S. W. and Isaac, S. P., "The Effect of Root Zone Composition on the Performance of Winter Game Pitches—II: Playing Quality," *Journal of the Sports Turf Research Institute,* Vol. 63, 1987, pp. 67–80.
[*22*] Holmes, G. and Bell, M. J., "Standards of Playing Quality for Natural Turf," The Sports Turf Research Institute, Bingley, West Yorkshire, England, 1987.
[*23*] Holmes, G. and Bell, M. J., "The Playing Quality of Association Football Pitches," *Journal of the Sports Turf Research Institute,* Vol. 64, 1988, pp. 19–47.
[*24*] Bregar, M. J. and Moyer, W. W., "An Automated System for Field Testing and Soil Impact Analysis," this publication, pp. 115–126.
[*25*] Rogers, J. N. III, Waddington, D. V., and Harper, J. C. II, "Relationships Between Athletic Field Hardness and Traction, Vegetation, Soil Properties, and Maintenance Practices," Progress Report No. 393, Pennsylvania State University, College of Agriculture, Agricultural Experiment Station, University Park, PA, 1988.

Richard J. Schefsky[1]

Benefits of Testing for the Owners of Artificial and Natural Turf

REFERENCE: Schefsky, R. J., **"Benefits of Testing for the Owners of Artificial and Natural Turf,"** *Natural and Artificial Playing Fields: Characteristics and Safety Features, ASTM STP 1073,* R. C. Schmidt, E. F. Hoerner, E. M. Milner, and C. A. Morehouse, Eds., American Society for Testing and Materials, Philadelphia, 1990, pp. 111–114.

ABSTRACT: Testing of artificial and natural turf should be an integral part of the purchasing process to maximize the cost-effectiveness of the purchase of these sports playing surfaces. Subsequently, annual testing of the installed surfaces is necessary to ascertain and control the safety performance of these systems. An additional benefit is that hard numbers are generated which can be used to project the usable life of the sports playing surface. These projections are useful for budgeting considerations.

KEY WORDS: playing fields, artificial turf, natural turf, sports playing surfaces, turf testing, shock attenuation testing, turf safety performance, injury prevention

It has been more than 20 years since the first artificial turf was installed to replace grass in the Houston Astrodome, in Houston, Texas, the first of many indoor facilities large enough to accommodate both baseball and football games. Since then, hundreds of facilities have installed artificial turf.

In 1967, Seattle was one of two cities that had installed artificial turf in an outdoor stadium.

Since these turfs were installed, many firms have entered and left the business of providing artificial turf. Many different concepts have been used to provide functional and economic padding systems. Likewise, many different concepts have been used for the playing surface itself.

Not all of these systems have satisfactorily met the performance anticipated for them, thus the dilemma for the purchasing agent trying to decide upon the best value.

The author's company, Northwest Laboratories, was originally requested to test artificial turf by a purchasing agent trying to decide between two competing bids for a replacement turf. Because the company has a textile testing department, he inquired whether we could assist him in providing data that would enable him to make an objective choice.

Based on the information provided by us, the purchasing agent determined that the more expensive playing surface system was actually a better value and therefore purchased it.

Procedure and Reasons for Testing Artificial Surfaces

The author proposes that the purchaser of sports playing surfaces view testing as a means by which he can optimize the cost-effectiveness of his purchase rather than as a means of providing grist for a potential lawsuit.

---

[1] President, Northwest Laboratories, Seattle, WA 98134.

The author is not privy to the installed price of sports playing surface systems. However, $300 000 to $500 000 is within the ball park range for these purchases. Many purchasers are looking for ten-year warranties, although there are usually insufficient actual use data to substantiate satisfactory performance for this length of time. What can be said for any system is that it will never be any better than when it was first installed.

Therefore, the purchasing process should start with potential vendors submitting samples of the system they propose to provide. The purchasing agent should submit these samples to an independent testing laboratory for evaluation testing. Using objective test data, the purchasing agent can make his value judgment and award the bid.

Next, samples of the actual product that has been manufactured for the site should be tested *before* it is shipped to the site. Again, this testing should be done by the same independent laboratory. This testing will ascertain if the vendor is actually providing the system that the purchasing agent ordered. The number of samples to be tested needs to be set forth as part of the award of the bid.

Finally, the installed sports playing system should be tested on-site to quantify the shock attenuating performance. Again, this is to ascertain if the system performs as purported. In addition, this testing will establish the baseline data with which future testing will be compared.

The Tests Used

The first and second round of testing usually encompasses the following tests:

Turf Fabric Measurements

The tests for turf fabric measure the following properties:

(a) total weight of the fabric, oz/yd^2 [ASTM Testing Woven and Tufted Pile Floor Covering (D 418-82)];
(b) average number of pile stitches per inch (ASTM D 418-82);
(c) average number of pile rows per inch (ASTM D 418-82);
(d) pile height, in. (ASTM D 418-82);
(e) tuft bind (ASTM Test for Tuft Bind of Pile Floor Coverings [D 1335-67(1972)];
(f) grab tear strength (ASTM Tests for Breaking Load and Elongation of Textile Fabrics [D 1682-64(1975)]; and
(g) flammability using a methenamine ignition source [ASTM Test for Flammability of Finished Textile Floor Covering Materials (D 2859-76)].

Pad Testing

The tests of the pad measure the following properties:

(a) density, lb/ft^3 (ASTM Specification for Flexible Cellular Materials—Vinyl Chloride Polymers and Copolymers (Closed-Cell Vinyl) [D 1667-76(1986)]);
(b) uniform thickness, in. [ASTM Testing Flexible Cellular Materials—Slab, Bonded, and Molded Urethane Foams (D 3574-86)]; and
(c) load to compress the mat to 25% of thickness, lbf [ASTM Tests for Rubber Property— Compression Set (D 395-85)].

Shock Attenuating Properties

The shock attenuating properties of the turf and mat as a system are tested by the ASTM Test for Shock Absorbing Properties of Playing Surface Systems and Materials (F 355-86).

Testing Natural Grass Surfaces

The benefits of testing are also available for those who utilize natural grass as the playing surface in their stadiums. These owners should have an ongoing program of test plots on practice fields to evaluate objectively new and existing grasses and maintenance practices for durability, esthetic values, and safety.

The evaluation of the plots can be made in-house. However, a rating system must be established to lend objectivity and consistency to the analyses.

Shock attenuation testing is the only testing that may require the assistance of an independent laboratory, and that is only because the instrumentation and testing experience may not be available in-house.

Shock attenuation is just as important to the owner of a natural playing surface as it is to the owner of an artificial playing surface. In fact, it may be more important because the shock attenuating properties of a natural field are not static. They vary with the season of the year, the temperature, the amount of use, the effects of watering and rain on the soil, and the maintenance practices.

Therefore, natural fields need to be tested to correlate the effects of the controllable variables on the shock attenuation. For example, a correlation between the soil moisture and the shock attenuating capabilities of the turf needs to be determined. These data, combined with the use of a moisture probe, can then be used to control the shock attenuating properties of the field.

The effect of thatching of the turf on shock attenuation can also be determined. If thatching or aeration improves the shock attenuation, then more frequent use of this may be warranted.

Functions of Playing Fields

Regardless of whether a sports playing surface is artificial or natural, its primary functions are the following:

1. It must be suitable for the sports that are to be played on it and for its other intended uses.
2. Its performance should not unduly affect the outcome of a sports contest. Rather, the outcome should be determined by the skill of the participants.
3. It must provide a safe surface that does not enhance the risk of serious or permanent injury to the participant.

The above functions are obvious and additional ones may be considered. In the author's opinion, the following fourth function should be added to the list:

4. It should be tested to mitigate the monetary consequences of a legal action when a participant experiences serious or permanent injury.

Safety and Liability

It is apparent that there is genuine concern on the part of institutions and owners of playing fields for the safety and well-being of the athletes that play on them. Tens of thousands of dollars each are spent by many institutions or organizations every year on pads, helmets, strength-building equipment, tape, liniment and Gatorade.

But, how many owners have an ongoing program to monitor and control the shock attenuating properties of the surfaces upon which these athletes participate? If there is no such program, the owner is seriously impairing his defense against possible legal action in the future. An annual monitoring of a playing surface for shock attenuations (practice fields as well) makes the owner defendable in a legal action. It demonstrates concern and provides hard numbers for comparison with recognized safety standards.

A spin-off economic advantage is that the owner or operator has hard numbers to project for budget planning when a field needs to be replaced or renovated (in the case of natural grass).

Cost Factors

Now, the question of major concern is this—how much is all of this testing going to cost? Is the cost of testing going to be cost-effective?

The cost of performing the qualification testing for potential vendors of artificial playing systems is in the neighborhood of $1700 to $2000 per vendor, depending upon the number of tests desired and the number of vendors. This is assuming that all of the products can be tested at one time; there are setup and break-down costs which are not duplicated if all of the products are tested at one time.

The shock attenuation testing costs $575, plus travel and instrument shipping costs and travel time charges. This is the standard pricing policy of this company. It provides measurements at three high-use locations on the playing field. Because travel, shipping, and travel time costs are frequently one or two times the actual cost of testing, there is a real opportunity to reduce the cost per field by coordination between purchasers in a given location. For example, all of the high school, college, and professional playing sites could be tested in one area during one trip.

These savings could lower the budget requirements for this type of testing below the amount currently budgeted for Gatorade.

Summary

In review, the use of a private, independent laboratory is a highly cost-effective technique for the purchaser to use in selecting a playing surface system and in monitoring this system once installed to ascertain whether it continues to function for the purpose for which it was intended, in accordance with recognized safety standards.

Mark J. Bregar[1] and William W. Moyer[1]

An Automated System for Field Testing and Soil Impact Analysis

REFERENCE: Bregar, M. J. and Moyer, W. W., **"An Automated System for Field Testing and Soil Impact Analysis,"** *Natural and Artificial Playing Fields: Characteristics and Safety Features, ASTM STP 1073,* R. C. Schmidt, E. F. Hoerner, E. M. Milner, and C. A. Morehouse, Eds., American Society for Testing and Materials, Philadelphia, 1990, pp. 115–126.

ABSTRACT: A sponsored effort was made to develop an automated system for determining the impact characteristics of soils and playing surfaces *in situ.* Most of the earlier measurements of this type yielded only information on peak deceleration. The equipment developed under this project consists of a portable measurement unit employed for data acquisition and a personal computer programmed for analysis of data from individual tests and for statistical analysis across an ensemble of tests. The data acquisition subsystem is comprised of an instrumented mass that is dropped from a fixed height through a guide tube and a battery-powered vibration analyzer that can capture the deceleration curve in memory for display or later recovery. The data set from each individual drop or averaged set of drops is downloaded to the computer and written to a Winchester drive. The analysis program uses a measured impact velocity and calculates maximum deceleration level, total duration of impact, several rates of change, and surface deformation. Recent additions to the program also provide determinations of severity index, rebound velocity, and rebound ratio when appropriate. The deceleration curve and all calculated parameter values are displayed on the system monitor; a hard copy of the display can be produced on a dot-matrix printer. A separate algorithm supports analysis of a set of data files selected by the operator; all selected files are combined into a single file on which statistical operations can be performed. Possible uses for the system include testing playing surfaces for injury potential and regular diagnostic testing of surfaces which must be maintained in a specific condition. The system uses widely available processing equipment and only the drop unit itself is custom made.

KEY WORDS: playing fields, soil impact, deceleration curve, accelerometer data

The Pennsylvania Turfgrass Council and the Agronomy Department of the Pennsylvania State University have jointly sponsored the development of intelligent instrumentation capable of measuring the impact characteristics of surfaces and analyzing the data collected. Interest in this development was based upon a desire to gain an ability to assess the shock absorbency of playing fields and a need to provide assistance for situations where surface consistency must be maintained. Earlier surface impact measurements were made using a Clegg Impact Soil Tester (CIT) [1], an instrument offered commercially by the Lafayette Instrument Company. This instrument has been widely accepted as a reference instrument and has been used extensively in studies of rugby playing surfaces. The CIT employs an accelerometer rigidly attached to a mass that is dropped from a fixed height through a guide tube to impact the surface under test. The deceleration signal produced by the accelerometer is amplified and filtered. The maximum level detected is retained by a peak detection circuit;

---

[1] The Applied Research Laboratory, The Pennsylvania State University, P.O. Box 30, State College, PA 16804.

a visible readout of the peak level, designated g-max, is generated. Although the Clegg was reliable, and a very similar drop mechanism was developed for further testing, the signal processing offered by the Clegg did not provide sufficient information to allow accurate characterization of surfaces. Assessment of parameters other than peak deceleration was deemed to be necessary.

Equipment

The instrumented drop mass, as represented by the test hammer on the Clegg instrument, was judged to be a reliable and practical mechanism for developing accurate deceleration data over the interval during which the test mass is in motion and in contact with the surface being evaluated. The preamplified output of the CIT sensor was used in early development of the instrumentation. An investigation of possible means of digitizing the temporal deceleration signal produced by the CIT sensor was initiated. The first attempt at digitization made use of an analog data acquisition card installed in an IBM PC/AT personal computer. This card, a Metrabyte Model Dash-16, permitted sampling the output of the accelerometer amplifier at rates up to 30 000/s and storing the samples in computer memory for subsequent analysis, which was done by a Lotus 123 routine. This initial attempt at digitization of the complete deceleration curve produced during an impact proved the viability of the approach. Although the system employed was suitable for the laboratory feasibility tests, it was not appropriate for field work. Consideration was given to a portable personal computer, but limitations on PC battery life and memory capacity proved to be disadvantages that could not be readily overcome.

A search for battery-powered instrumentation identified the Bruel and Kjaer Type 2515 (BK-2515) Vibration Analyzer as an appropriate choice for the application. The BK-2515 is a ruggedized analyzer intended primarily for use in investigating faults in gear boxes and bearings. It provides a preamplifier for direct connection of an accelerometer to the unit and contains a large nonvolatile memory that supports extensive data collection sessions. The sampling rate is variable through keystroke input between 100 samples per second (sps) and 20 000 sps. Memory storage for 1250 samples is available, supporting impact durations of 62.5 ms to 12.5 s. A sample rate of 20 kHz (62.5 ms duration) was found to be sufficient to capture the entire curve of interest. An adjustable trigger level, available on the vibration analyzer, is important for the impact analysis application. Collection of data over a selected sampling interval is initiated when the level of the signal produced by the accelerometer exceeds the trigger level chosen by the operator. The trigger level is selected to avoid both the recording of a false data block and the failure to collect data when a valid impact signal is received. An impact measurement apparatus very similar to the CIT was constructed. It consisted of a guide tube that accepted a cylindrical drop weight with an accelerometer mounted atop the weight. Three different drop weights (0.5, 2.25, and 4.5 kg) were used in the testing program. The output of the accelerometer was connected directly to the BK-2515 analyzer. All drops were made from a vertical distance of 45.7 cm (18 in).

The BK-2515 analyzer has the capability of averaging data over several collection intervals. Averaging is used for continuous sampling of a constant source such as vibration in a gear train and results in a measurement with noise or spurious signals suppressed. The BK-2515 can be commanded to average the data from a selected number of drops. The raw data sets are aligned at the initial threshold crossing, and the average of the measured deceleration levels in each time cell within the impact interval is determined. Most of the observed variation between drops occurs at the low g levels observed early in the impacts. The analyzer maintains a running average by performing the necessary calculations after each set of raw data is acquired. Averaged data is transferred from the memory of the BK-2515 to the com-

puter for storage on a floppy or Winchester disk. Similar data were grouped together in directories. The analysis routine was modified to process each data file and store the results in a
common file. A commercial statistics program (Lotus 123) was then used to categorize the
data. The display of the analyzer is calibrated in engineering units relating time to deceleration level. A typical display of a single drop produced from raw data by the BK-2515 is
reproduced as Fig. 1. The BK-2515 provides a cursor which can be manipulated by keyboard. This allows the operator to examine the data in the field and validate the reading
before storing. The unit has sufficient nonvolatile memory to store 50 data sets. Details of
the analyzer settings are stored together with the display and automatically recalled on the
analyzer. This feature allowed extended data collection trips. These trips were made over an
extended period of time in order to collect data from field playing and peripheral surfaces
over a range of weather conditions.

Analysis of the data collected in the field requires the capabilities of a general-purpose
computer with sufficient computational power for the processing and with significant mass
storage capabilities. An IBM PC/AT was chosen and fitted with a National Instruments
IEEE-488 interface card for communciations with the Vibrations Analyzer. A 568-byte file
is created within the analyzer to characterize each drop, and it is transferred across the bus
when processing by the IBM PC/AT is to be done. The first 52 bytes of any file contain
information concerning the setup of the analyzer for the corresponding drop. The remaining
bytes are the 12-bit data produced by the analog-to-digital converter (ADC) as the accelerometer output is digitized. Since there is little available documentation on the data protocol,
considerable experimentation was necessary to ascertain analyzer settings from the contents
of an individual file. This was accomplished by pacing the machine through each available
setting, recording the data, and then noting the changes in the data file. Most importantly,
the contents of the 19th and the 31st bytes of a file were found to carry information on
analyzer gain setting (sets absolute levels of measured data points) and sample time interval,
respectively. Once the parameters of the data sets were defined, an analysis routine was developed for the IBM PC/AT.

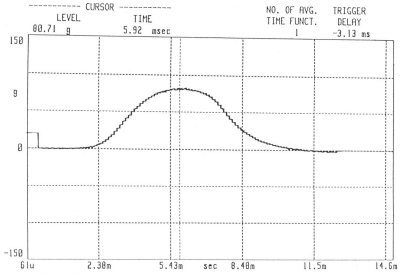

FIG. 1—*Typical drop test deceleration curve produced by BK2515 analyzer.*

Analysis Software

A menu-driven impact data transfer/data analysis program was written utilizing the Microsoft Quick Basic compiler. A flow diagram of the software is included as Fig. 2, with an enlargement of the analysis routine as Fig. 3. The final version of the program allows the operator to select the operation to be performed. Choices include transfer of data between the analyzer and the computer, performance of graphics routines on data sets, initiation of disk operations within the PC to check archived data sets, adjustment of analysis process parameters, and execution of the analysis routine itself. The last option is the most complex and is performed on one data set called by name from the memory of the computer. Over the course of the software development effort, the definition of the parameters to be determined in the analysis routine evolved. The intermediate choice was influenced to a considerable extent by Bell et al. [2] and consisted of the following:

(a) total duration of impact,
(b) time to reach peak deceleration,
(c) detected peak deceleration level,
(d) average deceleration during impact duration,
(e) rates of change of deceleration,
(f) area under the deceleration curve,
(g) maximum force exerted on the surface,
(h) deformation of the surface, and
(i) Gadd severity index.

The first five of these parameters can be evaluated directly from the time record of the deceleration produced during a test drop. As discussed, the raw data file generated by the BK-2515 during a single drop consists of 568 bytes of data that are transferred to the PC and recorded as a file on a Winchester or floppy disk. The gain of the BK-2515 preamplifier is coded into the data file. The analysis program evaluates this gain setting to convert each of the time samples of the deceleration curve to actual g values. The sampling interval is also coded into the raw data file and is decoded to provide timing from the start of the impact. This time value, the spacing between adjacent samples, is designated TUNIT and can take on discrete values between about 61 μs and 12 ms. The start of the impact is defined as the time of occurrence of the first sample that exceeds the threshold g level (GTHR) selected by the operator. A late addition to the parameter adjustment option of the routine allows the operator to select the threshold as a percentage of the peak deceleration found within a data file rather than as a specific g level. This facilitates direct comparison of results of drops made with different gain settings on the BK-2515.

The software provides an option to produce a graphic display of the deceleration curve, which is stored on a point-by-point basis in memory. Two graphic commands unique to QuickBasic and similar BASIC languages [3] simplify the computer code for graphics generation. The first of these commands, VIEW, allows setting the portion of the screen where the graphic will be displayed. One option displays the selected data set over the entire PC/AT screen. The more involved analysis option plots the data on the upper half of the screen with text containing the reduced data displayed on the lower half. The second important graphics command provided by BASIC is WINDOW, which allows working in engineering units with the conversion to screen coordinates done automatically by the computer. The actual curve is drawn by identifying each data point and drawing a line between consecutive points. Boundary points and several grid lines are drawn for reference. The graphic representation of the deceleration curve drawn in the analysis routine marks the peak deceleration and each end point, allowing visual assessment of the curve. A typical deceleration curve

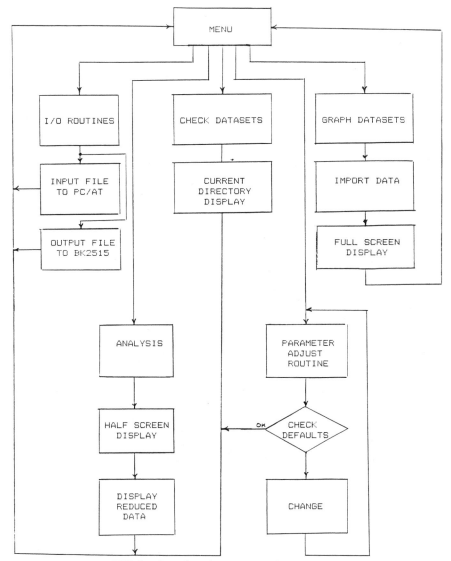

FIG. 2—*Overall analysis program flow diagram.*

produced by the full-screen plot option offered by the analysis program is reproduced as Fig. 4.

After a raw data file is transferred from the analyzer to the IBM PC/AT, each raw data sample is converted to a *g* level, and the display of the *g* curve is produced. The first pass through the ordered sequence of *g* values completes a search for the highest measured value. This value is designated GMAX; the number of the time interval in which it occurred is denoted BCNT. A search is conducted from interval BCNT backward (earlier in the time sequence), with each data point compared in turn to the threshold. The number of the time cell holding the first reading that falls below the threshold is designated LCNT and marks the start of the impact interval. A similar search forward in the time sequence determines

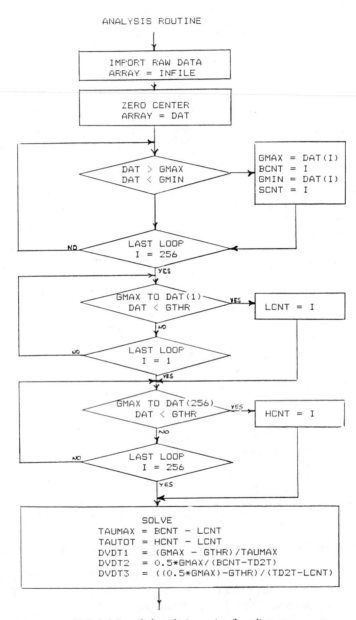

FIG. 3—*Detailed analysis routine flow diagram.*

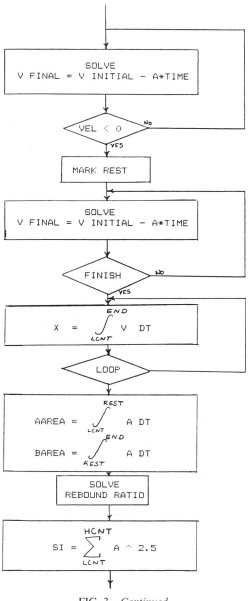

FIG. 3—*Continued.*

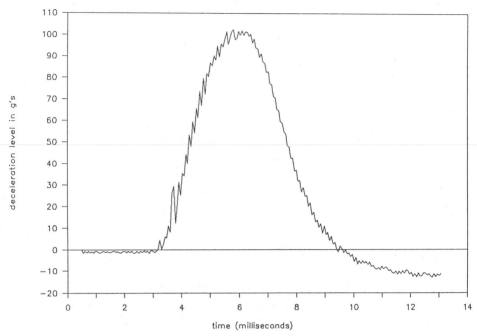

FIG. 4—*Typical full-screen deceleration plot produced by analysis program.*

the end of the impact, a time cell number denoted as HCNT. The first three analysis parameters, total duration of the impact interval (TAUTOT), the interval from the start of the interval to the point of maximum deceleration (TAUMAX), and the maximum level achieved (GMAX) are easily determined. GMAX is found directly, and the others are calculated by

$$TAUTOT = (HCNT - LCNT)*(TUNIT) \qquad (1)$$

$$TAUMAX = (BCNT - LCNT)*(TUNIT) \qquad (2)$$

Average deceleration is the simple average of all the sampled levels detected during the impact interval; this value was found to be of little interest since the average can be identical for many different shapes of impact deceleration curves. Therefore, the average was dropped from the list of parameters to be determined.

After some debate, a decision was made to calculate three average rates of change of deceleration. The first (DVDT1) extends over the entire rise of the deceleration curve (from LCNT to BCNT). A second (DVDT3) is the average rate measured from the time at which the threshold is exceeded (LCNT) to the time when half the GMAX level is reached; the time corresponding to this event is denoted as TD2T. The third rate of change (DVDT2) is that measured from TD2T to BCNT. These three rates of change are expressed as

$$DVDT1 = (GMAX - GTHR)/TAUMAX \qquad (3)$$

$$DVDT2 = 0.5*GMAX/(BCNT - TD2T)*(TUNIT) \qquad (4)$$

$$DVDT3 = ((0.5*GMAX) - GTHR)/(TD2T - LCNT) \qquad (5)$$

Maximum force exerted on the impact surface is determined simply by multiplying the maximum deceleration by the mass of the test projectile.

Conversion of the raw data in the file to g values produces an ordered sequence of readings that serves as a time history, or curve, of deceleration over time. Integration of this curve from a known initial condition, the velocity of the projectile at the start of the impact interval, or time cell LCNT, produces a velocity curve. The velocity decreases from the initial value with time as the impact progresses. A plot of one such curve is provided as Fig. 5. A second integration of the raw data (an integration of the velocity curve) produces a calculation of surface displacement from the start of the impact at time LCNT to the last data point in time cell HCNT. The displacement curve for the velocity history of Fig. 5 is represented as Fig. 6. The displacement curve goes positive in time cell LCNT, reaches a peak when downward velocity of the test mass reaches zero, and decreases as the mass rebounds. If the surface is sufficiently resilient, the drop mass remains in contact with the surface and the displacement returns to zero as the test mass passes through the original plane of impact while moving upward. Rebound velocity is the velocity observed or calculated as the mass returns to the point of original contact with the test surface. Rebound ratio, one of the parameters added to the analysis program, is defined as the ratio of the rebound velocity to the impact velocity, both measured at the plane of the initial impact. This ratio is also referred to as the coefficient of restitution. Many of the playing surfaces evaluated during this project deform to the extent that the test mass does not rebound to the original impact plane. For these surfaces, calculation of rebound ratio could not be done. Initially, the integrations needed to assess velocity and displacement were done by Simpson's rule which performs integration by approximating an analog curve with discrete points, creating weighted areas from those points, and summing the area under the curve over the range of interest. Since the value at each point and the time interval between points are known, an integration over

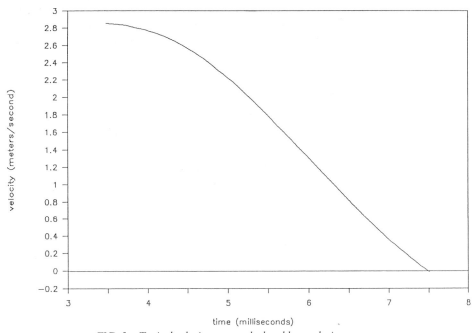

FIG. 5—*Typical velocity curve calculated by analysis program.*

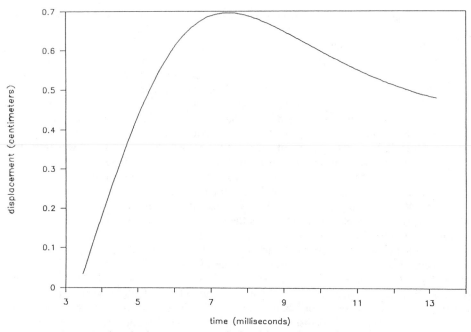

FIG. 6—*Surface displacement curve calculated from velocity information of Fig. 5.*

time can be very closely approximated as a sum of the products of points measured over the impact interval of interest and the time between successive samples.

Severity index assessment was initially investigated by Gadd [*4*]. This parameter is calculated as a weighted average of the area under the deceleration curve. The approach used within the analysis program is that stipulated by the ASTM Method for Shock-Absorbing Properties of Playing Surface Systems and Materials (F 355-86), with the exception that the sampling interval of the 2515 is employed in place of the millisecond interval dictated by the ASTM.

Experimentation

The velocity curve that pertains to a given impact is developed by integrating the deceleration from an initial velocity value until the test mass comes to rest. Since no practical way of measuring impact velocity for each drop was available, establishing a fixed value for this parameter was of some interest. Determination of the velocity attained by allowing the test mass to fall through the guide tube was necessary. This velocity was first calculated assuming free gravitational fall from a constant height of 45.7 cm in a vacuum. The value calculated (2.99 m/s) was perceived as an upper bound for the actual impact velocity since friction and interference in the guide tube were seen as velocity retardants. Experimentation to determine the importance of these factors was necessary.

Under the direction of Rogers and Waddington [*5*], two approaches were taken to making a reliable impact velocity determination. In the first of these attempts, a reflective tape of known width was wrapped around the cylindrical drop mass. An optical probe was mounted on the lower surface of the guide tube such that light produced within the probe was reflected to the detector within the probe when the tape caused sufficient reflection. The interval during which reflection persisted was measured and accepted as the time required for the width of the tape to pass the mouth of the guide tube. Twenty test drops were made with each of three drop weights. The average of these measurements indicated an exit velocity of 2.91 m/s. Variation with drop mass was negligible, and the velocities determined for 60 drops showed a standard deviation of 0.03 m/s. The second approach made use of high-speed photography. Motion pictures of two drops with each of the three weights were made, and the movement of the mass as it emerged from the guide tube was measured by comparison of successive frames. The rate of film advance was 1000 frames/s and shutter speed was 0.2 ms. No variation with drop weight was found; average velocity by this method was determined to be 2.79 m/s. Although the first of these methods was judged to be the more reliable, the average of the two determined values, or 2.85 m/s, was adopted for use in the analysis routine as the impact velocity, the initial value needed in the integration of the deceleration curve.

Ensemble Data Processing

Impact data were collected throughout the extended interval over which playing field surfaces were being investigated. Each drop was characterized by the school district to which the test surface belongs, the season during which the test was made, whether the drop was in the playing area or a peripheral area, and, in some cases, whether the goal or playing area was being tested. Each individual file was transferred to the Winchester disk on the IBM PC/AT. The analysis program was at first applied to individual files to produce information of the type illustrated by Fig. 7. This hard copy of a screen display was produced by activation of the Print Screen (PrtSc) key on the PC/AT keyboard. As the database archived on the disk grew, the need for better organization became apparent. A tree approach to structuring was adopted, with separate directories created for the different playing fields being tested. Subdirectories were created for the seasons of the test period.

When review of results across a cluster of files was first begun, a large file was created to hold the results of the application of the analysis routine to individual data files selected by the operator from memory by name. Processed results were added to this composite file as

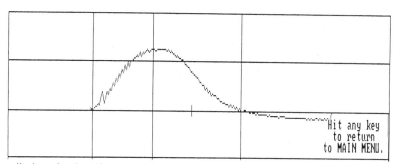

```
Maximum deceleration = 102.5 g
Total duration of impact = 6.1 milliseconds.
Max deceleration at 2.5 milliseconds after threshold exceeded
First rate of change = 40.32 g/millisecond.
Second rate of change = 33.06 g/millisecond.
Third rate of change = 51.67 g/millisecond
Impact velocity (assumed) = 2.85 meters/second.
Maximum force = 456.51 newtons. ( 102.62 pounds.)
Surface deformation= .69 centimeters.
Severity index= 242.72 seconds.    Rebound ratio: .18
```

FIG. 7—*Typical screen display of drop test results produced by analysis program.*

the data from each drop were analyzed. As directories grew, the use of this approach with its manual selection and the repeated delay in waiting for the analysis program to run became less attractive. A supplementary algorithm was developed that could be directed by the operator to a particular directory or subdirectory. The algorithm runs the analysis program on each data file in the designated directory, stores the processed results in a composite file, and provides a printout of the results for each file as the analysis of that file is completed. Sets of like parameters such as peak deceleration or severity index from the files of a directory can be subjected to a statistical analysis within a Lotus 123 program for examination in terms of mean and standard deviation. This supplementary program facilitates the examination of results of tests on a particular section of a given playing field during a selected playing season. Variations of the surface of an individual field with season or location or comparisons of different fields under similar conditions can be readily made.

Conclusions

The system discussed in this paper was developed to collect, store, and analyze accelerometer data acquired during impacts initiated to test characteristics of outside surfaces. This system performed well during the field trial period and subsequent analysis efforts in support of the main thrust of the research. The software routines developed for the surface analysis task are straightforward. Initial plans for processing to be carried out by the operating program were modified to accommodate the peculiarities of the particular drop test apparatus employed and were augmented over the course of the investigation to allow handling the large amount of data collected during the two-year period. The conclusions reached in interpretation of the drop data are discussed in detail in the Rogers and Waddington paper [5].

References

[1] Clegg, B., "An Impact Testing Device for In Situ Base Course Evaluation," *Proceedings of the Australian Road Research Bureau,* Vol. 8, 1976, pp. 1–5.
[2] Bell, M. J., Baker, S. W., and Canaway, P. M., "Playing Quality of Sports Surfaces: A Review," *Journal of the Sports Turf Research Institute,* Vol. 61, 1985, pp. 26–45.
[3] "BASIC Reference," third edition, International Business Machines Corp., Boca Raton, FL, May 1984.
[4] Gadd, C. W., "Use of a Weighted-Impulse Criterion for Estimating Injury Hazard," *Proceedings,* Tenth Stapp Car Crash Conference, 8–9 Nov. 1966, pp. 164–174.
[5] Rogers, J. N. III and Waddington, D. V., this publication, pp. 96–110.

Richard L. Henderson,[1] *Donald V. Waddington,*[1] *and Chauncey A. Morehouse*[2]

Laboratory Measurements of Impact Absorption on Turfgrass and Soil Surfaces

REFERENCE: Henderson, R. L., Waddington, D. V., and Morehouse, C. A., **"Laboratory Measurements of Impact Absorption on Turfgrass and Soil Surfaces,"** *Natural and Artificial Playing Fields: Characteristics and Safety Features, ASTM STP 1073,* R. C. Schmidt, E. F. Hoerner, E. M. Milner, and C. A. Morehouse, Eds., American Society for Testing and Materials, Philadelphia, 1990, pp. 127–135.

ABSTRACT: Soil and turfgrass surfaces prepared in wooden boxes were evaluated in the laboratory for peak deceleration and depth of penetration using Procedure A of ANSI/ASTM Test for Shock Absorbing Properties of Playing Surface Systems and Materials (F 355–86). A 9.1-kg missile with a flat surface (129 cm^2) was dropped three times from a height of 61 cm. The peak deceleration was greater and the penetration depth less with a soil depth of 7.5 cm than with depths of 15 cm or greater. This effect was attributed to the box bottom and heavy anvil on which the boxes were placed for testing. Peak deceleration was lower and penetration depth greater with turf cover than with bare soil and when soil was core cultivated. Each successive impact altered the results because of soil compaction. The limitations of this method were the small surface area (20 by 47 cm) available for testing (only three impact locations per box) and the lifting and transporting of soil-filled boxes.

KEY WORDS: playing fields, impact absorption, peak deceleration, penetration depth, turfgrass, soil properties

Playing quality is the main factor by which athletes judge athletic fields. Bell et al. [1] reported that the playing quality of fields is controlled by the physical properties of the immediate surface layer and underlying soil material. In the past, much of the research reported on these areas had dealt primarily with turfgrass or soil characteristics; however, in more recent studies, athletic fields have been judged by player/field interactions, and the main criteria for judging such interactions are hardness and traction.

Some degree of hardness is important for sports, but the optimum degree of hardness will vary among sports. Generally, an excessively hard surface will cause jarring of bones and muscle soreness, and increase the probability of injury in the event of a fall. If the surface is too soft, player fatigue, traction, and ball bounce properties will be affected [1]. Hardness of field surfaces has been measured using penetrometers and devices that detect impact or shock absorption properties. Van Wijk [2] used a penetrometer to assess playability of soccer fields and found soil water content and bulk density to be major factors affecting results. These soil properties also have considerable influence on impact absorption characteristics. Impact absorbing characteristics have been commonly assessed by measuring the deceleration upon

---

[1] Graduate research assistant and professor of soil science, respectively, Department of Agronomy, Pennsylvania State University, University Park, PA 16802.

[2] Professor emeritus of physical education, Department of Exercise and Sport Science, Pennsylvania State University, University Park, PA 16802.

impact of a falling missile (impact hammer). In 1968, Gramckow [3] reported on impact characteristics as affected by turfgrass and soil properties. Bowers and Martin [4] used this method to compare an asphalt surface and natural and artificial turf surfaces. Zebarth and Sheard [5] employed a similar procedure to assess impact characteristics of horse racetracks. In more recent studies, a portable impact hammer developed by Clegg [6] has been used to evaluate surfaces [7–15].

A standard test method of ASTM is ANSI/ASTM Test Method for Shock Absorbing Properties of Playing Surface Systems and Materials (F 355–86). Apparatus constructed by the Sports Research Institute at Penn State was designed to utilize this method. This apparatus is nonportable and was constructed on a steel anvil (base) weighing approximately 250 kg. It had been used primarily for testing of artificial playing surface materials. This study was conducted to determine the practicability of a laboratory procedure for evaluating soil and turfgrass surfaces utilizing this apparatus. Specific objectives were to determine the effect of soil depth, soil texture, turfgrass cover, core cultivation, and successive impacts on two impact characteristics: peak deceleration, g_{max}, and depth of penetration.

Procedure

Apparatus

Soils were packed into wooden boxes of different height, 20 cm wide by 47 cm long, constructed using 1.9-cm-thick pine boards. These boxes would fit between the missile guide rods on the impacting apparatus and could be positioned to obtain three impact locations on each surface. Procedure A of ANSI/ASTM F 355–86 was used for these tests. A 9.1-kg (20-lb) missile with a flat face of 129 cm^2 (20 in.^{2}) was dropped three successive times on each test location from a height of 61 cm (24 in.) above the surface. Peak deceleration was measured using a Kistler Model 801 linear accelerometer, and depth of penetration was determined using a linear variable differential transformer (Schaevitz Engineering Co.).

Experiment 1

The effects of soil depth, soil texture, turf cover, and successive impacts were determined in this experiment. With a shallow depth of soil, the bottom of the soil container and the anvil (base of the impact apparatus) will influence the measured impact properties; however, as soil depth increases, the effect of the container and anvil should be negligible.

The soil depths utilized were 7.5, 15.0, 23.0, 30.5, and 35.5 cm. Soils representing three textural classes were added to the boxes in 2-cm increments, which were packed to achieve the listed bulk densities:

1. Clay (8% sand, 35% silt, and 57% clay) was packed to a bulk density of 1.45 g/cm^3 and tested at a soil water content of 21% by weight.
2. Silt loam (13% sand, 60% silt, and 27% clay) was packed to 1.35 g/cm^3 and tested at a soil water content of 21% by weight.
3. Sand (100% sand, a coarse sand with 13% 2 to 1-mm, 46% 1 to 0.5-mm, 18% 0.5 to 0.25-mm, 11% 0.25 to 0.10-mm, and 12% 0.10 to 0.05-mm particles) packed to 1.58 g/cm^3 and tested at 7% water content by weight.

One of two boxes representing each depth-texture combination was sodded with two-year-old Kentucky bluegrass, *Poa pratensis* L., and the second had no vegetation. The boxes were placed outside and exposed to summer environmental conditions for three months prior to impact testing. Each box was split into three locations (middle and each end) for impacts, and three impacts were made at each location.

Experiment 2

In this experiment, the effects of coring (a widely used practice in the maintenance of athletic fields) were studied. The same silt loam as used in Experiment 1 was packed in boxes to achieve a 23-cm depth and a bulk density of 1.35 g/cm^3. The two coring treatments were noncored and cored to a depth of approximately 6 cm on 5-cm centers using 1.3-cm diameter hollow tines. Three replications were used, and each surface was tested as described previously at three locations with three impacts. Soil water content was 18% by weight prior to testing.

Experiment 3

The silt loam soil previously described was packed to a depth of 23 cm and to a bulk density of 1.35 g/cm^3. "Pennfine" perennial ryegrass, *Lolium perenne* L., was seeded and allowed to establish for 60 days in six boxes. Turf was cut as needed using a 4-cm cutting height. Three boxes were not seeded. The three vegetative treatments used for impacting were shoots plus roots, roots with no shoots (clipped prior to testing), and no roots or shoots (bare soil). Three replications were used, and each replicate was impacted three times at each of three locations.

Statistical Analyses

Data were analyzed using analysis of variance procedures, and treatment means were compared using the Waller-Duncan K Bayesian test with $k = 100$ [*16*].

Results and Discussion

Experiment 1

All factors except location within boxes significantly affected peak deceleration, depth of penetration, or both (Table 1). In all experiments, results were never significantly affected by location. Thus, impact in one location did not affect results on the next location to be tested, and impact results obtained were similar at the center location and the two end locations, which were close to three rather than two sides of the box. Peak deceleration was greatest and depth of penetration least with the 7.5-cm soil depth. Thus, this depth was not great enough to exclude effects from the box base and anvil of the apparatus. Each impact compacted the soil, and this effect was reflected in data from subsequent impacts at the same location.

With the bulk densities and soil water contents used, the clay soil gave the highest peak deceleration. These and other effects would be expected to vary with other densities and soil water contents. Turf cover caused lower peak deceleration and greater penetration. A cover by texture interaction indicated the effect of cover was greater on the clay and sand soils than the silt loam. Soil depth also produced significant interactions. For peak deceleration, the 7.5-cm depth was affected the greatest by the presence of turf (Fig. 1), and the differences due to texture were greater at the 7.5-cm depth (Fig. 2). The increase in peak deceleration with successive impacts was also greater with the 7.5-cm depth (Fig. 3). Another interaction showed that the increase in peak deceleration due to successive impacts was greater on bare than on turf-covered surfaces (Fig. 4).

TABLE 1—*Effects of soil depth, cover, soil texture, and impact on peak deceleration and depth of penetration.*

Soil Depth, cm	Peak Deceleration, g_{max}					Depth of Penetration, mm				
	Impact					Impact				
	All	1	2	3	All[a]	All	1	2	3	All[a]
7.5	63a[b]	47a	67a	75a	--	13b	17c	11a	10b	--
15.0	39b	27bc	42b	48b	39a	20a	22b	24a	15a	20a
23.0	36cd	29b	38cd	40c	36bc	17a	21b	16a	15a	17a
30.5	34d	24c	36d	43c	34c	19a	24a	17a	15a	19a
35.5	38bc	27b	41bc	44bc	38ab	17a	21b	16a	15a	17a
Cover										
Bare	50a	36a	55a	61a	42a	14b	16b	13b	12b	15b
Turf	34b	27b	36b	42b	32b	21a	25a	21a	16a	22a
Soil Texture										
Clay	47a	34a	51a	57a	36ab	17a	21a	20a	14a	18a
Silt loam	40c	29b	42c	48c	35b	17a	20a	15a	14a	17a
Sand	43b	31b	46b	50b	39a	16a	21a	16a	13a	20a
Impact										
1	31c				27c	21a				22a
2	45b				40b	17b				19a
3	51a				44a	14c				15b

[a]Data from 7.5 cm soil depth excluded.

[b]Treatment means within a column for a given factor followed by the same letter are not significantly different.

Results from each impact were analyzed individually (Table 1). The cover by texture, cover by depth, and texture by depth interactions for peak deceleration were also present for individual impacts.

It was concluded that the 7.5-cm depth was too shallow for this laboratory procedure, so results were also analyzed without the 7.5-cm data (Table 1). Although significant differences occurred among the 15.0 to 35.5-cm depths, all peak deceleration values were within a narrow 5 g range (34 to 39 g). A trend with increasing depth was not noted, and significant differences possibly were due to slight differences in packing or soil water content among the boxes. The only conclusion concerning other factors that was altered by eliminating the 7.5-cm data was that of the clay being the hardest surface. The effects of cover and impact number were still apparent, as was the previously discussed interaction of cover and texture.

PEAK DECELERATION, g $_{max}$

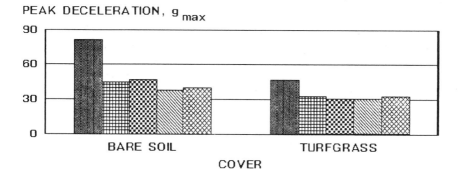

FIG. 1—*Effects of soil depth and cover on peak deceleration.*

PEAK DECELERATION, g $_{max}$

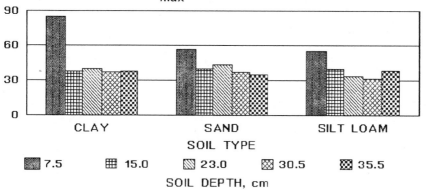

FIG. 2—*Effects of soil depth and soil type on peak deceleration.*

PEAK DECELERATION, g $_{max}$

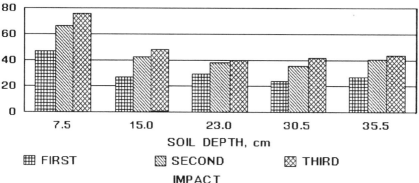

FIG. 3—*Effects of successive impacts and soil depth on peak deceleration.*

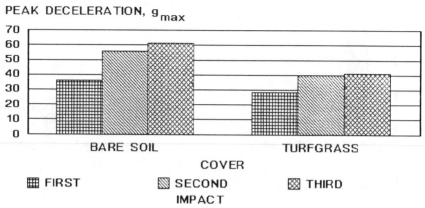

FIG. 4—*Effects of successive impacts and cover on peak deceleration.*

Experiment 2

Core cultivation significantly decreased peak deceleration and increased depth of penetration (Table 2). Results were altered due to the compacting effect of the first impact as indicated by a significant cultivation by impact interaction for depth of penetration (Fig. 5). With impact one, coring resulted in a large depth of penetration; however, due to the compaction produced by the first impact, the effect of coring was reduced considerably with the second and third impacts. Data from each impact were analyzed individually and are also shown in Table 2. Although peak deceleration increased with each successive drop, the differences between cored and noncored treatments remained about the same for all three impacts. The results show the value of core cultivation for reducing the hardness of a soil surface, and also that subsequent compaction can negate this beneficial effect.

TABLE 2—*Effects of core cultivation and impact on peak deceleration and depth of penetration.*

Cultivation	Peak Deceleration, g_{max}				Impact			
	All	1	2	3	All	1	2	3
Cored	36b[a]	25b	38b	42b	16a	23a	13a	13a
Non-cored	49a	39a	54a	56a	12b	14b	11b	11b
Impact								
1	32b	--	--	--	18a	--	--	--
2	46a	--	--	--	12b	--	--	--
3	49a	--	--	--	12b	--	--	--

[a]Treatment means within a column for a given factor followed by the same letter are not significantly different.

PENETRATION DEPTH, mm

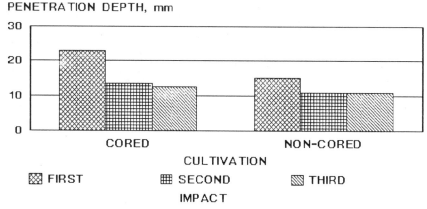

FIG. 5—*Effects of successive impacts and core cultivation on penetration depth.*

Experiment 3

Impact characteristics were significantly affected by vegetation and impact (Table 3). Peak deceleration was lowest and penetration greatest with shoots and roots present, and the presence of roots gave a softer surface than was obtained with bare soil. The greater effects of vegetation were due to shoots rather than roots. Differences observed could be partially explained by differences in soil water contents: bare soil, 22%; roots only, 28%; and shoots and roots, 27%. Although these soil moisture values, averaged over three replications, were not significantly different statistically, they may have affected results because higher peak deceleration and lower penetration values are associated with lower soil water contents.

TABLE 3—*Effects of vegetation and impact on peak deceleration and depth of penetration.*

Vegetation	Peak Deceleration, g_{max}				Depth of Penetration, mm			
	All	1	2	3	All	1	2	3
Shoots and roots	23c[a]	18c	24b	27b	18a	21a	17a	16a
Roots only	34b	26b	35a	40a	15b	17b	14b	13b
Bare soil	40a	32a	40a	47a	13c	14c	12b	12b
Impact								
1	26c	--	--	--	17a	--	--	--
2	33b	--	--	--	15b	--	--	--
3	38a	--	--	--	14c	--	--	--

[a]Treatment means within a column for a given factor followed by the same letter are not significantly different.

Greater moisture control may be required in these types of studies. Zebarth and Sheard [5] reported higher peak deceleration values with the presence of Kentucky bluegrass turf as compared with bare soil. The lack of agreement between their results and those in this study may be due to the differences in the turfgrass species used. Kentucky bluegrass has a rhizomatous growth habit, and the rhizomes (underground lateral shoots) may serve to increase soil strength. Perennial ryegrass is a bunch grass and does not have rhizomes or other extravaginal growth that could influence impact measurements. These aspects need further study. A survey of athletic fields by Rogers et al. [15] also showed turf cover to be negatively correlated with peak deceleration; however, field factors other than cover (soil moisture and bulk density) also varied on those sites.

Summary and Conclusions

A method for laboratory testing of soil and turfgrass surfaces was deemed to be practical. Peak deceleration was greater and penetration depth lower with a 7.5-cm soil depth than with depths of 15 cm or greater; thus, it was concluded that a minimum of 15 cm is needed to insure that impact measurements are not greatly influenced by the box bottoms or the anvil beneath the boxes when utilizing this procedure for the assessment of impact characteristics of turfgrass and soil conditions. In future laboratory evaluations with different soils, soil properties, or impacting energies, the critical soil depth for minimum base or anvil effect should be established. The depth effect was more apparent on bare than turfgrass-covered soil. The higher peak deceleration values at 7.5 cm suggest a practical significance to these results in cases where fields have been built with areas having a shallow soil covering over bedrock or other buried hard surfaces.

Peak deceleration increased and penetration decreased with each successive impact. The first impact more clearly reflected the characteristics of the surface under test, but the third impact provided information as to how the same soil would react to impact when in a severely compacted condition.

Peak deceleration was lower and penetration greater with turf on the soil and when the soil was core cultivated.

Limitations to this method were the small surface area within box areas that could be tested and the lifting and transporting of the filled boxes. Although no difference was found due to the three test locations in each box, these locations should be considered plot splits rather than replications in the experimental design because soil in each box may have its own slight variations in moisture and bulk density. Replication can be achieved by preparing additional boxes for each treatment.

Acknowledgment

This paper is contribution No. 8066 from the Pennsylvania Agricultural Experiment Station, Pennsylvania State University, University Park, PA.

References

[1] Bell, M. J., Baker, S. W., and Canaway, P. M., "Playing Quality of Sports Surfaces: A Review," *Journal of the Sports Turf Research Institute,* Vol. 61, 1985, pp. 26–45.
[2] van Wijk, A. L. M., "A Technological Study of Effectuating and Maintaining Adequate Playing Conditions of Grass Sports Fields," Centre for Agriculture Publishing and Documentation, Wageningen, The Netherlands, 1980.
[3] Gramckow, J., "Athletic Field Quality Studies," Cal-Turf Inc., Camarillo, CA, 1968.

[4] Bowers, K. D., Jr. and Martin, R. B., "Impact Absorption, New and Old AstroTurf at West Virginia University," *Medicine and Science in Sports,* Vol. 6, No. 3, 1974, pp. 217–221.

[5] Zebarth, B. J. and Sheard, R. W., "Impact and Shear Resistance of Turfgrass Racing Surfaces for Thoroughbreds," *American Journal of Veterinary Research,* Vol. 46, No. 4, April 1985, pp. 778–784.

[6] Clegg, B., "An Impact Soil Test for Low Cost Roads," *Proceedings,* Second Conference of Road Engineers Association of Asia and Australia, Manila, The Philippines, October 1978, pp. 58–65.

[7] Lush, W. M., "Objective Assessment of Turf Cricket Pitches Using an Impact Hammer," *Journal of the Sports Turf Research Institute,* Vol. 61, 1985, pp. 71–79.

[8] Holmes, G. and Bell, M. J., "Technical Note: Playing Surface Hardness and Tennis Ball Rebound Resilience," *Journal of the Sports Turf Research Institute,* Vol. 62, 1986, pp. 207–210.

[9] Holmes, G. and Bell, M. J., "The Playing Quality of Bowling Greens: A Survey," *Journal of the Sports Turf Research Institute,* Vol. 62, 1986, pp. 50–66.

[10] Holmes, G. and Bell, M. J., "A Pilot Study of the Playing Quality of Football Pitches," *Journal of the Sports Turf Research Institute,* Vol. 62, 1986, pp. 74–91.

[11] Baker, S. W., "Technical Note: Playing Quality of Some Soccer Pitches in Saudi Arabia," *Journal of the Sports Turf Research Institute,* Vol. 63, 1987, pp. 145–148.

[12] Baker, S. W. and Isaac, S. P., "The Effect of Rootzone Composition on the Performance of Winter Game Pitches: II—Playing Quality," *Journal of the Sports Turf Research Institute,* Vol. 63, 1987, pp. 67–80.

[13] Holmes, G. and Bell, M. J., "Standards of Playing Quality for Natural Turf," The Sports Turf Research Institute, Bingley, West Yorkshire, England, 1987.

[14] Holmes, G. and Bell, M. J., "The Playing Quality of Association Football Pitches," *Journal of the Sports Turf Research Institute,* Vol. 64, 1988, pp. 19–47.

[15] Rogers, J. N., III, Waddington, D. V., and Harper, J. C., II, "Relationships Between Athletic Field Hardness and Traction, Vegetation, Soil Properties, and Maintenance Practices," Progress Report 393, Pennsylvania State University, College of Agriculture, Agricultural Experiment Station, University Park, PA, December 1988.

[16] Waller, R. A. and Duncan, D. B., "A Bayes Rule for the Symmetric Multiple Comparisons Problem," *Journal of the American Statistical Association,* Vol. 64, 1969, pp. 1484–1503.

John N. Rogers III[1] and Donald V. Waddington[2]

Effects of Management Practices on Impact Absorption and Shear Resistance in Natural Turf

REFERENCE: Rogers, J. N. III and Waddington, D. V., **"Effects of Management Practices on Impact Absorption and Shear Resistance in Natural Turf,"** *Natural and Artificial Playing Fields: Characteristics and Safety Features, ASTM STP 1073,* R. C. Schmidt, E. F. Hoerner, E. M. Milner, and C. A. Morehouse, Eds., American Society for Testing and Materials, Philadelphia, 1990, pp. 136–146.

ABSTRACT: The Clegg impact soil tester (0.5 and 2.25-kg hammers), the Bruel & Kjaer 2515 vibration analyzer, and the Eijkelkamp Type 1B shear vane were used to evaluate effects of soil compaction, aeration, soil moisture, and thatch on impact absorption and shear resistance characteristics in several turfgrasses. Impact absorption characteristics were influenced most by soil moisture, soil compaction, and thatch. Peak deceleration decreased with increasing soil moisture and increased with compaction. Effects from aeration on peak deceleration were usually not significant; however, on several dates aeration significantly decreased the severity index and increased deformation. The presence of thatch on a surface improved shock attenuation under most conditions. Compaction increased shear resistance values. The effects on shear resistance from aeration and soil moisture were varied.

KEY WORDS: playing fields, impact absorption, shock absorption, shear resistance, traction, Kentucky bluegrass, *Poa pratensis* L., tall fescue, *Festuca arundinacea* Schreb., soil compaction, aeration, core cultivation, soil moisture, thatch

Most of the research to determine the quality of athletic fields has thus far been limited to developing portable methods for quantitative measurement of impact absorption and shear resistance [1–4]. While comparative studies between artificial and natural surfaces [5], natural surfaces themselves [6,7], and root zone composition [8–10] have been reported, there is a need for information on the relationships between these quantitative measurements and management practices on natural turf.

The objective of this research were (1) to determine the effects of compaction, aeration (core cultivation), and soil moisture on the impact absorption and shear resistance of Kentucky bluegrass (*Poa pratensis* L.) and tall fescue (*Festuca arundinacea* Schreb.) turf; and (2) to determine the effects of thatch and verdure of several turf species on impact absorption.

[1] Assistant professor, Department of Crop and Soil Science, Michigan State University, East Lansing, MI 48824.

[2] Professor of Soil Science, Department of Agronomy, Pennsylvania State University, University Park, PA 16802.

Procedure

General

Impact absorption was measured with a combination of the Clegg impact soil tester (Lafayette Instrument Co., Lafayette, IN) and the Bruel & Kjaer 2515 vibration analyzer (Bruel & Kjaer Instruments, Marlborough, MA). The surfaces were evaluated with two hammers (2.25 and 0.5 kg) in these studies. The hammers were dropped from a height of 45.7 cm, and the deceleration-time curves for plot surfaces were recorded and stored in the memory of the B & K 2515. The impact characteristics obtained were maximum or peak deceleration [in maximum gravity units (g_{max})], time to peak deceleration (in milliseconds), total duration of impact (in milliseconds), rate of change from the threshold to the point of maximum deceleration (rate of change 1) (in gravity units per millisecond), rate of change from the threshold to the 0.5-point of maximum deceleration (rate of change 2) (in gravity units per millisecond), rate of change from the 0.5-point to the point of maximum deceleration (rate of change 3) (in gravity units per millisecond), surface deformation (in centimetres), Gadd severity index (in seconds) [11], and rebound ratio. The surface deformation, severity index, and rebound ratio were calculated from the deceleration-time curve. More detail on this method and correlations between impact characteristics have been reported [12,13].

Shear resistance was measured with an Eijkelkamp Type 1B shear vane (Eijkelkamp, Giesbeek, The Netherlands). Shear strength, calculated as the quotient of the maximum torque (in newton metres) and the constant of the apparatus (2.285×10^{-4} m^3), was recorded as the average of four measurements.

Data were analyzed using analysis of variance and Fisher's least significant difference (LSD) procedures.

Experiments 1 and 2

Experiments 1 and 2, conducted on tall fescue and Kentucky bluegrass turf, respectively, were initiated in April 1986 at the Joseph Valentine Turfgrass Research Center, University Park, PA, to evaluate the effects of compaction and core cultivation on impact absorption and traction. The experimental sites were located adjacent to each other, and the soil type was Hagerstown silt loam (17.2% sand, 62.2% silt, and 20.6% clay). Direct comparisons between the tall fescue and Kentucky bluegrass were not included because each turf had been established at a different time, and it was assumed that soil structural differences could exist. Fertilization and weed control were used as needed. The turf was mowed at a height of 2.5 cm and received no water other than rainfall.

A split plot design of a 2 × 2 factorial experiment with three replications was used. Main plots (2.1 by 21.5 m) were either aerated or not aerated, and they were split for compaction treatments (compacted or noncompacted). The treatments were identical for each experiment. The areas were aerated on 27 May 1986, 9 November 1986, and 4 June 1987 by using 8 to 10 passes with a pull-behind Ryan Renovaire Model No. 544317 aerator with 1.9-cm-diameter tines. Compaction was applied using a clay tennis court riding compactor (364 kg). Approximately 40 passes were made from May through November 1986, plus another 30 passes from April through July 1987, when soil moisture conditions were conducive to soil compaction.

Six impacts at different areas on each plot surface were used to obtain an average deceleration-time curve, which was stored in the B & K 2515.

Impact absorption and shear resistance measurements were made on 20 September and 16 November 1986; on 14 April, 1 July, 25 August, and 16 October 1987; and on 24 June 1988. The percentage by weight of the soil moisture of the surface 5.0 cm was determined

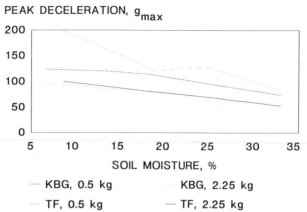

FIG. 1—*The effect of soil moisture on peak deceleration measured on tall fescue and Kentucky bluegrass turf using 0.5 and 2.25-kg hammers.*

on each date. The bulk density of the surface 5.0 cm was measured on 13 June 1986 and 28 August 1987. All data were statistically analyzed for each data collection date.

Soil moisture was not significantly affected by treatments on any of the sampling data; however, differences among the sampling dates gave a range of soil moisture contents (Fig. 1) at which data were collected. In June 1986, compaction had increased the bulk density of the tall fescue area from 1.20 to 1.27 g/cm^3; in August 1987, measurements showed an increase from 1.24 to 1.34 g/cm^3. On the bluegrass area, the compaction effect was significant only in 1987 (1.12 versus 1.26 g/cm^3). Significant changes due to aeration were not detected.

Experiments 3 and 4

Experiments 3 and 4 were conducted on four separate sites to determine the effect of thatch on impact absorption. The first site was a fine fescue (*Festuca rubra* L.) plot located in a residential lawn in Centre County, PA. Sites 2 and 3 were on Kentucky bluegrass turf at the Joseph Valentine Turfgrass Research Center, with one site (Kentucky bluegrass-A) being a five-year-old stand and another site (Kentucky bluegrass-B) a three-year-old stand. The final site was a zoysia grass (*Zoysia* sp.) plot located in a residential lawn in Centre County. For each site the design was the same.

Experiment 3 was a randomized complete block with three treatments and four replications. Treatments represented surfaces comprised of (*a*) full turf or verdure (top growth remaining after mowing), (*b*) thatch (organic layer beneath verdure and above soil surface), and (*c*) bare soil obtained by removing top growth and thatch. The B & K 2515 recorded an average of two impact measurements on each plot. Soil moisture and thatch depth were measured for each replication for all sites.

Experiment 4 was also conducted at the sites described earlier. The 10-cm-diameter thatch + top-growth plugs removed in Experiment 3 served as surfaces for this experiment. The plugs were placed on a section of running track padding for impact measurements. The three treatments in this randomized complete block design with four replications were grass + thatch on the pad, thatch on the pad, and the pad alone. For all measurements the pad was placed on a concrete surface. The B & K 2515 recorded an impact measurement for each treatment using both the 2.25 and 0.5-kg hammers.

Data for both experiments at the fine fescue, Kentucky bluegrass-A, Kentucky bluegrass-B, and zoysia grass sites were collected on 3 September, 25 September, 12 October, and 10 September 1987, respectively. The data were analyzed separately for each site.

TABLE 1—*Effect of compaction on impact characteristics of Kentucky bluegrass and tall fescue turf (average of all sampling dates).*

Treatment	Peak Decel	Tot Time	Peak Time	Rate of Change[a]			Deform	Sev Index	Reb Ratio
	g_{max}	ms	ms	1	2	3	cm	s	
				----g/ms----					
Kentucky bluegrass									
				0.5 kg Hammer					
Noncompacted	89	7.7	4.7	19.6	23.9	16.8	1.05	206	0.22
Compacted	105	6.6	3.9	28.4	33.2	25.1	0.88	250	0.21
				2.25 kg Hammer					
Noncompacted	65	9.1	5.4	12.5	12.1	13.1	1.23	135	0.18
Compacted	78	7.9	5.0	17.8	17.1	18.5	1.05	177	0.21
Tall Fescue									
				0.5 kg Hammer					
Noncompacted	108	6.0	3.6	37.1	38.7	36.2	1.09	192	0.12
Compacted	125	5.3	3.1	47.2	49.0	46.2	1.00	238	0.16
				2.25 kg Hammer					
Noncompacted	62	8.8	5.1	13.4	10.9	17.2	0.88	211	0.18
Compacted	75	7.7	4.4	17.6	15.2	21.6	0.77	271	0.18

[a] 1, 2, and 3 are rate of change from threshold to peak deceleration, from threshold to one-half of peak deceleration, and from one-half of peak deceleration to peak deceleration, respectively.

Results and Discussion

Experiments 1 and 2

The effects of compaction on impact characteristics for Kentucky bluegrass and tall fescue turf are presented in Table 1. Averages over all sampling dates were used in this table to condense the manuscript; however, trends due to compaction are readily seen in this condensed form. Tables showing data and statistical results from each sampling date are available from the authors. Compaction increased the peak deceleration, severity index, and rates of change for the leading edge of the deceleration-time curve. The total impact time, time to peak deceleration, and deformation were decreased by compaction. Significant differences occurred on a majority of sampling dates except for the severity index and rebound ratio obtained with the 2.25-kg hammer on tall fescue and the rebound ratio using the 0.5-kg hammer on Kentucky bluegrass. High correlations between these impact characteristics measured on these and other areas have been reported [12,13].

In June 1988, no significant effect of compaction was obtained for any of the measured criteria. An explanation for this result could be the lack of any compaction treatment to the area for an eleven-month period, and alleviation of compaction by frost action. Also, soil moisture was extremely low on this date: 6.4 and 8.3% for the Kentucky bluegrass and tall fescue areas, respectively. Soil moisture on other dates ranged from 13 to 33%.

There was a relationship between the soil moisture on each sampling date and the impact characteristics. As the soil moisture decreased, the peak deceleration (Fig. 1), rates of change, and severity index increased, and the time periods and deformation decreased. Any inferences concerning differences in impact characteristics between the tall fescue and Kentucky bluegrass turfs should be made with caution because establishment methods and times were not the same for each grass. However, peak deceleration values, as measured with the 0.5-kg hammer, that were lower for Kentucky bluegrass than for tall fescue appeared to reflect a softening effect from the thatch layer (approximately 6 mm) present in the Kentucky bluegrass.

Few significant effects due to aeration were detected. Only in October 1987 was peak deceleration significantly lower with the aerated treatment ($g_{max} = 58$) than with the nonaerated

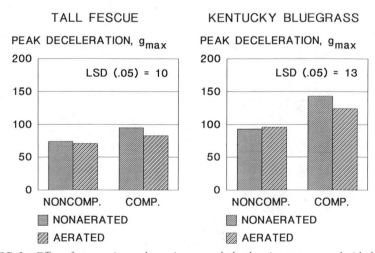

FIG. 2—*Effect of compaction and aeration on peak deceleration as measured with the 0.5-kg hammer on tall fescue in September 1986 and on Kentucky bluegrass in July 1987.*

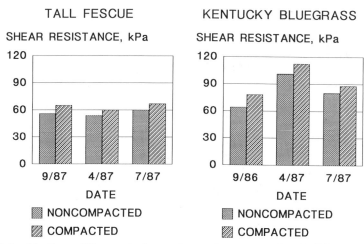

FIG. 3—*Significant differences in shear resistance due to compaction of tall fescue and Kentucky bluegrass turf.*

treatment (g_{max} = 63), as measured with the 0.5-kg hammer. Other characteristics were measured 20 times (2 grasses, 2 hammers, and 5 dates). Significant differences were measured only once for time periods, four times for rates of change, twice for the severity index, three times for deformation, and once for rebound ratio. Significant compaction by aeration interactions indicated that aeration effects were greater on compacted areas. Significant interactions occurred twice for peak deceleration (Fig. 2), four times for the three rates of change, twice for severity index, three times for deformation, and once for rebound ratio.

A reason for the general lack of effect from the aeration is the nature of aeration or core cultivation in turfgrass. It takes time for soil undisturbed during aeration to move laterally into the holes produced. Initially, the undisturbed soil may be just as dense as it was before aeration. The turfgrass manager aerating a field for the first time should be warned not to expect immediate benefits in alleviating hardness. Another reason for the lack of effect of aeration was the methodology of the experiment. During 1986, the plots were aerated and then compacted, while in 1987 the majority of compaction was done prior to aeration. The combination of compaction and aeration resulted in a harder surface than was detected on the noncompacted, nonaerated plots.

Significantly higher shear resistance due to compaction was measured on three of six dates (Fig. 3). Although aerated treatments had lower shear values, they were not significantly different from those on nonaerated areas. Shear values for compacted areas receiving aeration were equal to or less than values for untreated areas. On two dates, the compaction by aeration interaction was significant (Fig. 4), but only with Kentucky bluegrass. Aeration had a greater effect on compacted areas. The holes created during aeration had a greater effect on shear values than on impact characteristics. Moisture fluctuations did not affect shear resistance values as they did impact absorption characteristics. Overall, the Kentucky bluegrass turf had higher shear resistance values than tall fescue turf. Because of its rhizomatous growth habit, Kentucky bluegrass had formed a tighter, more dense turf than the tall fescue.

Experiment 3

The purpose of this experiment was to determine the effects of thatch and verdure on impact absorption characteristics in several species. The respective ranges for uncompressed

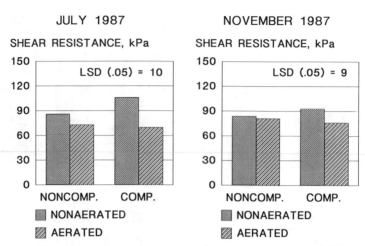

FIG. 4—*Effect of compaction and aeration on shear resistance of Kentucky bluegrass turf on two dates.*

and compressed (beneath a 1-kg weight) thatch thickness for the fine fescue, the Kentucky bluegrass-A, the Kentucky bluegrass-B, and the zoysia grass sites were 12 to 28, 17 to 38, 16 to 28, 14 to 30 mm and 9 to 26, 14 to 24, 11 to 23, 13 to 27 mm. Blocks were arranged to remove variation due to thatch depth; however, block differences were never significant in the statistical analyses.

0.5-Kilogram Hammer—The effects of thatch and verdure on the impact characteristics are presented in Table 2. To condense the manuscript, values were averaged over the four sites. Tables showing data and statistical results of each site are available from the authors. The peak deceleration values measured on bare soil treatments were significantly higher than full turf treatments in all species and higher than thatch treatments in all but the zoysia grass. There were significantly shorter duration times and times to peak deceleration for all bare soil treatments. Full turf treatments had lower peak deceleration values than thatch treatments, but they were not significantly lower. However, significantly longer time periods were associated with treatments of full turf than with thatch. Bare soil treatments had significantly higher rates of change than thatch and full turf treatments. Although rates of change for full turf were lower than for thatch treatments, only one signficant difference occurred. Significantly higher deformation values and rebound ratios and lower severity index values occurred for full turf in comparison with bare soil treatments. With some exceptions, thatch treatments differed from bare soil in a similar manner. Except for fine fescue, deformation and rebound ratios were greater with full turf than with thatch.

2.25-Kilogram Hammer—Differences due to treatments were not as great when measured with the 2.25-kg hammer (Table 2). Significant differences in peak deceleration due to treatment existed only at two sites. At these sites, bare soil treatments had higher peak deceleration values. There was no significant difference in any of the measured parameters between thatch and full turf treatments. Although no differences between treatments existed in peak deceleration in the zoysia grass, bare soil had significantly shorter time periods than the other treatments. In measurements of this type (including both bare and turf surfaces), the importance of measuring more than one impact characteristic became apparent. A significant difference in duration of impact in these species shows that the turf is acting as an impact

TABLE 2—*Effect of thatch and verdure on impact characteristics (averaged over four turfgrass sites).*

Treatment	Peak Decel	Tot Time	Peak Time	Rate of Change[a] 1	2	3	Deform	Sev Index	Reb Ratio
	g_{max}	ms	ms	-----g/ms-----			cm	s	
In situ									
Bare Soil	118	5.3	2.6	0.5 kg Hammer 47.8	41.2	82.5	0.63	287	0.15
Thatch	86	8.5	4.8	17.2	19.1	15.7	1.07	178	0.27
Full Turf	76	10.1	6.0	12.6	14.6	11.3	1.30	152	0.28
Bare Soil	67	8.4	4.2	2.25 kg Hammer 16.8	12.4	29.5	1.02	136	0.19
Thatch	63	10.0	5.6	10.7	9.9	11.8	1.24	124	0.26
Full Turf	65	10.1	5.7	10.6	10.1	11.3	1.27	130	0.28
Plugs									
Pad	185	4.4	2.1	0.5 kg Hammer 80.2	73.7	89.4	0.42	705	0.12
Thatch on Pad	78	9.6	5.7	13.4	15.7	11.7	1.23	164	0.30
Turf on Pad	71	10.3	6.2	11.7	13.4	10.3	1.34	141	0.30
Pad	140	5.6	3.1	2.25 kg Hammer 41.4	45.2	38.5	0.65	434	0.14
Thatch on Pad	73	10.1	5.7	12.4	12.8	12.2	1.26	160	0.35
Turf on Pad	68	10.5	6.0	10.5	10.8	10.2	1.30	139	0.35

[a] 1, 2, and 3 are rate of change from threshold to peak deceleration, from threshold to one-half of peak deceleration, and from one-half of peak deceleration to peak deceleration, respectively.

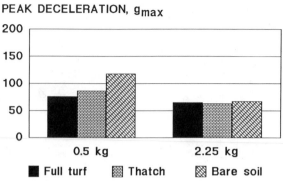

FIG. 5—*The effect of thatch and turf on peak deceleration as measured with 0.5 and 2.25-kg hammers (averaged over four sites).*

absorbent in lengthening the impact, even though there was no significant difference in peak deceleration values. In most instances, rate of change and severity index were greatest with bare soil, and no difference occurred between thatch and full turf. Deformation and rebound ratio were usually lowest on bare soil.

The results show that the presence of thatch reduced peak deceleration values. Although verdure did not significantly lower peak deceleration beyond the thatch effect, the 0.5-kg hammer detected nonsignificant differences between the thatch and full turf treatments that the 2.25-kg hammer did not (Fig. 5). The greater sensitivity with the lighter hammer agrees with results of previous experiments. It is logical to speculate that differences due to vegetation would be greater for drier soil conditions. Even though thatch is typically not a problem in athletic fields, further study should be conducted to assess any benefits of thatch.

Experiment 4

This experiment was a continuation of Experiment 3 in which the objective was to determine the effect of thatch and verdure on impact characteristics. The plugs removed to measure the bare soil treatment in Experiment 3 were placed on a pad and measured for their ability to absorb energy of impact. Thus, any inherent variability in soil was removed for this testing. As with Experiment 3, results have been averaged over the four sites (Table 2).

0.5-Kilogram Hammer—Placement of thatch + verdure and thatch plugs on a pad significantly lowered peak deceleration values and increased duration of impact and time to peak deceleration periods in comparison with the pad-only treatment in all species. Only with Kentucky bluegrass-A was there a significant difference in impact values and time periods between full turf and thatch treatments.

In all species, lower rates of change were associated with full turf and thatch plugs in comparison with the rates of change on the pad only. There were also higher deformation values and rebound ratios and lower severity index values calculated for those measurements made on the plugs.

2.25-Kilogram Hammer—Measurements made with the 2.25-kg hammer resulted in the same trends as those made with the 0.5-kg hammer (Table 2). However, the results with the 0.5-kg hammer showed a greater sensitivity to the presence of thatch and verdure. These results are for the most part consistent with those found in Experiment 3.

Conclusion

Compaction of turfgrass areas caused a significant change in impact characteristics obtained with both hammers. On most dates, peak deceleration and rates of change increased with compaction, while the time to peak, total impact time, and deformation decreased. Impact characteristics were influenced by the soil moisture content, which varied with the dates of impact measurements. Aeration affected impact characteristics on fewer occasions than compaction, and effects of aeration were often more apparent on compacted plots. Studies evaluating different types of aerators are warranted; however, investigators should be certain to include in their trials compacted areas in need of aeration.

Thatch increased shock attenuation over the value for bare soil. Although effects of thatch or full turf were not always significant when measured in place, significant effects were always obtained from plugs of thatch or full turf that were removed and tested on a uniform surface. Although thatch is not typical for intensively used athletic fields, an advantage in absorbing impact would be given to those fields that had just been sodded with a turf containing a slight to moderate thatch layer as opposed to a new turf stand obtained through seeding. Studies are needed to measure impact characteristics on an area as thatch develops over a number of years.

Compaction tended to increase shear resistance. Under the conditions of this research, soil moisture changes did not affect shear resistance values. Compacted areas that received aeration had lower shear resistance values than compacted areas without aeration. Research is needed to measure the effects of thatch on shear.

Acknowledgment

This paper is contribution No. 8016 from the Pennsylvania Agricultural Experiment Station, Pennsylvania State University, University Park, PA.

References

[1] Lush, W. M., "Objective Assessment of Turf Cricket Pitches Using an Impact Hammer," *Journal of the Sports Turf Research Institute,* Vol. 61, 1985, pp. 71–79.
[2] Canaway, P. M. and Bell, M. J., "Technical Note: An Apparatus for Measuring Traction and Friction on Natural and Artificial Playing Surfaces," *Journal of the Sports Turf Research Institute,* Vol. 62, 1986, pp. 211–214.
[3] Holmes, G. and Bell, M. J., "Standards of Playing Quality for Natural Turf," The Sports Turf Research Institute, Bingley, West Yorkshire, England, 1987.
[4] Holmes, G. and Bell, M. J., "The Playing Quality of Association Football Pitches," *Journal of the Sports Turf Research Institute,* Vol. 64, 1988, pp. 19–47.
[5] Bowers, K. D., Jr., and Martin, R. B., "Impact Absorption, New and Old AstroTurf at West Virginia University," *Medicine and Science in Sports,* Vol. 6, No. 3, 1974, pp. 217–221.
[6] Baker, S. W., "Technical Note: Playing Quality of Some Soccer Pitches in Saudi Arabia," *Journal of the Sports Turf Research Institute,* Vol. 63, 1987, pp. 145–148.
[7] Holmes, G. and Bell, M. J., "A Pilot Study of the Playing Quality of Football Pitches," *Journal of the Sports Turf Research Institute,* Vol. 62, 1986, pp. 74–91.
[8] Baker, S. W. and Isaac, S. P., "The Effect of Rootzone Composition on the Performance of Winter Game Pitches: II—Playing Quality," *Journal of the Sports Turf Research Institute,* Vol. 63, 1987, pp. 63–80.
[9] Gramckow, J., "Athletic Field Quality Studies," Cal-Turf Inc., Camarillo, CA, 1968.
[10] Zebarth, B. J. and Sheard, R. W., "Impact and Shear Resistance of Turfgrass Racing Surfaces for Thoroughbreds," *American Journal of Veterinarian Research,* Vol. 46, No. 4, 1985, pp. 778–784.
[11] Gadd, C. W., "Tolerable Severity Index in Whole-Head Non-Mechanical Impact," *Proceedings,*

15th Stapp Car Crash Conference, Society of Automotive Engineers, New York, 1971, pp. 809–816.

[*12*] Rogers, J. N. III and Waddington, D. V., in this publication, pp. 96–110.

[*13*] Rogers, J. N. III, "Impact Absorption and Traction Characteristics of Turf and Soil Surfaces," Ph.D. thesis, Pennsylvania State University, University Park, PA, 1988.

State-of-the-Art Natural and Artificial Surfaces

William H. Daniel[1]

Prescription Athletic Turf System

REFERENCE: Daniel, W. H., **"Prescription Athletic Turf System,"** *Natural and Artificial Playing Fields: Characteristics and Safety Features, ASTM STP 1073,* R. C. Schmidt, E. F. Hoerner, E. M. Milner, and C. A. Morehouse, Eds., American Society for Testing and Materials, Philadelphia, 1990, pp. 149–153.

ABSTRACT: A root zone for natural grass of sports fields (planted surfaces) based on suction applied to a water control system has been developed and patented. Controlled water management by surface and/or subirrigation, conservation, and suction removal is automatically regulated by soil moisture sensing. The availability of sports fields for scheduled events regardless of weather is enhanced and wear tolerance increased. The Prescription Athletic Turf system is patented by Purdue Research Foundation as USA 3908385, 13 SE 75 and Canada 985516, 16 MR 76.

KEY WORDS: playing fields, natural turf, root zone, moisture sensing, suction on drains, subirrigation

For years we accepted the fact that poor turfgrass for sports events was at times inevitable—muddy fields that offered poor or inadequate footing for the players—were a common sight. That is why in 1967 artificial turf was welcomed. It provided a clean look for the players and TV audience. It also provided the business office with increased revenue.

So the question became how to provide an alternative to artificial turf—a natural turf field with a consistently uniform playing surface that provides traction and improved safety for players.

Development of the System

The Prescription Athletic Turf system (Fig. 1) commonly called the PAT system, was developed during 1971 as a direct result of this search for an improved natural turf surface. Research showed that the speed of normal drainage could be reduced from 6 h to 6 min by using suction.

The system provides moisture control including the addition, conservation, and removal of excess water through three unique features.

1. Soil moisture sensing and automatic controls provide both surface and subsurface irrigation as needed.
2. A plastic barrier provides for isolation of the subgrade and for maximum water conservation in a sand root zone.
3. Excess water is removed from the surface and root zone by uniform suction.

To maintain the high quality of workmanship necessary to a PAT system, competitive bidding is not acceptable. The innovative technology of the system qualifies for single-bid

---

[1] Turfgrass Services Co., W. Lafayette, IN 47906

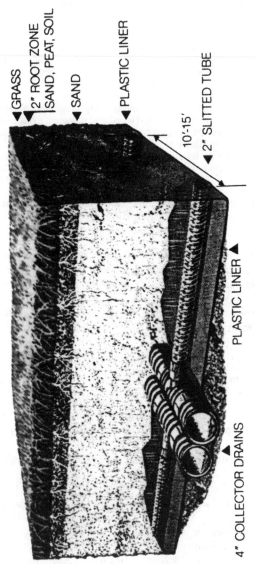

GRASS

2" ROOT ZONE
SAND, PEAT, SOIL

SAND

PLASTIC LINER

10'-15'

2" SLITTED TUBE

PLASTIC LINER ▲

4" COLLECTOR DRAINS ▲

FIG. 1—*The Prescription Athletic Turf system.*

installation by public institutions. Experienced regional licensees assist architects in developing custom plans and provide "turnkey" installations.

Installation

The patented system is built over a flat subgrade that allows for maximum uniformity and conservation of water. Excess water applied at any point will move toward equalized distribution.

Trenches are made in the subgrade to accommodate and protect the drains during placement of sand, but more importantly they increase the efficiency of the subirrigation and suction as well as reduce the amount of sand fill required. A uniform series of trenches, 3.1 m (10 ft) apart and 10 to 15 cm (4 to 6 in.) deep are cut to accommodate the 5-cm (2-in.) inside diameter (ID) drains. Trenches are cut 20 to 30 cm (8 to 12 in.) deep for the collectors and mains.

Plastic sheeting is spread, overlapped, and taped to create a seal or waterproof barrier. The edges are extended upward to the turf surface to isolate the entire root zone from the subgrade.

The drainage system utilizes narrow 5-cm (2-in.) slitted drains connected to collector drains which are joined to the mains that junction with the suction tank. Each "main" (three to seven per field) is equipped with an isolation valve which permits water retention or which can be closed to concentrate suction in selected areas.

After the plastic barrier is in place, the drain pipes are installed into the previously cut trenches, and all snap fittings are double taped to prevent sand inflow. All irrigation pipe and control wires are placed onto the barrier. Sand is delivered to the edge of the field and pushed over the surface. A minimum depth of 30 cm (12 in.) of sand is firmed and leveled to grade.

Additives such as peat, slow release nitrogen, and complete fertilizers are mixed into the upper surface. Sprinkler heads are attached to pipes in the desired locations. Pairs of moisture sensors are located in each irrigation zone and attached to wires extending to the controllers.

After the final grade is approved, the preferred grass is sodded, sprigged, or seeded. Components for automatic water management are assembled in a control center adjacent to the field.

A sealed concrete tank capable of holding 5.7 m^3 (200 ft^3) of air in the upper portion and 11.4 m^3 (400 ft^3) of water in the lower portion is connected to the main drains which also have a holding capacity of 5.7 m^3 (200 ft^3) of water. Inside the tank are two 10-cm (4-in.)-pipe submersible pumps. Each is capable of expelling 2.7 m^3 (700 gal.) or 100 ft^3 per minute. As excess water accumulates, the sensitive probes in the tank activate one or both pumps.

Moisture sensors located below the turf surface are attached to a controller which activates the air suction pump. As air is expelled at 2.7 m^3/min, water is drawn from the sand through the slits of the 5-cm-ID drains into the collectors, mains, and tank and then expelled. The combined suction of both air and sump pumps can remove more than 7.6 m^3 (2000 gal)/min.

Subirrigation is achieved by a water charge directly into the suction tank through the drainage system. All water exchange is made through narrow slits in the drains. The sensors automatically control suction, subirrigation, and surface irrigation.

Performance of System

Water infiltration into the surface has been measured by the use of a double ring infiltrometer at 60 cm (24 in.) per hour. The system was proven at the Robbie Stadium of Miami,

Florida in 1988. Overnight 86 mm (3.4 in.) of rain fell while all drains were closed. At 8:00 a.m. water was 0.5 m (16 to 20 in.) deep over the entire field because trash had blocked the drains in the stands, and all the water from the stands (70 000 seats) had shed onto the field. Valves were opened and the pumps operated; 6 h later the field was judged playable. The system effectively disposed of 7.6 mm (3 in.) of water per hour.

Water Management

Automatic water management is basic in design to the PAT system. The system used at the Crane High School of Chicago, built in 1979, has been maintained with only subirrigation for the past ten years. Vandalism was the reason for eliminating all sprinkler heads. The soil moisture probes and controllers automatically operate subirrigation.

Water Conservation

The plastic barrier which isolates the subgrade from the root zone provides for water control. Optimum amounts of rainfall, nutrients in dilute solution, and all applied irrigation can be conserved.

The severe drought of 1988 caused a ban restricting irrigation in Findlay, Ohio. The turfgrass above the PAT system stayed uniformly green while the surrounding turf died or became dormant.

Durable Turf Cover

The original sod continues to serve well on the first PAT system field installed in 1972. Areas of bent grass infestation have been chemically irradicated and reseeded. Turf-type ryegrasses have been overseeded into existing bluegrasses for increased wear tolerance in some fields. Periodic resodding may be advisable where intense wear destroys the sod. Such was the case for the landing areas of jumping horses following a two-day show in Cincinnati, Ohio.

Mile High Stadium in Denver is used for a variety of activities—more than 100 per year. In preparation for football following baseball, some sodding is required. However, 50% of the PAT system turf has been in place since 1976.

When Purdue University had a traditional "soil" football field, it was customary to replace divots following each game—using up to 1000 plugs of 10 cm (4 in.) each. The manager reports that with a PAT system the damage to the turfgrass is much less and instead of replacing plugs they now spread a mixture of sand and pregerminated seed as needed.

Maintenance Cost

The Cincinnati Bengals' 10 000 m² (107 600 ft²) PAT system practice field is used from June to December. Ninety percent of practice time for the team is spent on the PAT field, while adjacent artificial turf is used the other 10%. The contract price for annual turfgrass maintenance and painting averages $30 000.

Records for the Ross Ade Stadium of Purdue University show all direct turf care costs for three years averaged $2000 for material and $4000 for services. In contrast, the paint material for the field cost more than $2000, and application costs were more than $4000. Painting costs exceed turfgrass care each year.

Conclusions

Prescription Athletic Turf systems are home fields to seven professional, nine National Collegiate Athletic Association (NCAA), and five high school teams, plus two sports fields within city parks.

The one generally agreed upon fact is that wear-tolerant, uniform grass requires a consistent and wise management program of maintenance.

The search for innovative and creative ideas for improving sports turf continues.

References

[1] Daniel, H. W., "New Natural Turf—PAT System," *Proceedings,* Midwest Regional Turf Conference, Purdue University, W. Lafayette, IN, 1973, pp. 65–69.

[2] Daniel, W. H., Freeborg, R. P., and Robey, M. L., "Prescription Athletic Turf System," *Proceedings,* Second International Turf Grass Research Conference, American Society of Agronomy, 1973, pp. 277–281.

[3] Daniel, W. H. and Freeborg, R. P., "Root Zone Moisture Measurement," *Proceedings,* Fourth International Turf Grass Research Conference, American Society of Agronomy, 1981, pp. 554–555.

J. B. Beard[1] and S. I. Sifers[1]

Feasibility Assessment of Randomly Oriented, Interlocking Mesh Element Matrices for Turfed Root Zones

REFERENCE: Beard, J. B. and Sifers, S. I., **"Feasibility Assessment of Randomly Oriented, Interlocking Mesh Element Matrices for Turfed Root Zones,"** *Natural and Artificial Playing Fields: Characteristics and Safety Features, ASTM STP 1073*, R. C. Schmidt, E. F. Hoerner, E. M. Milner, and C. A. Morehouse, Eds., American Society for Testing and Materials, Philadelphia, 1990, pp. 154–165.

ABSTRACT: Turfgrass injury and reduced playing surface quality are increasing problems on intensively trafficked turfs such as sports fields and race courses. Feasibility investigations were conducted concerning the use of randomly oriented, interlocking mesh element root zone matrices for the purpose of providing reduced divoting, better soil-turf stabilization, increased traction, and improved uniformity of ball bounce. Mesh element inclusion substantially reduced divot opening width and length and lateral cleat tear. This resulted in twice as rapid divot recovery. The mesh element matrices had no effect on ball bounce resiliency, but substantially enhanced the consistency of ball bounce. The traction and compression displacement results were variable. Soil moisture levels were consistently higher in the mesh element matrices treatment. This feasibility investigation revealed that augmentation with mesh element inclusions provided significant benefits in reduced turfgrass injury and a more uniform playing surface.

KEY WORDS: playing fields, ball bounce, bermuda grass, compression displacement, divot size and recovery, sport fields, tear resistance

Historically, greens and sports fields were constructed with high clay content soils. This practice was followed for two primary reasons: (*a*) better stability of the surface for sports use and (*b*) better water holding characteristics of the high clay soil which assisted in sustaining an actively growing green turf in the early days when there was no irrigation capability.

The late 1940s and early 1950s introduced an era of increasingly intense traffic, public demand for higher quality turfed sports fields, and the use of overhead sprinkler irrigation systems for sports fields and greens. The increasing intensity of traffic combined with the traditional construction approach of relatively high clay soils led to soil compaction problems which became the limiting factor in turfgrass culture on recreational surfaces [1].

Because of an increasing soil compaction problem which was seriously limiting turfgrass growth, experimental work and practitioner trial-and-error approaches with high sand content root zones evolved. The primary objective in using coarser textured soils was to provide adequate drainage of excess water and the resultant aeration needed to support rooting and overall healthy turfgrass growth. This early interest in sand root zones for sports fields was pioneered in the United States [2]. The first root zone construction system developed which was soundly based on scientific principles and backed by thorough research was the U.S.

---

[1] Professor and research associate, respectively, Department of Soil and Crop Sciences, Texas A&M University, College Station, TX 77843.

Golf Association (USGA) Green Section Method of root zone construction developed at Texas A&M University [3–7]. For the first time, detailed specifications and a soil physical testing procedure were established for greens and sport field root zone construction. Sand is a major component of this root zone mix, with detailed specifications for particle size distribution, infiltration rate, porosity, bulk density, and a pea gravel layer below the sand root zone possessing a particle size differential which produces an innovative perched water table. This USGA Green Section Method of root zone construction has been proven by the test of time with numerous successful root zones having been in place over 30 years. The key is proper construction that follows all the specifications in detail.

While there have been a number of other high sand content root zones proposed, many being modifications of the USGA Green Section Method, they tend to be deficient in sound science with inadequate fundamental research to support the concept [1]. Many proposed root zone mixes are only slight modifications of the USGA Green Section Method, but they result in significant changes from a soil physical principles standpoint. Among all these proposed root zone mixes, none have proven as successful and reliable under a diverse range of climatic and soil conditions throughout the world as the USGA Green Section Method.

For those sports fields properly constructed to the USGA Green Section Method specifications, the scene of mud-covered football players is history. This success has led to an even greater intensity of use of individual sports fields. The primary problem now developing is not the underground limitations of poor drainage and lack of aeration characteristic of the finer textured root zones, but rather the severe divoting and turfgrass wear of above ground shoots. Under intense traffic, this latter problem eventually leads to turf thinning and bare areas. The use of improved turfgrass cultivars with more rapid shoot growth rates, a greater green biomass, better recuperative potential, and disease resistance has partially assisted in solving the problem.

Stabilization of sand root zones and the allied turf have also been attempted via textile fibers and nettings of various compositions that are placed horizontally near the surface of the root zone. These horizontally oriented inclusions rely on simple friction. There is a lack of published research concerning the performance of these horizontally oriented materials. Under intense turfgrass wear they tend to rise to the surface, become torn, interfere with ball roll and running of players, and prove very unsightly.

The feasibility studies reported herein assess the use of randomly oriented mesh element inclusions in high sand turfed root zones. In this system the stress transfer mechanisms between and among the soil particles and the mesh elements rely upon an interlocking dimension. Mesh element studies have been conducted with clay soils utilized in roadbed construction. These experiments emphasized soil stabilization through the use of randomly oriented tensile inclusions in order to alter the stress-strain behavior of granule soils [8–10]. The interlock occurs in two dimensions, with the ribs of discrete mesh elements interlocking with groups of soil particles to form aggregations of particles and then adjacent mesh element-aggregations interlocking to form a coherent matrix. Since this system has proven very effective in roadbed construction, feasibility investigations were initiated concerning the use of randomly oriented interlocking mesh elements in turfed sports field and race track root zones for the purpose of providing (a) reduced divoting and tear, (b) better overall soil-turf stabilization, (c) increased traction, and (d) improved uniformity of ball bounce.

The terminology used in this paper for traffic stress is as follows [1]. Specifically, traffic consists of two primary components. One is turfgrass wear, which involves the above ground injurious effects of concentrated traffic on the turf [11]. The turfgrass wear component is characterized by divot, tear, and bruising dimensions. The second component, soil compaction, is a more indirect hidden effect involving the pressing together of soil particles into a more dense soil mass, typically resulting from mechanical pressure applied by human or vehicular traffic. In terms of playing surface characteristics, assessments such as traction, ball bounce resiliency, and compression displacement can be made.

Procedures

The feasibility assessment study was initiated in 1985 with two basic treatments. No mesh element versus mesh element augmentation of a high sand root zone. The mesh inclusions consisted of discrete 50 by 100-mm rectangular elements with open ribs extending from the perimeter, as manufactured by the Netlon process from high-density polypropylene. The square aperture between individual ribs of the extruded mesh element was 10 mm. The concept is that the soil particles form aggregates through the apertures in the mesh elements creating a stable layer adjacent to and within the mesh [10]. Other particles become oriented with the primary layer to form a stable assemblage of particles. In addition, the individual aggregations randomly formed around the meshes interlock together with adjacent mesh-particle systems to isotropically stabilize and strengthen weak soils.

The mesh treatment consisted of 2.5 kg·m^{-3} of mesh elements mixed in the upper 15 cm of root zone with a 2.5-cm layer of root zone mix distributed over the top. The two treatments were arranged in a randomized block design with four replications. The plot size was 2.4 by 4.5 m, subdivided into four 0.6 by 1.1-m subplots.

The completely modified soil consisted of a high sand root zone mix meeting USGA Green Section specifications with 10-cm-diameter subsurface drainage lines in a gridiron arrangement of 4.5-m spacing. The root zone-mesh element matrices were mixed off site using a small capacity rotating drum mixer in which the drum was closed by a lid and positioned horizontally to achieve maximum uniformity of mixing. The root zone mix components were premixed off site prior to addition of the mesh elements. The treatment involving no mesh consisted of the same high sand root zone mix added to the four replicated plots to a comparable depth as that described for the mesh element-high sand root zone matrices treatment.

Turf Establishment

The plot area was established with Tifway bermuda grass (*Cynodon dactylon* × *Cynodon transvaalensis*) in August of 1985. A preplant fertilization was applied at a rate of 1 kg each of nitrogen, phosphorus, and potassium/100 m^2 (are). The vegetative sprigs were planted by broadcasting across the area at a rate of 0.4 m^3·are^{-1}, lightly topdressed, and fertilized with 1 kg phosphorus/100 m^2 to encourage rapid establishment. The experimental site was irrigated via perimeter pop-up gear-driven sprinkler heads positioned at 3.5-m spacings. Turf establishment was achieved in six weeks.

Cultural Practices

The cultural practices imposed on the experimental area were representative of hybrid bermuda grass sports fields. Mowing consisted of a 2.5-cm cutting height practiced twice weekly using a three-gang reel mower with clippings returned. The nitrogen fertilization rate was 0.4 kg of actual nitrogen/100 m^2/growing month, which typically extended from April through September. Phosphorus and potassium were maintained in the high range, based on soil tests conducted annually. Irrigation was practiced as needed to prevent visual wilt. No pesticides were applied to the experimental area during the study, which avoided any potential confounding effect in terms of toxicity to the roots. Also, no turf cultivation or vertical cutting was practiced.

Assessments

The methods used to assess the influence of randomly oriented interlocking mesh element-turfed root zone matrices for overall turf-soil stabilization are described in this section. Assessments were accomplished in early summer and in early fall of 1986, 1987, and 1988, plus at six-week intervals during 1988 starting in May.

Divoting

One of the more destructive dimensions on turfs where sports, such as American football or golf, are played is divot removal. A divot simulation apparatus was designed, constructed, and successfully tested to assess divot opening size and recovery rate. It consisted of an adjustable horizontal swinging pivot bar positioned above the soil surface by a metal frame. Attached to the center pivot is a 140-cm-long bar of 25 mm diameter. Attached to the lower end of the free swinging bar was a nine iron golf club, above which was fixed a 22.5-kg weight. The free swinging divot apparatus was dropped from a set height of 200 cm above the soil surface, producing a divot typically ranging from 40 to 300 mm in length and 30 to 90 mm in width. To produce this range in divot sizes, the base of the divot stimulation device was originally set at 30 mm for 1986, and it was adjusted to swing 25 mm below the soil surface for 1987 and 20 mm below the soil surface for 1988. Three individual divot simulations were imposed within each subplot. The length, width, and depth of the divot opening was measured at the soil surface immediately. The divot openings were not repaired and were subsequently assessed for recovery rate at weekly intervals using the same measurement technique.

Compression-Tear-Traction Apparatus

Traction encompasses the properties of a turf which enables a player with footwear having studs, spikes, or cleats to obtain a grip on the turf surface. An apparatus for the assessment of compression displacement, lateral tear, and traction of a cleated plate simulating the sole of a football shoe was designed, constructed, and successfully tested. The apparatus consists of a two-level, four-legged bench of 45 by 25 cm, with the individual metal benches positioned 90 and 40 cm above the soil surface. A 15-mm hole was drilled in the center of each bench through which an 8-mm-diameter by 80-cm-long metal rod was vertically positioned. A small platform, designed to hold 33-cm-diameter metal weights, was attached to the upper end of the vertical rod. Positioned at the lower end of the vertical rod was an attachment to which could be fixed a cleated plate or similar device, depending on the specific assessments desired. The plate used was an oblong shape of 26 by 10 cm with five cleats each of 5 mm long and 1.5 mm in diameter with 4-cm spacings between cleats. A 28-cm-long bar was attached perpendicular to the center vertical bar at a height of 28 cm from the base. A metal cable was attached to the end of the horizontal bar and extended through a series of pulleys to a scale attached to a winch.

Compression Displacement

The apparatus was used for assessment of compression displacement by dropping the cleated plate from a height of 30 cm. The depth of soil displacement was measured from the soil surface downward in a centered position. The apparatus was moved and releveled for three replicate tests within each subplot. There were two weights of 4.5 and 11.25 kg utilized in each compression displacement drop test.

Lateral Tear

The tearing of sport turfs due to the twising action of cleated shoes is a very stressful dimension of turfgrass wear. Traction and extent of turf tear were assessed using the apparatus previously described. After dropping the cleated plate from a height of 30 cm, a uniform pull was applied via a winch, and the force required to rotate the cleated plate over 90° was monitored as traction in pounds per square inch. The length of turf tear produced by the outermost cleat was measured at the soil surface. Two different weights of 4.5 and 11.25 kg were utilized in each of the 30-cm drops. Three replicates each of traction and tear length were assessed within each subplot. The apparatus was moved and releveled after each test.

Traction

An additional type of traction assessment apparatus was employed in 1987 and 1988. Traction was measured by a technique involving a 1.5-cm-diameter steel disc with studs positioned at the base of a 32.5-cm-long shaft at the top of which was positioned a two-handled torque wrench [12]. Six football studs, each 1.2 cm in diameter, were positioned in a circle 4.6 cm from the center of the disc. A 40-kg weight was placed above the steel disk, giving a total weight of 47.8 kg. The apparatus was dropped from a controlled height of 60 mm. Traction was assessed as the torque required to turn the studded plate planted in the turf through 90°. Three traction assessments were made within each subplot.

Ball Bounce

In sports involving the bounce of a ball, the effects of the playing surface characteristics are an important dimension. The assessment methodology used involved a vertical support device which released the ball from a height of 3 m [12,13,14]. The ball release mechanism dropped the ball without impulse or spin. The soccer ball used was approved by the Federation Internationale de Football Association (FIFA), and it was inflated to 0.61 bar. The results were based on ball bounce resiliency expressed as the ratio of height bounced to height dropped.

Soil Moisture

Following the assessments conducted during 1986, it became apparent that some variability among assessment dates was the result of varying soil moisture levels. Thus, starting in 1987, soil moistures were assessed at depths of 5.0, 10, and 15 cm at the time the assessment parameters were made. A standardized soil sampling procedure was used to determine the soil moisture content. Each wet soil sample was transferred in air-tight containers, weighed, dried in an oven at 105°C for 24 h to remove water, and weighed again. The loss of weight on drying is the weight of water originally present, and it is expressed as a percentage of the oven dry weight of the soil.

Results and Discussion

The turfgrass quality was assessed visually in terms of a uniform cover with a high shoot density at 15-day intervals throughout each growing season. No differences were noted between the no-mesh and mesh element-root zone matrices treatments throughout the study. Further, there were no visual symptoms of turfgrass injury caused by disease or insect activity.

Turfgrass Injury

The dimensions of turfgrass injury associated with traffic assessed in this study were (*a*) divot opening, length, size, and width; (*b*) the associated rate of recovery of the divot openings; and (*c*) the lateral tear, as affected by the presence of the mesh element in the root zone matrices.

There is a trend in all cases for reduction in both divot length and width as a result of the mesh element inclusions (Tables 1 and 2). For summer and fall assessments in 1986 through 1988, the divot length and width were significantly reduced by the presence of a mesh element matrices in the root zone, except for the October 1986 and September 1988 assessments. Even in the latter case, the trends remain the same as for the other dates. In the case of divot depth, the presence of mesh element matrices resulted in a significant reduction in divot depth, except at the July 1986 assessment. The reduced divot size may result from the turfgrass roots being better anchored in and around the mesh.

The most striking evidence for the importance of these divot size differences between treatments is illustrated by the recovery rate of the divot openings. Generally, there was a 25 to 50% reduction in the time required for the turf to reestablish in the divot openings where the mesh element-root zone matrices were present, in comparison to a root zone without mesh elements (Table 2). This translates to the potential for doubling the intensity of use on sports fields where the mesh element-root zone matrices system is utilized.

The presence of a mesh element matrices significantly reduced the length of tear at the 4.5-kg test weight positioned above the cleated plate, except for September 1988. The treatment comparisons at the 11.25-kg weight test varied, although the trends still reflected similar responses to those at the 4.5-kg test.

A significant reduction in divot opening lengths and widths was observed for all assessments dates during 1988 except for 15 September when a high soil moisture level existed (Table 2). There also was a significant reduction in depth of divoting for two of the four assessment dates where mesh element matrices were present. The rate of divot opening recovery through the season responded similarly to the annual assessments in that the presence of mesh elements in the root zone resulted in a 33 to 66% reduction in time required for full recovery of the turf. This is a very significant response in terms of the increased intensity of play that could be permitted on sports fields without reducing the turf quality characteristics of the playing surface.

Playing Surface Characteristics

The playing surface characteristics assessed in this investigation included ball bounce resiliency, traction, and compression displacement. The findings are summarized in Tables 3 and 4.

No differences in ball bounce resiliency, as measured with a soccer ball dropped from a standard height of 3 m, were found between no-mesh and mesh element inclusion in the turfed root zone. These findings were consistent throughout the summer and fall assessments for the years of 1986 through 1988 (Table 3) and also for the 4 six-week seasonal assessments in 1988 (Table 4). These findings were based on a 2.5 kg·m^{-3} rate of inclusion with a 2.5-cm layer of root zone applied over the surface of the mesh element matrices. It's possible that the comparative ball bounce results might change if the mesh element inclusion rate was increased or if the mesh element inclusion was extended to the soil surface. However, under the mesh element installation specifications conducted in this study, the variability in bounce height was much less than that occurring with no mesh.

TABLE 1—Annual summer and fall assessments** for the years 1986 through 1988 concerning the effects of randomly oriented, interlocking mesh element-root zone matrices on turf injury and soil moisture.

Assessment Parameter	July 1986		Oct. 1986		Oct. 1987		June 1988		Sept. 1988	
	Mesh	No Mesh	Mesh	No Mesh	Mesh	No Mesh	Mesh	No Mesh	Mesh	No Mesh
Divot Opening Size:										
Length (mm)	287.3b*	327.0a	208.8a	248.4a	119.8b	173.3a	38.6b	67.3a	57.5a	63.0a
Width (mm)	64.6b	90.9a	71.1a	76.7a	40.9b	46.5a	30.3b	36.4a	34.8a	37.9a
Depth (mm)	33.7a	37.0a	18.3b	23.2a	30.0b	39.6a	9.3b	12.8a	17.4a	12.9b
Divot Recovery (days to):										
50%	--	--	16.0b	21.0a	14.0b	21.0b	7.0b	14.0a	7.0b	14.0a
75%	--	--	21.0b	29.0a	21.0b	28.0a	14.0b	21.0a	14.0b	21.0a
Lateral Cleat Tear (mm):										
4.5 kg weight	44.5b	54.8a	48.5b	59.3a	28.3b	39.3a	--	--	13.0a	0.0b
11.25 kg weight	60.8a	67.0a	71.3a	75.7a	58.3b	64.5a	--	--	13.9a	3.9b
Soil Moisture %										
5 cm depth	--	--	--	--	36	32	12	9	46	38

* Means followed by the same letter in the same row within a date are not significantly different, LSD T Test, alpha = 0.05.
**Except for means for early summer of 1987.

TABLE 2—*The 1988 seasonal assessments concerning the effects of randomly oriented, interlocking mesh element-root zone matrices on turf injury and soil moisture.*

Assessment Parameter	May 1		June 15		August 1		September 15	
	Mesh	No Mesh	Mesh	No Mesh	Mesh	No Mesh	Mesh	No Mesh
Divot Opening Size:								
Length (mm)	48.6b*	82.9a	38.6b	67.3a	58.1b	71.5a	57.5a	63.0a
Width (mm)	37.1b	50.9a	30.3b	36.4a	36.7b	44.9a	34.8a	37.7a
Depth (mm)	10.1b	15.0a	9.3b	12.8a	14.8a	13.6a	17.4a	12.9b
Divot Recovery (days to):								
50%	7.0b	16.0a	7.0b	14.0a	7.0b	21.0a	7.0b	14.0a
75%	10.0b	28.0a	14.0b	21.0a	14.0b	28.0a	14.0b	21.0a
Soil Moisture %:								
5.0 cm depth	35	31	12	9	29	21	46	38
10.0 cm depth	25	19	14	13	22	21	44	38
15.0 cm depth	26	21	13	13	24	22	41	37

* Means followed by the same letter in the same row within a date are not significantly different, LSD T Test, alpha = 0.05.

TABLE 3—Annual summer and fall assessments** for the years 1986 through 1988 concerning the effects of randomly oriented, interlocking mesh element-root zone matrices on turfed playing surface characteristics.

Assessment Parameter	July 1986		Oct. 1986		Oct. 1987		June 1988		Sept. 1988	
	Mesh	No Mesh	Mesh	No Mesh	Mesh	No Mesh	Mesh	No Mesh	Mesh	No Mesh
Ball Bounce Resiliency (% of drop height)										
Mean	--	--	--	--	17.6a*	22.2a	20.1a	20.8a	15.0a	14.6a
Maximum	--	--	--	--	19	27	23	29	17	23
Minimum	--	--	--	--	16	14	17	13	13	7
Traction (kg for 90° turn)										
4.5 kg	18.8a	19.4a	17.7a	12.9b	17.3b	19.4a	--	--	2.6a	2.0b
11.25 kg	22.7+	22.6	22.7+	21.2	22.7+	22.7+	--	--	3.1a	3.5a
44.5 kg	--	--	--	--	--	--	16.8b	18.8a	14.1a	13.9a
Compression Displacement (mm)										
4.5 kg	25.1b	29.6a	26.7a	19.5b	28.2a	30.7a	--	--	8.9a	4.7b
11.25 kg	35.7a	36.8a	34.2a	28.0b	35.3b	44.8a	--	--	10.1a	5.0b
44.5 kg	--	--	--	--	16.9a	13.1b	11.3a	11.4a	17.1a	13.3b

* Means followed by the same letter in the same row for each year are not significantly different, LSD T Test, alpha = 0.05, confidence = 0.95.
**Except for means for early summer of 1987.

TABLE 4—*The 1988 seasonal assessments concerning the effects of randomly oriented, interlocking mesh element-root zone matrices on turfed playing surface characteristics.*

Assessment Parameter		May 1 Mesh	May 1 No Mesh	June 15 Mesh	June 15 No Mesh	August 1 Mesh	August 1 No Mesh	September 15 Mesh	September 15 No Mesh
Ball Bounce Resiliency (% of drop height)	Mean	26.8a*	28.6a	20.1a	20.8a	17.3a	18.9a	15.0a	14.6a
	Maximum	36	37	23	29	19	27	17	23
	Minimum	20	19	17	13	15	10	13	7
Traction (kg for 90° turn):	4.5 kg	--	--	--	--	--	--	2.6a	2.0b
	11.25 kg	--	--	--	--	--	--	3.1a	3.5a
	44.5 kg	27.9a	25.1b	16.8b	18.8a	16.1a	14.4b	14.1a	13.9a
Compression Displacement (mm):	4.5 kg	--	--	--	--	--	--	8.9a	4.7b
	11.25 kg	--	--	--	--	--	--	10.1a	5.0b
	44.5 kg	12.3a	12.5a	11.3a	11.4a	15.3a	11.4b	17.1a	13.3b

*Means followed by the same letter in the same row within a date are not significantly different, LSD T Test, alpha = 0.05.

One other dimension of ball bounce resiliency is the repeatability or uniformity of the turf surface. The range in percent of drop height from the maximums to the minimums was found to be three to four times greater where no mesh element was present in the root zone versus the presence of a mesh element-root zone matrices (Tables 3 and 4). This consistency in ball bounce of mesh element augmented turf root zones is a significant component of the surface quality for sports use.

Results from traction assessments, which simulated the grip achieved by a cleated shoe, were variable in comparisons between no-mesh and mesh element inclusion in the turfed root zone. At the 4.5-kg test weight, traction was greater for the mesh element inclusion treatment on October 1986 and September 1988, whereas the reverse occurred in October 1987, with no difference being evident in July 1986. At the 11.25-kg test weight, no differences were noted at any of the five assessment dates. In the case of the 1988 seasonal assessments over four dates using the 40-kg test weight, there was greater traction on the root zone without mesh treatment on 1 May and 15 June, but the reverse occurred on 1 August, with no differences evident on the 15 September date. The reasons for this wide variability in findings are not clear. More detailed mechanistic studies must be conducted relative to the dimensions contributing to traction before a correct interpretation can be accomplished.

Results of the compression displacement assessments on the turfed root zone varied between the two treatments. In the 4.5-kg weight test, greater displacement occurred in the mesh element treatment on October 1986 and September 1988, while the reverse occurred in July of 1986; no difference was noted for the October 1987 assessment. In the case of the 11.25-kg test weight, compression displacement was greater in the no mesh treatment on July 1986 and October 1987, while the reverse occurred in October 1986 and September 1988. For the 1988 seasonal assessments at the 40-kg test weight, there were no differences between the two treatments for the 1 May and 15 June assessments, while the mesh element treatment exhibited slightly greater compression displacement on 1 August and 15 September.

Soil Moisture

When the authors observed that soil moisture content differentials might exist between the treatments, specific measurements were initiated in 1987. Throughout the subsequent observation period of 1987 through 1988, including the four seasonal assessments during 1988, the soil moisture contents of the mesh element-root zone matrices were higher than for the no mesh treatment (Tables 2 and 4). This higher soil moisture could be attributed to the increased aggregation of soil particles between the apertures in the mesh so that the aggregate enhances overall moisture retention of the root zone. The higher soil moisture retention was found to occur at all three depths of 5.0, 10, and 15 cm below the soil surface. Thus, the use of mesh element inclusions has an additional benefit in terms of a reduced irrigation water requirement for turfs grown on high sand root zones.

Acknowledgments

This article is Journal Article No. 24321 from the Texas Agricultural Experiment Station. This research was partially supported by a grant from Netlon Ltd., Blackburn, England.

References

[1] Beard, J. B., "Turfgrass: Science and Culture," Prentice Hall, New York, 1973, pp. 368–380.
[2] Lunt, O. R., "A Method for Minimizing Compaction in Putting Greens," *Southern California Turfgrass Culture,* Vol. 6, No. 3, 1956, pp. 17–20.

[3] Kunze, R. J., "The Effects of Compaction of Different Golf Green Soil Mixtures on Plant Growth," M. S. Thesis, Texas A&M College, College Station, TX, 1956, pp. 1–75.

[4] Howard, H. L., "The Response of Some Putting Green Soil Mixtures to Compaction," M. S. Thesis, Texas A&M College, College Station, TX, 1959, pp. 1–97.

[5] Ferguson, M. H., Howard, L., and Bloodworth, M. E., "Laboratory Methods for Evaluation of Putting Green Soil Mixtures," *USGA Journal and Turf Management,* Vol. 13, No. 5, 1960, pp. 30–33.

[6] Anonymous, "Specifications for a Method of Putting Green Construction," *USGA Journal and Turf Management,* Vol. 13, No. 5, 1960, pp. 24–28.

[7] Ferguson, M. H., "After Five Years: The Green Section Specification for a Putting Green," *USGA Green Section Record,* Vol. 3, No. 4, 1965, pp. 1–7.

[8] Mercer, F. B., Andrawes, K. Z., McGown, A., and Hytiris, N., "A New Method of Soil Stabilization," *Proceedings,* Conference on Polymer Grid Reinforcement, Thomas Telford, London, 1984, pp. 244–249.

[9] McGown, A., Andrawes, K. Z., Hytiris, N., and Mercer, F. B., "Soil Strengthening Using Randomly Distributed Mesh Elements," *Proceedings,* XI International Conference S.M.F.E., Balkema, San Francisco, 1985, pp. 1735–1738.

[10] Andrawes, K. Z., McGown, A., Hytiris, N., Mercer, F. B., and Sweetland, D. B., "The Use of Mesh Elements to Alter the Stress-Strain Behavior of Granular Soils," *Proceedings,* Third International Conference on Geotextiles, Vienna, Vol. 3, April 1986, pp. 103–116.

[11] Shearman, R. C. and Beard, J. B., "Turfgrass Wear Tolerance Mechanisms: I. Wear Tolerance of Seven Turfgrass Species and Quantitative Methods for Determining Turfgrass Wear Injury," *Agronomy Journal,* Vol. 67, No. 2, March–April, 1975, pp. 208–211.

[12] Canaway, P. M. and Bell, M. J., "Technical Note: An Apparatus for Measuring Traction and Friction on Natural and Artificial Playing Surfaces," *Journal of the Sports Turf Research Institute,* Vol. 62, 1988, pp. 211–214.

[13] Bell, M. J., Baker, S. W., and Conaway, P. M., "Playing Quality of Sports Surfaces: A Review," *Journal of the Sports Turf Research Institute,* Vol. 61, 1987, pp. 26–45.

[14] Winterbottom, W., "Artificial Grass Surfaces for Association Football: Summary Report and Recommendations," Sports Council, London, May 1985, pp. 26–37.

T. A. Orofino[1] *and J. W. Leffingwell*[2]

Selection of Materials for Artificial Turf Surfaces

REFERENCE: Orofino, T. A. and Leffingwell, J. W., **"Selection of Materials for Artificial Turf Surfaces,"** *Natural and Artificial Playing Fields: Characteristics and Safety Features, ASTM STP 1073*, R. C. Schmidt, E. F. Hoerner, E. M. Milner, and C. A. Morehouse, Eds., American Society for Testing and Materials, Philadelphia, 1990, pp. 166–175.

ABSTRACT: Characteristics of diverse polymers used as pile ribbon, backing yarns, and shock-absorbing pads in artificial turf systems are examined. Particular attention is directed toward end-use performance in the major commercial systems of polypropylene or nylon 66 pile ribbon combined with polypropylene or polyethylene terephthalate backing yarns and with shock-absorbing pads of cross-linked polyethylene or polyvinyl chloride/rubber interpolymer. As with most applications of plastics, inclusion of various additives is necessary for key performance. Data on the effect of carrier resins, used to conveniently introduce additives into nylon 66, on the frictional characteristics of the final pile ribbon are presented. The role of turf ribbon friction as it may relate to wear resistance of the pile, monitored in the laboratory by the ASTM Schiefer and Taber abrader tests, and to shoe traction is examined.

KEY WORDS: playing fields, nylon 66, polypropylene, frictional coefficient, fabric wear testing, polymer properties, polymer additives, artificial turf, artificial surfaces

The objectives of this paper are to examine the general characteristics of plastics and resins as they apply to optimum performance in artificial turf sports surfaces [*1*]. Particular emphasis is placed on the major components of the two important commercial systems, polypropylene and nylon 66 artificial turf laid over polyethylene or polyvinyl chloride/rubber shock-absorbing pads. Laboratory data on frictional characteristics of nylon 66 also are presented, and their roles in turf wear and sports shoe traction are investigated.

Basic Polymer Technology

The pile fiber of artificial turf, the shock-absorbing underpad, and the various ancillary components of the typical field system are selected from the broad class of high-polymer materials with specific performance attributes in mind. The basic considerations in selection are the choices between thermoplastic and thermosetting materials, choices between crystalline and amorphous physical forms, the temperature transitions characteristic of the particular polymers, and the presence of certain key additives essential or desirable for optimum performance of the plastic.

Thermoplastics consist of high-polymer molecules unrestrained by cross-linkages. They are comparatively easy to process at elevated temperatures, where viscous flow occurs, and thus are the materials of choice for extrusion of continuous sheets or filaments used in arti-

---

[1] Department of Chemistry, University of Tennessee at Chattanooga, Chattanooga, TN 37403.
[2] EG & G Mound Applied Technology, Miamisburg, OH.

ficial turf pile and backing construction. Thermosets, on the other hand, are cross-linked polymers, very form stable, but difficult to process unless the cross-linking is introduced subsequent to forming at the (thermoplastic) precursor stage. The stability introduced by cross-linking is especially important in elastomers for shock-absorbing pads where, lacking crystalline structure, the materials would otherwise permanently deform under repeated impacts.

Virtually all so-called crystalline polymers are semicrystalline in the sense that the highly ordered crystalline regions, characterized by a thermodynamic melting point, seldom comprise all of the material. The percent of crystallinity in a final product depends very much on the conditions of processing, such as the extent of orientation (fiber drawing) and rate of cooling. The noncrystalline regions are termed amorphous. Here, crystalline order and crystalline interchain forces are absent, and the regions have the characteristics of a liquid. This liquid, however, possesses a unique property, the glass transition temperature, T_g, different for different polymers, which plays a role somewhat analogous to that of the melting point for the crystalline portions. The value of T_g, relative to use temperature, determines whether the amorphous portion of the polymer is soft and rubbery (use temperature above T_g) or hard and brittle (below T_g).

In the case of filament extrusion to make turf ribbon and backing yarns, a phase transition between use temperature and processing temperature is required so that the extrusion can proceed under flow conditions and the final product will be form stable. Both polypropylene and nylon 66 are semicrystalline and have melting points in a useful range (Table 1). Both also are extruded above their glass transition temperatures. At use temperature, the crystalline structure augmented by drawing of the yarn and reformed during cooling provides good form stability and strength. In the case of nylon 66, stability is further enhanced in the amorphous region as well, by virtue of its T_g being well above ambient temperatures for turf applications.

The location of T_g may be a further important consideration in the turf ribbon texturizing process often used to impart a kind of crimped physical form to the ribbon beneficial for traction uniformity and surface appearance. In this process, the extruded and subsequently cooled continuous filament is again heated to a temperature approaching the melting point, formed into the crimped configuration by various mechanical means, then cooled again. The crystalline transition (melting point) is sufficient to "set" the crimp in both polypropylene and nylon 66. However, in the case of nylon 66, a similar stability again is imparted to the amorphous region through the corresponding passage through and return below the glass transition.

In the case of backing yarns, high filament strength and low shrinkage are the main considerations. The highly drawn, semicrystalline polymers polypropylene and polyethylene terephthalate (polyester) are the principal choices for commercial turf systems. Nylon 66,

TABLE 1—*Some physical properties of semicrystalline polymers used in artificial turf construction.*

Property	Polypropylene	Nylon 66	Polyethylene Terephthalate
Melting point, °C	170	265	250
Glass transition, °C	−18	50	69
Density, g/cm³	0.91	1.14	1.38
Breaking strength, N/tex[a]	0.22	0.31	0.18 to 0.35
Moisture regain, % at 65% relative humidity, 21°C (70°F)	0.1	3 to 4	0.4

[a] To convert N/tex to g/denier multiply by 11.33.

although offering excellent strength, is subject to a certain degree of undesirable shrinkage and expansion in outdoor use, owing to its relatively high moisture regain (Table 1).

Elastomers, ideally, should be entirely noncrystalline, used at temperatures above their T_g, and be formed stabilized by chemical or physical cross-linkages. Important commercial applications include polyethylene foams, chemically cross-linked by reactive additives or by irradiation, and polyvinyl chloride/rubber interpolymer foams, utilizing conventional sulfur vulcanization (cross-linking) of the rubber component.

The requirement that plastics serving as elastomers be well above their T_g values, a necessity for efficient energy absorption, also leads to a tendency for a certain degree of unrecoverable strain, i.e., permanent set. Cross-linking reduces the tendency to a minimum, but the effect remains a shortcoming of concern in practical applications. Polyethylene foams offer a fairly good combination of energy absorption and recoverable strain (elasticity), but they tend to be rather firm materials for sports field applications. Incorporation of some vinyl acetate, copolymerized with the ethylene units, softens the pad but also increases the permanent set. Polyethylene foams are noteworthy in possessing rather flat shock-absorbency-temperature response. The polyvinyl chloride/rubber foams offer a good combination of shock-absorbing properties, by virtue of the hysteresis of the un-cross-linked polyvinyl chloride component, and resilience, through the cross-linking of the rubber component which is physically intermixed with the other polymer.

The various physical forms for a generalized semicrystalline polymer and its associated temperature transitions are depicted in Fig. 1.

Additives of one kind or another are so common in plastics that end-use properties normally associated with particular polymers are rather better considered to be characteristic of the formulated systems. Polyethylene and polypropylene, for example, are highly sensitive to chemical degradation from exposure to light. Over the years, various stabilizers have been

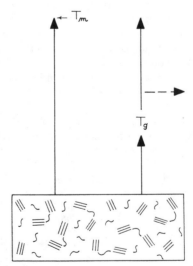

FIG. 1—*Relationships among the physical forms of semicrystalline polymers with temperature. The left vertical shows the transition of the crystalline regions (hard, strong) to the liquid polymer (flow) at the melting point T_m. The right vertical shows the difference in the amorphous regions below the glass transition temperature T_g (hard, brittle) and above it (soft, elastic). Above T_m (and T_g) the crystalline and amorphous regions are indistinguishable. Cross-linking (dashed arrow) makes the rubbery state of the amorphous region permanent. Polymers may be essentially all crystalline, all amorphous, or a mixture of both forms.*

developed to thwart the sequence of chemical reactions involved in chain scission and, as a result, the commercial forms of these polyolefins can be quite resistant to effects of outdoor exposure. Typical polymer additives, in addition to UV stabilizers, include plasticizers (to soften, by lowering T_g, such plastics as polyvinyl chloride), blowing agents (to make foams), cross-linking chemicals, processing aids, and pigments/colorants.

In many applications, a number of polymer additives are required, and it is sometimes convenient to introduce them into the principal resin through use of a second, carrier polymer in which the additives may be more readily dispersed. Nylon 66 for turf ribbon is an example of such a system in which stabilizers, pigments, and dyes are introduced [2]. An incidental property affected by the additives is coefficient of friction, μ, influencing some end-use properties. In the sections following, some estimates of μ from laboratory data are given, and their roles in turf wear and shoe traction are examined.

Estimation of Frictional Coefficients of Nylon 66 Turf Ribbons

Experimental

A number of experiments were carried out in the laboratory of AstroTurf Industries, Inc., to assess the importance of relatively small changes in coefficient of sliding friction of turf ribbons in contact with some bearing surfaces. The principal objective in that work was to develop a method for assessing directly the effects of various additives on ribbon wear; however, the data also can be used to estimate values for the coefficients μ. The abrasive surfaces selected were the H-18 grinding wheel from the Taber Abraser, described in ASTM Test Method for Abrasion Resistance of Textile Fabrics (Rotary Platform, Double-Head Method) (D 3884–80), and a cylindrical section of a polyurethane sports shoe cleat. These two surfaces should be relevant in analysis of accelerated turf pile wear via the Taber method and to levels of shoe traction, respectively. Some literature data on μ for nylon 66 and polyethylenes against steel will have relevance to analysis of accelerated turf pile wear via the Schiefer method, ASTM Test Method for Abrasion Resistance of Textile Fabrics (Oscillatory Cylinder and Uniform Abrasion Methods) (D 1175–80.)

In all cases of the laboratory investigations, the method of measurement was the "slipping belt" model [3] depicted in Fig. 2. In this experiment, a length of the test ribbon is placed

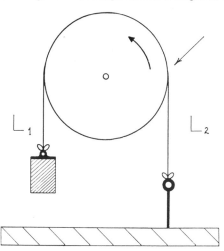

FIG. 2—*Schematic of "slipping belt" model used in two variations for calculation of coefficients of sliding friction. Point of eventual ribbon failure is indicated by arrow.*

over a radial angle θ around the partial circumference of the abrasive wheel or cylinder, and a fixed load, L_1, is attached to the free ribbon end. As steady slipping motion between ribbon and wheel is induced, a load (tension), L_2, develops at the fixed ribbon end according to the relationship

$$L_2 = L_1 \exp{(\mu\theta)} \tag{1}$$

The ribbon experiences resistance and abrades away at all points of contact and, if the slipping continues long enough, finally breaks at the last point of contact with the wheel at the fixed end, where both wear rate and tension on the ribbon are maximum. Two variations of this method were used to investigate μ.

In one set of experiments utilizing the polyurethane cleat, the cylindrical surface was stationary, and the ribbon was steadily pulled over the cylinder, retarded by the free-end load L_1. The tension L_2 was measured directly in this case by attachment of the "fixed" ribbon end to an Instron load cell carried by the crosshead. Load L_1 was varied from 10 to 50 g, ribbon speed over the surface was 25 cm/min (10 in./min) and contact angle θ was π radians.

In the more extensive set of experiments utilizing the Taber grinding wheel, the arrangement of Fig. 2 consisted of a stationary ribbon and rotating wheel. Abrasion was continued until the ribbon failed. Some measurements of L_2 were made directly, but in most cases the only recorded experimental observation was cycles-to-break, c_B. Various loads L_1 were investigated. It was also established that over a range of 12 to 55 cpm, the c_B value for a given ribbon type was constant (coefficient of variation, 8%), without trend, a condition implicit in use of Eq 1. Ribbon samples were washed, and the abrading wheel was cleaned with an air stream and dressed as required with the Taber Abraser refacing tool. Values of c_B with the 2-in.-diameter H-18 wheel ranged from about 100 to 10 000.

To permit extraction of μ values from the Taber wheel experiments, the reasonable assumption was made that ribbon denier, d, varies in a linear fashion with grinding surface exposure (cycles, c), i.e., with time at given wheel revolutions per minute.

$$d = A - Bc \tag{2}$$

The value for A was taken as 56 tex (502 denier), the initial average denier of all ribbons made according to the standard extrusion conditions employed. The parameter B is assumed to be proportional to the product of normal force per unit ribbon length pressing the ribbon against the wheel at the fixed end and frictional coefficient μ. The former is proportional to L_2, and therefore B may be equated to $K\mu L_1 \exp{(\mu\theta)}$, where the proportionality constant K incorporates various quantities such as the ribbon width and wheel diameter, which are the same in all experiments. Also constant is angle θ, which is equal to π radians. Denier may be expressed as the quotient of load at the point of failure, L_2, and ribbon tenacity, s, expressed in grams per denier. Combination with Eq 1 gives

$$L_1 \exp{(\pi\mu)} \left(\frac{1}{s} + K\mu c_B \right) = 502 \tag{3}$$

Results

Coefficients of friction for various nylon 66 ribbons sliding against the polyurethane cleat material, calculated directly from Eq 1, are given in Table 2. The values do not appear dependent upon load L_1. Somewhat higher friction is noted for the ribbons incorporating low-density polyethylene carrier resin.

TABLE 2—*Calculated frictional coefficients of various nylon 66 ribbons against polyurethane sports shoe cleat material.*

Nylon 66 Ribbon Type[a]	L_1, g	L_2, g $\pm$ Standard Deviation	μ (Eq 1)
1% LDPE	10	213 $\pm$ 91	0.97
	50	1130 $\pm$ 322	0.99
1% HDPE	10	172 $\pm$ 73	0.91
	50	958 $\pm$ 340	0.94
1% N	10	173 $\pm$ 82	0.91
	50	840 $\pm$ 322	0.90

[a] All ribbons were made from nylon 66 with the standard colorants and stabilization additives introduced through a polymeric carrier. LDPE is low-density polyethylene, HDPE is high-density polyethylene, and N is a nylon copolymer carrier. Each L_2 entry is an average of 25 to 35 observations.

For the series of friction experiments utilizing the H-18 Taber wheel, the data were interpreted according to Eq 3. For the value of s, 0.071 N/tex (0.8 $\pm$ 0.1 g/den) was used, calculated from observed denier at break and L_2 measured directly in some of the experiments. (We note in passing that ribbon tenacity measured under standard Instron tensile test conditions is about 0.3 N/tex (3 g/den) for all these ribbons; the lower, effective value in the friction experiment is attributed to an observed fibrillation mode of failure.)

Equation 3 permits calculation of μ from observed cycles-to-break, c_B, once the value of K has been established. For that purpose, data at $L_1 = 50$ g and 100 g on one ribbon class were used to solve Eq 3 for K (and the corresponding μ). This gave $K = 4.57 \times 10^{-4}$. All subsequent applications were for $L = 98$ to 100 g. Results for commercial nylon 66 ribbon samples and for a more extensive set of additive combinations in which the ribbons were produced on a laboratory equivalent of the production extruder are given in Table 3.

TABLE 3—*Frictional coefficients of various nylon 66 ribbons against the Taber H-18 grinding wheel.*

Nylon 66 Ribbon Type[a]	L_1, g	μ (Eq 3)
Production ribbons		
S,C,LDPE	50	0.43[b]
	100	0.43[b]
	150	0.31
S,C,HDPE	50	0.32
	100	0.33
	150	0.27
Laboratory ribbons		
. . .	97.9	0.43
S	97.9	0.29
S,LDPE	97.9	0.38
S,HDPE	97.9	0.21
S,LLDPE	97.9	0.27
S,PP	97.9	0.27
S,C,LDPE	97.9	0.44
S,C,HDPE	97.9	0.30
S,C,LLDPE	97.9	0.34

[a] Indicated additives and polymeric carrier, if any of either, are S (standard stabilizer additives), C (standard colorant additives, LDPE (low-density polyethylene), HDPE (high-density polyethylene), LLDPE (linear low-density polyethylene), and PP (polypropylene).

[b] The reference set used for calculation of K; see text.

Inspection of Table 3 shows, first of all, good agreement in μ values between production ribbon and laboratory samples for the two cases where stabilizer additives, colorants, and either low-density polyethylene (LDPE) carrier or high-density polyethylene (HDPE) carrier resin were incorporated. The laboratory set permits systematic analysis of the apparent effects of the various additives on coefficient of friction. As with the polyurethane cleat material (Table 2), μ for LDPE carrier is consistently higher than that for HDPE, other additives being equal. Linear low-density polyethylene carrier (LLDPE) is in between. Evidently, incorporation of the (inorganic) stabilizer additives sharply reduces μ from its value for nylon 66 alone, and subsequent introduction of the carrier resin may either increase it again (LDPE) or decrease it further. Introduction of the pigment/dye colorant additives systematically increases μ, other additives being held constant. To the extent that μ values are important at all in end-use properties, the last three entries of Table 3 probably are the most helpful, as options for carrier resins are more readily available than for the other additives.

Laboratory Tests of Accelerated Fabric Wear

The expected lifetime of artificial turf surfaces exposed to multipurpose sports usage, often under harsh environmental conditions, is of considerable interest. Two laboratory tests for turf pile wear under accelerated conditions are the Taber and Schiefer methods referenced earlier. While certainly useful for laboratory comparisons among fabrics of similar construction, the tests may or may not relate in a simple way to actual turf pile deterioration in the field. There, among other differences, abrasion occurs concurrently with ultraviolet exposure.

Typical laboratory results for polypropylene and nylon 66 pile fabrics via Taber and Schiefer testing are given in Table 4. Note that for these two principal commercial systems, one appears superior according to the Taber test and the other superior according to the Schiefer method. Interpretations here are confined to how results from either method may relate to turf ribbon friction.

With respect to the Taber results of Table 4, there appears to be a small but definite penalty in performance for nylon 66 fabrics incorporating LDPE carrier resin, compared with results for the HDPE counterpart. (All other aspects of turf construction are identical.) It is tempting to account for this difference through the corresponding difference in calculated frictional coefficients (Table 3), as the change in Taber wear for LDPE (10%) is in the same direction as that for μ (30 to 50%). Conceivably, a difference in frictional coefficient could also account for reduced Taber wear of polypropylene compared with either nylon 66 fabric. Unfortu-

TABLE 4—*Data for accelerated fabric wear according to the Taber and Schiefer laboratory methods.*

Fabric[a]	Taber Wear, g/500 Cycles, H-18 Wheel	Schiefer Wear, g/50 000 Cycles
Nylon 66 (LDPE)	1.10	0.067
Nylon 66 (HDPE)	1.00	0.048
Polypropylene	0.53	3.38

[a] Nylon 66 fabrics contain standard additives and are of textured ribbon, knitted construction. Polypropylene fabric utilizes "fibrillated" slit film ribbon and tufted construction.

nately, our data do not include estimates of μ for the former and, in any case, the substantial difference in fabric construction is likely to be a major complicating factor.

Turning next to the results in Table 4 for Schiefer wear, the reader will observe a similar penalty for the nylon 66 incorporating LDPE carrier. Here, the relevant comparison would be μ values for ribbons against steel. We do not have the frictional coefficient data needed, but results [4] reported for μ with *pure* HDPE against steel (0.23) and LDPE against steel (0.33 to 0.6) are again in the right direction. The polyethylenes incorporated in nylon 66 ribbon exist as separate phases [2], and one might expect additive contributions from the mixed polymers. The excessive Schiefer loss for polypropylene fabrics seems unaccountable by frictional coefficient differences and, more likely, results from occasional, gross loss of fiber pieces in this test due to the "fibrillated" blade geometry, tufted fabric construction, or both.

Sport Shoe Traction

Traction level and, especially, traction uniformity are key performance considerations for artificial turf surfaces [1]. Traction may be defined as the coefficient of friction between a specified sports shoe sole surface and the playing surface. It is expressed in the customary manner as the ratio of pulling force to initiate (static) or sustain (sliding) motion divided by the vertically applied force (weight). The value of the coefficient will in general depend upon the direction along the fabric, for example, the direction in which the fabric was produced by knitting or tufting. As a laboratory or field method, traction is conveniently measured with the selected shoe sole flattened and attached to a rigid support upon which a weight can be placed. A spring gage can be used to measure pulling force parallel to the playing surface.

Traction level, $\overline{T}$, may be defined as the average of four measured coefficients of friction (normally, against the pile angle induced by manufacture, with the pile, and two at cross directions). Differential traction, ΔT, is defined

$$\Delta T = \frac{\Sigma |T_i - \overline{T}|}{4} \tag{4}$$

where T_i is coefficient of friction measured in one of the four principal directions. An ideal surface would have $\overline{T}$ at a useful level and ΔT at or close to zero. It should be noted that $\overline{T}$ depends entirely upon the choice of shoe/turf combination selected and thus must be appropriately specified. Surfaces with values of ΔT greater than about 0.1 are likely to exhibit nonuniformity noticeable to the player. Effects on trueness of ball roll could be apparent at values of $\Delta T < 0.1$. Some values are listed in Table 5 for comparison.

It is apparent from entries of Table 5 that turf materials and construction, together with the characteristics of the sports shoe itself, are dominating factors in determining shoe traction. Differences in μ for the materials involved of the magnitude of those measured and reported in Table 2 are likely to have a minor influence on traction. Indeed, measurement of traction levels for a number of specific nylon 66 turf constructions revealed no dependence on the presence of various carrier resins such as LDPE *versus* HDPE. That basic frictional characteristics are important, given large enough variation in them, is however clear from the readily observed decrease in traction level for wet nylon 66 surfaces and, interestingly, a corresponding increase for the polypropylene systems. Total effective coefficient of friction for turf/shoe interaction $\overline{T}$ exceeds μ by 50 to 150%, depending upon sports shoe construction. Therefore, factors of fabric construction remain the practical means for good surface design.

TABLE 5—*Shoe traction[a] for artificial turf surfaces.*

| Turf | Traction Level (Dry) | | Traction Level (Wet) | | Differential Traction |
	High Traction Shoe[b]	Low Traction Shoe[c]	High Traction Shoe	Low Traction Shoe	
Knitted nylon 66, untexturized	1.8 to 2.0	1.2 to 1.4	1.6 to 1.8	1.2 to 1.4	0.1 to 0.3
Knitted nylon 66, texturized	1.9 to 2.1	1.3 to 1.5	1.7 to 1.9	1.3 to 1.5	0 to 0.1
Tufted polypropylene	1.7 to 2.0	. . .	1.8 to 2.1	. . .	0.1 to 0.2

[a] Sliding friction for normal force in the range 12 to 15 kg.
[b] Adidas Gripper, American football, circa 1980.
[c] Hyde 440, soccer, circa 1980.

Conclusions

In the general discussion of plastics, some key properties desirable in particular artificial turf system components were identified. It appears that the characteristic properties of polypropylene, nylon 66, polyethylene, and polyvinyl chloride all are used to advantage in the major commercial systems, although trade-offs are evident in most cases.

Nylon 66 pile materials, for example, are strong and possess good natural ultraviolet resistance. The relatively high moisture regain of the polymer causes noticeable change in traction under wet *versus* dry conditions (sometimes used to advantage in optimizing artificial turf fields for certain sports.) The inherent instability of polypropylene to ultraviolet exposure would be a prime concern, except that the additives incorporated in the turf ribbons apparently are quite effective for long periods of time.

The polyvinyl chloride/rubber interpolymer foam probably offers the most attractive material for shock-absorbing pads, owing to the excellent combination [5] of hysteresis and elasticity of its components. Energy absorption is efficient, the pad is comfortable underfoot, and a desirably low ball bounce from the surface is characteristic. Polyethylene pads are durable and the shock-absorbing properties vary little with temperature in the range of −18°C (0°F) to 49°C (120°F). A tendency toward firmness and excessive ball bounce are disadvantages. Both polyvinyl chloride/rubber and polyethylene use the concept of crosslinking to optimize performance.

The work on determination of frictional coefficients of turf ribbons appears to show relevance to some end-use properties of the sports surfaces. Accelerated fabric wear, sports shoe traction, and other operations on the turf clearly have to do with complex forms of resistance, and it is not obvious that classical sliding friction of the materials involved would play an important role. In the case of Taber and Schiefer testing, this indeed appears to be the case. In the case of shoe traction, simple friction plays a role, but mechanical resistance of the cleats is the major factor. The overall results suggest that coefficient of friction can be a useful primary physical property in selection of materials.

Most of the μ values discussed here were derived indirectly from a novel technique for determination of turf ribbon lifetime under abrasive exposure. That method together with the referenced procedures developed previously to characterize the main elements of shoe traction may contribute to a battery of tests, dedicated to artificial surfaces, needed to describe these unique products. The recently issued ASTM Standard for Relative Abrasiveness of Synthetic Turf Playing Surfaces (F 1015-86) is a good beginning.

References

[1] Orofino, T. A., *Polymer News,* Vol. 10, 1985, pp. 294–300.
[2] Orofino, T. A. and McNeely, R. L., *Journal of Macromolecular Science-Physics,* Vol. 327, No. 1, 1988, pp. 31–39.
[3] Broxon, J. W., *Mechanics,* Appleton Century-Crafts, Inc., New York, 1960, pp. 40–41.
[4[Nielsen, L. E., *Mechanical Properties of Polymers,* Reinhold, New York, 1962, p. 226.
[5] Hamner, W. F. and Orofino, T. A., "Recreational Surfaces," *Kirk-Othmer Encyclopedia of Chemical Technology,* Vol. 19, third edition, 1982, pp. 926–927.

Richard D. Breland[1]

Performance Standards for Artificial Turf Surfaces

REFERENCE: Breland, R. D., **"Performance Standards for Artificial Turf Surfaces,"** *Natural and Artificial Playing Fields: Characteristics and Safety Features, ASTM STP 1073,* R. C. Schmidt, E. F. Hoerner, E. M. Milner, and C. A. Morehouse, Eds., American Society for Testing and Materials, Philadelphia, 1990, pp. 176–182.

ABSTRACT: A set of test methods and some minimum standards have evolved which synthetic turf surfaces should meet or exceed, including proof by performance testing in the field before these materials and systems are offered in the marketplace.

Various technical properties and ASTM testing methods are described for use in compiling a complete, consistent artificial turf surface system. The minimum or limiting values for performance levels required, as well as typical or recently measured values for individual samples of synthetic playing surfaces systems and components, are described in this paper. The typical values are just that, and of course are subject to normal variations both in production control and in testing, especially when different testing laboratories are involved.

Laboratory testing conditions are controlled at between 20 and 22°C (68 and 72°F) and between 60 and 65% relative humidity, unless otherwise noted. These are essentially the standard textile laboratory test conditions specified in the ASTM Practice for Conditioning Textiles for Testing (D 1776-85), which calls for 65 ± 2% relative humidity and a temperature of 21 ± 1°C (70 ± 2°F). Testing in laboratories under markedly different conditions and techniques may give different test results in some cases.

The objective of this paper is to provide an overview of the test methods adopted for characterizing and documenting the performance properties of artificial turf, turf systems, and system components.

KEY WORDS: playing fields, artificial turf, nylon 6,6, football, performance standards, ribbon pile fiber, pile wear, grab tear testing, tuft bind, flammability, relative abrasiveness, shock absorbency, compression resistance, compression set, synthetic turf surface

Pile Fiber

The pile fiber in a synthetic, grasslike, playing surface provides the wear and weather-resisting portion of the system. As such, the author's company, AstroTurf Industries, Inc., has stabilized the fiber in its surfaces for resistance to heat and ultraviolet radiation, designed it to balance drainage and cleaning properties, and colored it with durable pigments suspended in the fiber during its manufacture. The company's current products incorporate these properties in the pile fiber, as measured by the following test methods:

1. *Filament Size* [Test: ASTM Test for Linear Density of Textile Fibers (D 1577-79)]

    The denier, a measure of weight per unit length of the pile fiber, is a big factor in its texture, strength, drainage rate, resistance to weathering, and ease of cleaning. Deniers were tested, ranging from normal carpet fiber levels up to the 1100 denier level, and it

---

[1] Director of technology, AstroTurf Industries, Inc., Dalton, GA 30720.

was found that deniers in the middle of the tested range provide the best balance of these properties.

The denier of the AstroTurf[2] pile ribbon exceeds 500, and typically averages 550 denier. (The denier is the weight in grams of a single filament of yarn 9000 m long).

2. *Breaking Strength and Elongation* [Test: ASTM Test for Breaking Load (Strength) and Elongation of Yarn by the Single-Strand Method (D 2256-80)]

The tensile properties of the fiber used are a direct measure of how strong it is and how far it will stretch before it breaks. The stronger the fiber and the more elastic, the better it will resist wear.

The breaking strength for nylon 6,6 pile fiber exceeds 3.0 g per denier. Typical production data indicate an average of 3.5 g per denier.

The breaking elongation (an indication of elasticity and resilience of the fiber) must exceed 25% to meet the ASTM D 2256 standard. Typical production data for the ribbon used in AstroTurf[2] surfaces average 40% elongation before breaking.

Significance: The combination of fiber strength and filament size used on nylon 6,6 fields gives the user the best balance of drainage, cleanability, wear, and weather resistance available, along with the aesthetic properties of a permanently pigmented, non-glare fiber that stays attractive for years of heavy athletic usage.

3. *Melting Point* [Test: ASTM Tests for Determination of Relative Viscosity, Melting Point, and Moisture Content of Polyamide (PA) (D 789-86)]

The melting point of the pile fiber is related to its composition, chemical properties, and flammability. The minimum standard for the melting point of synthetic turf pile fiber is at least 250°C. The normal melting point for nylon 6,6 is in the range of 260°C.

4. *Density (Specific Gravity)* [Test: ASTM Test for Specific Gravity (Relative Density) and Density of Plastics by Displacement (D 792-86)]

The density of the fiber is related to its chemistry as well as its physical properties—low-density materials provide good "cover" but may offer less strength. Higher density materials tend to be stronger but require more weight of material per unit of area for the same amount of "cover" or "apparent value." The company has found that the best performance is obtained with high-density fibers. Tests of nylon 6,6 used for synthetic surfaces show a density of 1.14 g/cm^3.

Significance: Both the melting point and the density of nylon 6,6 AstroTurf[2] ribbon are set by the physics and chemistry of the material used. The high melting point means that the fiber will hold its properties well in the heavy scuffing of athletic traffic and will be less affected by the heat of a dropped match or cigarette. Strength, durability, ease of cleaning, and resistance to weather are all benefits of 500-denier nylon 6,6 pile fiber.

5. *Glass Transition Temperature* (T_G)

This is the temperature at which plastic materials change from a crystalline to an amorphous state. Below this temperature the plastic has an ordered structure which gives it "memory" and, in the case of synthetic fibers, makes them resistant to matting or crushing under traffic. Above the glass transition temperature, synthetic fibers are easily deformed and have no tendency to recover their original, untrafficked condition.

---

[2] AstroTurf is a registered trademark of AstroTurf Industries, Inc.

For synthetic turf surfaces, the company feels that only fibers having T_G values above 50°C should be used. The T_G for nylon 6,6 is 70°C, which is well above any temperatures usually encountered in outdoor synthetic turf application.

Fabric

Experience shows that the integrity of the fabric component of the playing surface system is a vital element in the performance of the total system. The properties listed below are the ones regarded as most important for surfaces used for heavy-duty athletic fields.

1. *Construction* [Test: ASTM Methods of Testing Woven and Tufted Pile Floor Covering (D 418-82)]

   Carpets are made by a number of manufacturing methods. Weaving is the traditional method, and was used for early AstroTurf surfaces. It is now seldom used because of its slow production rates and high costs. Tufting is the most common method of carpet manufacture today. It is inexpensive and fast, but the carpet is limited in strength, tuft bind, and resistance to rips and tears. The carpet knitting process produces fabrics as strong and durable as woven ones, but more resistant to wrinkles and puckers. Knitting requires specially modified equipment to handle the sizes and weights of fabric for synthetic turf playing fields.

   In designing fabrics, a number of balances must be struck. If the surface pile is too sparse, its wear and weather resistance are affected. Pile fiber that is packed too tightly will be abrasive and harsh, difficult to clean, and slow to drain.

   AstroTurf fabric is knitted, using all-synthetic materials, with a pile fiber content exceeding 50 oz/yd². The backing fabric weighs in excess of 8.0 oz/yd², and the fabric contains 4.0 oz/yd² of precoat resin, for a total weight of 62 oz/yd².

2. *Grab Tear Strength* (Test: ASTM Tests for Breaking Load and Elongation of Textile Fabrics [D 1682-64(1975)])

   The "grab tear strength" method measures the tear resistance of the total fabric structure rather than the strength of the fabric components taken independently. The grab tear strength of recreational surface fabrics should average at least 350 lb when tested both along and across the fabric.

   Knitted nylon 6,6 fabrics are more resistant to damage from rips and tears than materials of lower strength. Tests of surfaces in both the company's own and outside laboratories have frequently run above 385 lb.

3. *Resistance to Tuft Pullout* (Test: ASTM Test for Tuft Bind of Pile Floor Coverings [D 1335-67(1972)])

   The tufts should be securely attached to the backing fabric, and it should require at least 25 lb of force to pull them out. Recent reports from independent test laboratories have shown tuft-bind values of greater than 25 to 30 lb for knitted nylon 6,6 surfaces.

   Actually, tuft failure in this test with knitted fabrics includes destruction of the backing yarns.

Significance: The combination of materials used, the knitted construction, exceptional fabric strength, and exceptional tuft-bind properties of AstroTurf fabric means that the fields resist rips, tears, and mechanical damage better than any other synthetic turf. The knitting design used produces a fabric that is manageable and that can be securely bonded to the underpad.

4. *Fabric Flammability* [Test: National Bureau of Standards Flooring Radiant Panel Test, ASTM Test for Critical Radiant Flux of Floor Covering Systems Using a Radiant Heat Source (E 648-86) NFPA 253]

Artificial turf surfaces are exposed to abuse both from carelessly dropped cigarettes and deliberate acts of vandalism. Knitted nylon 6,6 surfaces have an excellent record of resisting both kinds of event. The flooring radiant panel method tests the heat flux required to maintain combustion in a floor covering, reporting it as "critical radiant flux" in watts per square centimeter.

The company designed its surface fabrics for synthetic turf to have critical radiant flux values in excess of 0.3 W/cm^2. Independent laboratory results for the company's synthetic turf fabrics range from 0.47 to 1.05 + W/cm^2.

Significance: Knitted nylon 6,6 fabrics are less likely to be severely damaged by the heat or fire from dropped matches, cigarettes, or even the attacks of vandalism than synthetic turfs made of other materials or by other methods.

5. *Pile Height* [Test: ASTM Methods of Testing Woven and Tufted Pile Floor Covering (D 418-82)]

The company has found that the pile height of a fabric should be great enough to provide good cover, minimize "brushiness," and give good wear resistance but should not be so high that drainage is retarded excessively, cleaning is made more difficult, or traffic patterning is more apparent. Pile heights between 0.47 and 0.51 in. appear to balance these properties well. The nominal pile height for a stadium surface is ½ in. Shorter pile fabrics tend to become more abrasive to players.

6. *Abrasion Resistance* [Test: ASTM Test for Abrasion Resistance of Textile Fabrics (Uniform Abrasion Method) (D 4158-82)]

The correlation between laboratory abrasion tests and field performance is affected by many factors not found in the laboratory, including soilage, air pollution, and types of traffic found on the field (for example, baseball spikes versus multicleated soccer shoes). Tests for abrasion resistance should ensure, however, that the fabric system falls into the "highly resistant to abrasion" category. The "uniform abrasion method" of ASTM D 4158 gives a good basis for making this judgment. A surface should lose less than 0.05 g from the abraded area (4 in.^{2}) when subjected to 1000 cycles of the spring steel blade abradant under a 10-lb load before being regarded as highly abrasion resistant. When nylon 6,6 surfaces are subjected to this test, the weight loss is usually less than 0.01 g. (See Table 1).

Note: the ASTM test methods for abrasion resistance all contain warnings against using them to compare textile materials with different types of fiber or different construction, unless the test in question has been validated by correlation with wear data from actual usage.

Significance: The AstroTurf nylon 6,6 surface fabric design has evolved through years of testing and development to provide a proven record of exceptional strength, durability, and performance in heavy athletic field usage.

7. *Relative Abrasiveness* [Test: ASTM Test for Relative Abrasiveness of Synthetic Turf Playing Surfaces (F 1015-86)]

The properties of resistance to abrasive wear and minimal abrasiveness to players, apparel, and equipment tend to oppose each other. ASTM Test F 1015 measures the

TABLE 1—*Abrasion resistance to surface wear: ASTM uniform abrasion method (D 4158-82).*

Pile Ribbon/Fabric	Surface Wear, g/50 000 Cycles
Nylon 6.6/stadium[a]	0.67
Polypropylene/stadium[b]	3.38

[a] Nylon stadium fabric is made up of 500-denier/continuous-filament ribbon in knitted construction.
[b] Polypropylene stadium fabric is tufted with fibrillated slit film.

ability of a synthetic turf surface to wear away a standard synthetic polymer foam during sliding weighted contact and correlates well with both subjective and other objective measures of abrasiveness. AstroTurf surfaces typically show abrasiveness index values of less than 40 under standard laboratory conditions and even lower values under typical game conditions in most locations.

Shock Absorbing Underpads

The underpad in the surface system is designed to provide both comfort and cushioning properties for athletes. It must do so throughout the range of weather conditions likely to be encountered in athletic usage. To meet these demands, the company has provided a closed-cell synthetic foam material of high mechanical strength that resists the loss of properties due to wear, mechanical abuse, and weather. The current pad system has been thoroughly tested in a wide range of climates and uses and has performed well even under occasional traffic of lightweight pneumatic-tired motor vehicles, normally found at athletic fields.

1. *Shock Absorbency* [Test: ASTM Test for Shock Absorbing Properties of Playing Surface Systems and Materials (F 355-86)]

   "Softness," "hardness," and "comfort" are difficult to measure by any single test. "Shock absorbency" is the ability of a playing surface to spread out the time and lessen the force of a blow or fall onto a playing surface. The referenced test requires dropping a heavy weight onto the playing surface and using electronic equipment to record how hard it hits the surface.

   The company has tested the impact values of the AstroTurf system using Procedure A of ASTM Test F 355. Newly manufactured samples of the stadium surface system test below 100 g_{max}, and typically 75 g_{max}, when tested at 70 to 75°F and 60 to 65% relative humidity, and they show modest change in impact values when tested at pad temperatures as low as 32°F or as high as 120°F.

2. *Compression Resistance* (Test: ASTM Specification for Flexible Cellular Materials—Vinyl Chloride Polymers and Copolymers (Closed-Cell Vinyl) [D 1667-76(1987)])

   This test measures the force required to compress the pad to 75% of its original thickness (25% compression). Our experience has shown that values between 7 and 10 psi provide good player comfort values in most applications. Values for AstroTurf pad material run at approximately 8.5 psi when tested at standard laboratory temperature and humidity.

Significance: The underpad was designed to give the best balance of comfort and cushioning properties under the conditions encountered in heavy outdoor athletic usage.

3. *Compression Set Under Constant Load* [Test: ASTM Tests for Rubber Property—Compression Set (D 395-85)]

For full usefulness of a playing field, it is sometimes necessary to erect temporary stands, drive vehicles on the field, or otherwise put loads on the surface for hours, days, or even longer. This compression set test measures the loss of pad thickness following exposure to a constant load of 100 psi for a period of 22 h, with a 24-h recovery period afterward, and with the test made at standard laboratory temperature and humidity (70 to 75°F and 60 to 65% RH). The high permanent set values for closed-cell pads suggest poor durability. The pads used for AstroTurf surfaces normally have 20 to 30% set under this severe test.

4. *Tensile and Elongation Properties* [Test: ASTM Tests for Rubber Properties in Tension (D 412-87)]

Low mechanical strength makes the pad subject to delamination and tearing in service. The company's tests show that, for good performance, the pads used under its heavy-duty athletic fields should have tensile strengths exceeding 90 psi and breaking elongations above 125%. Typical values for the pad used under AstroTurf fields run at about 115 psi breaking strength and 130% elongation before breaking.

5. *Stability to Heat and Moisture* [Test: ASTM Test for Response of Rigid Cellular Plastics to Thermal and Humid Aging (D 2126-75)] Environmental Aging Chamber, 150°F, and 98% RH for 28 days).

The company has found that all closed-cell foam systems tend to lose their properties through gas diffusion from the cells under hot, wet conditions. Exposure of the pad to 150°F and 98% RH for 28 days will reveal the tendency for gas loss in service. The company does not consider pad systems that lose more than 25% of their volume following such exposures acceptable. Typical values from independent laboratory tests for closed-cell pads show volume losses of only 4 to 5% after 28-day environmental aging.

Significance: The pad system used under AstroTurf surfaces can take the loads required for many different activities—both static and moving. Synthetic turf nylon 6,6 surface systems are truly multiple-use facilities. Their ability to withstand outdoor exposure is the best available, and this ability has been proven both in the laboratory and in actual field service.

Installation

Seams and joints in synthetic turf systems represent potential weak spots for wear and vandalism and should therefore be minimized. All surfaces should be installed by experienced crews using materials suitable for the climate of the installation site and for the designed uses of the installation.

1. *Seam Frequency*

   (*a*) Side seams in the fabric are at 15-ft intervals, matching the 5-yd lines on a typical football field. Fewer seams means less chance of problems.

   (*b*) All seams are sewn with a double-locked stitch to give excellent strength and durability.

   (*c*) There are no "cross" or "head" seams on the playing surface for normal football/ soccer fields.

TABLE 2—*Summary of performance test methods for synthetic turf surfaces.*

Standard	Property Tested
Pile fiber	
ASTM D 1577-79	linear density of textile fibers (denier)
ASTM D 2256-80	breaking strength and elongation
ASTM D 789-86	melting point
ASTM D 792-86	density (specific gravity)
Fabric	
ASTM D 418-82	pile fiber construction
ASTM D 1682-64(1975)	grab tear strength
ASTM D 1335-67(1972)	resistance to tuft pullout
ASTM D 648-86	critical radiant flux (flooring radiant panel test)
ASTM D 418-82	pile height
ASTM D 4158-82	abrasion resistance (uniform abrasion method)
ASTM F 1015-86	relative abrasiveness
Shock absorbing underpads	
F 355-86	shock absorbency
D 1667-76(1986)	compression resistance
D 395-85	compression set under constant load
D 3574-86	tensile and elongation
D 2126-75	hydrolytic stability

2. *System Bonding*

   (*a*) The AstroTurf underpad is installed over the asphalt substrate in a uniform manner, with no visible bubbles or areas that show up as "soft spots" or trap water.

   (*b*) The fabric is bonded to the underpad with no visible wrinkles, ripples, or bubbles. If any such bubbles occur, they are repaired by the installers in such a way that the strength of the fabric system is not impaired. Slits in the surface fabric to relieve wrinkles are not permitted.

3. *Painting*

   The fields are painted with the markings required for the principal game to be played. The paint materials used should be compatible with the turf, give good resistance to the wear of the game traffic, and provide good visibility for players, officials, and spectators.

Significance: No synthetic turf is better than the job done in its installation. AstroTurf fields are well made, carefully installed, and supported by a full-time, year-round professional service organization with the experience of installing over 500 playing fields worldwide.

Conclusions

The performance standards described in this paper for artificial turf surfaces (Table 2) are a bench mark for characterizing and communicating the properties of synthetic turf. The ASTM procedures and test methods described herein should be considered for adoption to establish minimum standards and properties for synthetic turf components and systems.

Edward M. Milner[1]

Selecting a Synthetic Turf Surface

REFERENCE: Milner, E. M., "**Selecting a Synthetic Turf Surface,**" *Natural and Artificial Playing Fields: Characteristics and Safety Features, ASTM STP 1073,* R. C. Schmidt, E. F. Hoerner, E. M. Milner, and C. A. Morehouse, Eds., American Society for Testing and Materials, Philadelphia, 1990, pp. 183–187.

ABSTRACT: The author discusses factors to be considered when selecting a synthetic turf surface. These include factors related to the playing of the game, as well as factors related to the cost, durability, and value of the synthetic surface.

KEY WORDS: playing fields, synthetic turf, standards

Every design or purchase decision involves trade-offs, balances, and compromises. The decision to buy and install a synthetic turf playing surface is no exception. Those steeped in the traditions of a game may say, "Never change my game," while the athletic director of a "landlocked" public school or college may say, "How can I accommodate too many participants for too many hours on too little land and still provide a safe and pleasant place to play?" Properly designed and selected synthetic turf systems can meet the needs of both— and it is only after looking at these needs, in the light of the needs of those who actually play on the surfaces, that detailed, numerically precise specifications should be drawn. Such specifications then become the bases on which intelligent design and purchase decisions can be made.

Game Factors

From the standpoint of the users of playing surfaces several concepts come quickly to the fore:

(*a*) *The surface should perform—and allow users to perform on it—in ways similar to traditional, well-maintained natural grass surfaces.*

- *The surface should be "nondirectional."*

  Natural grass is inherently nondirectional. While golfers may pride themselves on being able to "read the grain" on a grass putting green, exhaustive measurements on actual putting greens have shown that "grain" does not exist. Instead, skilled golfers read the smallest changes in elevation and slope of the green, and adjust their putting strokes accordingly. Synthetic turf surfaces should be similarly nondirectional in relation to ball roll and ball bounce, as well as to player footing or traction.

- *The synthetic surface should accept moisture.*

  Natural grass gains many of its desirable properties from its ability to aspirate moisture from the surrounding soil in through its root structure and out through its leaves. The grass surface is cooled in the process and made less abrasive, at the expense of

---

[1] President, Astroturf Industries, Inc., Dalton GA 30720.

being torn apart more easily or abraded away in game traffic. An ideal synthetic surface should regain enough moisture to absorb and release ambient moisture in normal use conditions if it is to approximate good-quality natural grass. The synthetic surface should wet easily and drain rapidly to permit ease of cleaning, early usage after rain, and ease of temperature control at the air-surface interface.

(b) *The ideal synthetic surface should not change the fundamental nature of the games played on it.*

The ball management properties, such as rolling speed and bounce, should be similar to those for traditional surfaces. Ball roll should be "true" as to both distance and direction.

A great deal of work in the area of ball roll and bounce properties has been done by the Sports Council (United Kingdom)[2] in their efforts to develop standards for soccer and field hockey surfaces. In both these sports the ball is on the surface for most of its time in play, so rolling characteristics are important.

(c) *The surface should be a safe and enjoyable one on which to play.*

The term "user friendly" has been overworked in the field of electronic data processing and personal computers, but it is highly appropriate in describing the quality of well-designed playing fields.

- *The surface should provide shock absorbency or cushioning properties similar to those of traditional surfaces at their best.*

    While there are no exact standards which say that impact values above a certain level are unsafe, it is reasonable to assume that there are impact properties that players of individual sports have come to accept as "normal." A packed clay baseball infield is much harder than a well-prepared grass football field. Soccer, hockey, and lacrosse players prefer a firmer surface than do players of American football or rugby. The ASTM Test for Shock-Absorbing Properties of Playing Surface Systems and Materials (F 355-86) provides a simple and reliable way to measure the impact properties of both natural and synthetic turfs. The principle in ASTM Test F 355-86 of dropping an object of specified weight from a specified distance and reporting its impact deceleration performance in units of gravity (g) values is straightforward and understandable. The approach of the Sports Council and the Rubber and Plastics Research Association (RAPRA), in which the drop height of the dropped object is adjusted to reach some preselected maximum g value, brings in the need for repeated impacts as the drop height is adjusted and also the possibility of errors in setting and controlling the actual drop height or the resulting impact velocity. Along with loss of accuracy and precision, the use of varying drop heights adds to the cost and time required for testing.

- *The players' footing, or traction, should be uniform, predictable, and within traditional ranges.*

    Here, both the selection of shoes and the nature of the surface come into play. On natural surfaces, player traction results from both the shoe/surface coefficient of friction and the mechanical interlocking of cleats, studs, or spikes that penetrate into the surface. Such penetration on natural turf varies widely with the surface moisture content, grass type, grass density, and soil type. Cleat penetration is a major factor in the wear and tear of heavily used natural grass.

---

[2] Winterbottom, Sir Walter, "Artificial Grass Surfaces for Association Football: Report and Appendices," The Sports Council, London, May 1985.

On synthetic surfaces, player traction is the result of friction between the shoe sole and the surface. Controlling factors include the material from which the sole is made, its relative hardness, its relationship to the turf surface material, and its configuration, along with the kinds of movements made by the wearer in the course of his game. A well-designed synthetic surface should give consistent traction at "normal" levels without requiring shoes that are exotic in appearance or unduly expensive.

- *Synthetic surface properties should be more uniform than those of natural turf.*

Herein lies one of the principal reasons for the use of synthetic turf. Natural grass wears out in heavy use during a single season and must then be nursed back to health before the next year's season. Synthetic surfaces should show minimal changes in player performance over wide extremes of heat, cold, sun, and rain. The surface configuration itself should hold no surprises for the player—no puddles, chuckholes, mud, stones, ruts, or other anomalies that cause changes in impact properties, player footing, or ball management. The character of the seams in the synthetic surface should be carefully checked to be sure that they do not provide unusual levels of hardness, abrasiveness, or difficulty in ball management.

- *Synthetic surfaces should not be unduly abrasive.*

With some materials, traction comes only with the disadvantage of increased abrasiveness to the player, his apparel, and his equipment. The development of the ASTM Test for Relative Abrasiveness of Synthetic Turf Playing Surfaces (F 1015-86) offers a major step forward in quantifying the relative abrasiveness of synthetic turf playing surfaces. This test should be more often used in specifying the properties of turf surfaces. The relative abrasiveness of the surface should not be confused with abrasion resistance, or the wearing resistance of the surface itself.

(*d*) *The synthetic turf surface should be well suited for practicing and teaching game skills.*

A synthetic turf surface should favor normal game skills, including team play. It should be suitable for play at all levels of skill and for both male and female players. Skills and tactics developed on the synthetic surface should be applicable to other surfaces without changing the game in undesirable ways.

(*e*) *The synthetic turf surfaces should be excellent for competitive play.*

Players should not be distracted by the surface used, and should be free to concentrate on the game being played. The surface should favor the more skilled, the more fit, and the team with more effectively coordinated tactics. It should not give an undue "home field advantage."

Value Factors

Those who purchase and maintain playing surfaces must add the concerns of cost, durability, and value to those related to the play of games. Accordingly, synthetic turf surfaces should be long-lasting and require minimum maintenance under almost constant usage.

(*a*) *The synthetic turf surface should have as few seams as possible.*

It is well established that problems with textile systems—whether they are garments, protective covers, carpets, or synthetic playing surfaces—tend to be concentrated at the seams. Wider fabrics have fewer seams than narrower ones and should be favored. Textile structures that minimize the risk of unraveling at the edges and consequent seam failure should be favored. The ease of seam repair should be considered. *All* seams are subject to eventual failure. The durability, simplicity, and speed of repair of seams are important value factors in turf selection.

(b) The game line-marking systems for synthetic turf should be both durable and easy to change.

Game rules regarding field markings change from time to time, but game boundary and other markings should be clear and distinct. Field decorations have become an important part of the ambiance of major sports competition—but need to be changed from one event to another. The turf supplier should provide clear directions for the application and removal of both decorations and game markings. Proper precautions to avoid "caking" or the use of excessive paint, which may create hard or excessively abrasive surfaces at marked areas, should be indicated by the turf supplier.

(c) The synthetic turf system should drain rapidly and be easy to clean.

Residential and commercial carpets wear out first near entrances, where grit and dirt are deposited from the shoes of pedestrians, which then proceed to wear away the carpet pile fiber. Carpet life is extended by the use of "walk-off mats" to collect this dirt before it reaches the floor covering and by frequent and thorough cleaning. On outdoor synthetic turf playing fields, the soiling from foot traffic is augmented by airborne dust and pollutants, as well as by sand and dirt that may be kicked out of jump pits or washed in by rainwater. The surface should not trap such abrasive materials and must be easy to clean using readily available materials and equipment such as fire hoses and plenty of clean water.

(d) A synthetic turf surface must be a truly "all-weather" surface.

The playing field should drain rapidly after a rainstorm or snowmelt and should not be damaged by usage in bad weather. The fibers chosen for synthetic turf should retain their strength and "memory" in hot weather to minimize matting or pile crushing in summertime usage.

(e) A synthetic turf surface should last for many years in its intended location and with its intended usage with minimal change from wear and weather.

- *All materials exposed to the weather should be well stabilized to resist ultraviolet radiation, heat, and air pollution.*

  Laboratory methods for predicting resistance to ultraviolet and weathering factors are still few, and their results are uncertain. The experience of similar installations under similar conditions of climate and usage is the best guide to the performance of a projected new installation. Well-planned inspections of existing fields will be extremely helpful in this area, but prospective buyers should remember that all synthetic fields look as if they will last forever when new. Buyers should make a point of looking at fields that have been in use for five or more years, as well as ones that are brand new. New installations offer opportunities to evaluate the installer's workmanship but give few clues as to the material's longevity.

- *Consistent with resistance to ultraviolet radiation and weathering, synthetic turf surfaces should be resistant to both wear from usage and abuse or vandalism.*

  Such wear may show up in the form of matting and fibrillation at sites of concentrated usage (goal mouths, batting boxes, midfield, etc.). The "skinned area" of a traditional grass baseball field exhibits the wear pattern inherent in the game of baseball. Wear patterns for soccer, lacrosse, and American football are well defined on natural grass fields. With synthetic surfaces, the usage patterns will be the same as those on natural turf, but the rate of differential wearing should be far less severe.

Traffic simulators—including the WIRA dynamic loading machine, described in British Standard 4052,[3] and the Tetrapod Walker test[4]—are useful laboratory methods for simulating the relative effects of repeated foot traffic on playing surfaces.

The issue of vandalism cannot be ignored, and shows up most often in the forms of fire and graffiti. Fire resistance is most dependably measured using the ASTM Test for Critical Radiant Flux of Floor Covering Systems Using a Radiant Heat Energy Source (E 648-86), which determines the radiant energy flux required to maintain combustion of the turf system in its normal horizontal configuration with face fibers up and fire loading from the top. Where the turf is to be installed indoors, its fire properties become even more important as a matter of occupant safety.

Graffiti from canned spray lacquers may be encountered in some situations. Turf suppliers should supply instructions for the removal of paint—whether applied for field decoration and line marking or by pranksters or vandals.

(f) *The turf fabric should be resistant to rips, tears, and physical damage.*

Baseball players traditionally wear steel cleats. Heavy equipment may be used to remove snow. Athletes wearing track spikes may choose the synthetic turf to do their stretching and warm-up excercises. These insults to the turf surface may hit it in any direction.

The "grab tear" method of the ASTM Test for Breaking Load and Elongation of Textile Fabrics [D 1682-64(1975)] gives an indication of the resistance of the entire fabric structure to rips and tears from any of the types of insult just described. Traditional tensile strength methods are limited in that they measure the strength of the turf fabric in either the warp or the filling direction. Wear from normal foot traffic is difficult to estimate, but the "uniform abrasion method" of the ASTM Test for Abrasion Resistance of Textile Fabrics (Uniform Abrasion Method) (D 4158-82) is a useful way to compare the resistance of various turf systems to a specified abradant which attacks all parts of the exposed turf system from all possible angles. Special attention should be paid to the caveats in all tests for abrasive wear regarding the need for correlation between laboratory wear simulations and real-world wear and weathering.

Conclusions

Buyers, users, and the spectator public all have specific interests in the choice of synthetic turf materials and product systems. While there are no known laboratory methods which will exactly simulate either game use requirements or the effects of traffic, wear, and weathering, existing ASTM methods are available with which useful comparisons can be made. In the selection of a system and the methods used to test it, it is important to be aware of the sometimes conflicting needs of users, owners, and the public, and of the balances which must be made by turf designers and buyers to meet these needs in the best way.

Synthetic grasslike turf surfaces have been in commercial service since 1966. While there is no one ideal surface that will be best for every application, synthetic turf has found widespread acceptance where people are plentiful, land is scarce, and inclement climates and heavy usage make the growth and maintenance of natural grass surfaces expensive, difficult, or impossible.

---

[3] British Standards Institution, BS 4052: 1972 Method for Determination of the Thickness Loss of Textile Floor Covering Under Dynamic Loading.

[4] International Organization for Standardization, Tetrapod Walker Test, ISO Document DTR 38/12 N 119, 1980.

Indexes

Author Index

Subject Index